SAFFRON INCORPORATED

Also by Stuart Coupe

Paul Kelly: The Man, the Music and the Life in Between

Roadies: The Secret History of Australian Rock'n'Roll

Gudinski: The Godfather of Australian Rock

The Promoters: Inside Stories from the Australian Rock Industry

SAFFRON INCORPORATED

THE FIRST KING OF THE CROSS AND FIFTY YEARS OF SEX, MURDER, MUSIC AND MAYHEM

STUART COUPE

Published in Australia and New Zealand in 2025
by Hachette Australia
(an imprint of Hachette Australia Pty Limited)
Gadigal Country, Level 17, 207 Kent Street, Sydney, NSW 2000
www.hachette.com.au

Hachette Australia acknowledges and pays our respects to the past and present Traditional Owners and Custodians of Country throughout Australia and recognises the continuation of cultural, spiritual and educational practices of Aboriginal and Torres Strait Islander peoples. Our head office is located on the lands of the Gadigal people of the Eora Nation.

A catalogue record for this book is available from the National Library of Australia

ISBN: 978 0 7336 4823 6 (paperback)

Cover design by Luke Causby, Blue Cork Designs
Cover photograph courtesy of State Library of NSW Digital Collections, reference number 9628875, call numbers ON 388/Box 077/Item 279
Typeset in Adobe Garamond Pro by Kirby Jones
Printed and bound in Australia by McPherson's Printing Group

The paper this book is printed on is certified against the Forest Stewardship Council® Standards. McPherson's Printing Group holds FSC® chain of custody certification SA-COC-005379. FSC® promotes environmentally responsible, socially beneficial and economically viable management of the world's forests.

For Susan – always.

And in memory of Cleo (the Wonder Dog), a fine companion and confidante during the writing of eight books.

CONTENTS

CONTENTS

PREFACE

The infamous Sydney organised crime boss Abe Saffron was no saint, but he didn't have a reputation for being physically violent or bloodthirsty. He wasn't a pugilist. He did have a pistol (and a fur-lined whip), but he wasn't known for using the pistol – the whip was another story.

While there were always the hard men, the savages and thugs, the downright dangerous and desperate within Saffron's generation and milieu of criminal activity, he was never within that class. But his hands weren't clean. If you order someone to be killed or bashed you might not register the bloodstains on your hands or clothes, but it registers on your soul, if you have one.

In comparison to Mafia godfathers, perhaps Abe wasn't anywhere near winning Organised Crime Figure of the Year, but he was always a cut above the wannabes and those who followed on who hadn't yet learned the lessons he'd learned – and maybe never would.

The man known as Mr Sin ruled Kings Cross from the 1940s until well into the '80s and the myths and legends and stories about him are many. But was he really as bad as some say?

Most people who were there are dead, but there are enough who have chronicled bits and pieces of his life in anecdotes, newspaper articles, books, court transcripts and whispers in my ear that I wanted to gather them all together and see the full portrait of Abe Saffron and his times.

For almost two decades I reviewed crime fiction for the *Sydney Morning Herald*, co-edited three fiction crime anthologies, founded *Mean Streets* (Australia's first crime and mystery fiction magazine), co-founded the Ned Kelly Awards and received a Ned Kelly Lifetime Achievement Award in 2005.

So, for me it makes perfect sense to combine my dual passions of music and crime writing, and I imagine others might be intrigued by that mix, too – all the glamour and the grit. As time has collected days and years in my own life, and I have been asked to recall events, people and places in the Australian music and entertainment industry I am still part of, I now often think more expansively about where I was and what was happening beyond me in those moments. It's just something you don't do when you are fully immersed in your own work and your own life.

I mean, when you are bounding down Darlinghurst Road with Tom Waits, you're hardly thinking about the owner of the Pink Pussycat and exactly what kind of life he was living. You're not paying much, if any, attention to the person behind you in line waiting for a teller at the ANZ bank in the main strip of Kings Cross. You're not wondering if it's the revered figure who rules the area.

PREFACE

At any given moment there are millions of stories unfurling around us. The context of the streets we all walked, the venues and the shows we saw or read about, the deals, and the news headlines we chatted about during meetings is, when I reflect upon it, endlessly curious and revelatory.

And, Abe Saffron, for better or worse, was one of the people who shaped a time and a place, and would set the stage for others to follow.

INTRODUCTION

BRIGHT LIGHTS, BIG CITY

The first time I saw the place nicknamed Sin City was in 1976 on my second-ever visit to Sydney. Driving down the main drag of Kings Cross at around 10 pm my head took flight in many directions. I was 19 years old and awestruck. There were cars and people everywhere, the kinds of people I'd never seen before, amid a sea of neon lights that I expected might be visible from Mars. But it was more than that. There was also an energy, an anticipation, an expectation of possibility, a rush. It was at once exciting and dangerous.

As a kid who'd grown up in Launceston, Tasmania, then only slightly bigger than a country town, before a stint at university in the staid and far-from-glitzy Adelaide, I was experiencing a complete revelation. Did places like this actually exist? Apparently, they did.

This was a world that seemed to be teeming with excitement, glamour, thrills and vicarious and real pleasures like I'd never imagined. I wanted in.

But I'd have to wait another two years before I moved to Sydney, and Kings Cross would become an almost daily part of my world. Soon after I moved to Sydney in August 1978 to work for *RAM* (*Rock Australia Magazine*) one of the first share households I moved into was in Brougham Street in Kings Cross. Yes, I was actually living in the Cross and walking its streets every day and night.

After a while I moved to the suburban inner-west world of Stanmore, which was closer to *RAM*'s offices, but then *RAM* moved from the not-altogether unhip Glebe to Darlinghurst and the Cross was just a stroll up William Street. I played Space Invaders in amusement parlours on the Strip for hours on end. I hung out watching rock'n'roll bands at the Manzil Room, the Rex Hotel and numerous other venues in and around the Cross.

As a fledgling rock'n'roll journalist, I ventured through the Cross what seemed like every other day to the more gentrified Elizabeth Bay, where on the dividing line between the two worlds was the Sebel Townhouse. Seemingly every international rock star stayed and held court there for the never-ending parade of journalists, groupies and other hangers-on. The Sebel epitomised much of the Cross in those days in so far as anything – and I mean pretty much anything – was permitted within its walls just as long as no one was (badly) hurt and the police didn't need to be called.

I recall one evening in the early 1980s after I'd interviewed the Beat Generation–inspired singer Tom Waits, a fellow journalist friend and I suggested to Waits that we take a stroll through the Cross. That we did, with Waits taking in the sights and sounds and characters of the Strip as it was then. He posed next to neon-lit outlines of women at the front of strip clubs and chatted to spruikers plying their trade on the pavement. For him it was the Australian equivalent of the seedy but exciting Hollywood Boulevard, which was his turf in Los Angeles. I hadn't been to Hollywood, but for me the Cross was as glamorous and squalid as I'd first seen it five years earlier.

Up close and outside of the protective cocoon of the car that had taken me through there in 1976, I realised pretty quickly that it wasn't all harmless glamour. People everywhere were clearly heavily affected by drugs. The street-walking women didn't look that fabulous the closer you got, often make-up covering their bruises, and there was a constant air of tension.

Aside from the drug intake, many of those walking the streets were clearly inebriated, some swaying noticeably, others exuding the body language of those who'd consumed four too many drinks and had convinced themselves the night was still young and there was more drinking and fun to be had. There were groups of males with an air of potential trouble about them. You sensed that some were more than slightly unenlightened in how to treat and respect women and that, combined with a pent-up aggression, meant that one slight provocation could set them off.

It could be something small that quickly escalated. Giving one of the street spruikers outside a strip club a bit too much lip could instantly turn nasty. Trying to get into bars and clubs when those four drinks too many had put you clearly over the limit but you were beyond realising it could be the catalyst. An off-colour or derogatory comment to a woman – working or just also out for a good time – could bring on a fire of verbiage and fists.

Other figures moved furtively up and down the streets creating a sense that something *could* happen at any moment and in any form. Was someone about to get stabbed? Would a gunshot ring out? Was a melee about to break out? Were there scores about to be settled? I always walked the streets of Kings Cross wide-eyed at the glitz and glamour but with my senses sharpened because the contrast between the bright lights and superficial good times and what might happen in a split second was often palpable.

I thought I was relatively street smart and savvy but there were clubs and bars that I simply was not game to venture inside and I avoided the back streets and alleys altogether. Nothing good was going to happen to a guy like me on those streets. There was a distinct air of danger there.

Back then, I spent as much time in and around the Cross as I could. I loved it and also had a perverse attraction to the edginess of it – just so long as I didn't get toooo close. I ate focaccias and drank coffee at the Tropicana in Victoria Street on the border of Darlinghurst and the Cross. I hung out at Mamma Maria's cafe in William Street before it moved up and across the road. I spent goodly amounts of money at Nicholas Pounder's tiny, well-organised antiquarian bookshop at 298 Victoria Street and ate many meals at Pinocchio's on the Strip and schnitzels at Una's, which again was technically Darlo but felt like Kings Cross.

After interviews at the Sebel Townhouse or just because we felt like it, a group of us would often go to a small Indian restaurant just down the road from the hotel where often one of my friends would have called up the day before and ordered a Derek Special. Derek, a mild-mannered Englishman, and his wife ran the restaurant. A Derek Special was a curry prepared to a level of heat that was so intense that only the hardy could ever finish one. I never tried. And a few doors further down was the occult bookshop with all sorts of fascinating books and knick-knacks. I bought Aleister Crowley and Colin Wilson books there.

I hung out with a bunch of friends who worked at Double J radio before it went national. I had frequent drinking sessions with presenter George Wayne at a hotel across the road from their studios in William Street and did double-takes at the sex workers plying their trade in St Peters Lane behind the ABC building. I was still naive about a lot of things then.

St Peters Lane was also where author Peter Corris located the fictional offices for his weather-beaten private investigator Cliff Hardy, a character who spent a lot of time treading the mean streets of Kings Cross and surrounding areas, where particularly the criminal element gave Corris plenty of fodder for his novels.

In the early 1980s I moved from Stanmore to Cathedral Street in Woolloomooloo, so the streets of the Cross were just a simple but daunting almost straight-line walk up the McElhone Stairs connecting Brougham and Victoria streets, which had been built in 1870. I've subsequently learned that it's 113 steps but of course I didn't count them, and far preferred returning home to climbing up them, no matter what promised good times awaited.

Soon afterwards, when I began managing the Hoodoo Gurus and later Paul Kelly, I had a management office in Victoria Street above a cafe called Toppers. Technically this was also Darlinghurst, but in those days it all felt like one character-filled, hip but edgy area.

When I moved into the office, I was bemused by the number of mirrors in the rooms I was renting – including a couple attached to the ceiling. What was this all about, I wondered. Remember – kid from Tasmania here. Eventually someone pointed out that my space had been a brothel in a rather recent life.

A little later I lived in Elizabeth Bay for a time and took weekly strolls up the hill to the Cross to eat at a Japanese restaurant around the corner from the Coca-Cola sign. Japanese restaurants weren't everywhere then as they are now. Artist Brett Whiteley knew about the place too and we'd often be there at the same time, nodding in recognition as we seemed to be the only diners who weren't Japanese tourists.

Close to this time I co-promoted a tour by the American actor and musician Harry Dean Stanton who had starred in *Paris Texas*, *Repo Man* and many other cult films. Harry Dean and his band stayed in the Cross and wandered around the streets regularly during their time in Sydney. No one ever said a word to or recognised Stanton.

When I told friends this they gasped, 'Why didn't anyone recognise him!' I explained that every second person walking the streets of Kings Cross had that down-on-their-luck look that Harry Dean cultivated.

The Cross – then and now – was peopled by the most astonishing array of characters. Actors, musicians, drug addicts, street hustlers, bankers, tourists from around the globe, police, bohemians … they all mixed together on those streets.

Everything about the Cross and its surrounds thrilled me. It felt like freedom if you could feel such a thing. For the first time in my life I felt totally enlivened, as if anything was possible. Kings Cross stimulated my senses – and sense of possibility – in ways that I'd never felt in Launceston or as a university student in Adelaide. This was urbane city living with all its extremes and I was totally enraptured and embracing of all that it offered.

I first visited New York City in 1981, and Kings Cross was as close to the hipness and edgy cool of Manhattan in that era as you were likely to find in Australia. Well, there was Fitzroy Street in St Kilda in Melbourne, which definitely rivalled Kings Cross for edgy seediness, I guess. But it lacked the neon glamour that hid the cracks common to both.

Looking back through the prism of today, the latter 1970s and early 1980s in Sydney – and in Kings Cross in particular – were another time and place, a seemingly alien landscape of drugs, street walkers, shady characters and rock'n'roll. But there were also continental delicatessens, cafes, restaurants and the legacy of the bohemian cohort from an even earlier time that added to the sparkle. Besides the European refugees, it was a place that attracted the intellectuals, artists, music makers, writers and poets – all adding light to the dark and making the dark more pronounced and intense.

I can only imagine what it was like for people in Sydney in the 1950s and 1960s, particularly people from the suburbs who were drawn there on a Friday or Saturday night.

This was a long time before the advent of real suburban nightlife. If you lived anywhere in Sydney or its surrounds and you wanted bright lights, you had to head to the Cross.

In the 1980s Kings Cross became my entertainment playground. I had no idea that a man called Abe Saffron probably owned half the establishments I frequented. I may well have passed him in the street and not have recognised him. But I would come to know his name and his reputation fast. People talk and I am a good listener.

* * *

Kings Cross was full of possibilities in the second half of the 1940s. World War II was over, and the world felt different. Relief fuelled optimism. Australia was not going to be taken over by foreign forces; our cities were not going to be decimated by bombs. There was a desire for escapism and good times. People wanted to go out, enjoy themselves and spend their money.

It was a time and place that was ripe for the picking by people like Abe Saffron, and he'd run his first business there in the 1940s. Within two decades, he'd play a big part in changing the nature of organised crime in Sydney, and define, influence and partially dominate the Australian entertainment landscape. He had his fingers in more pies than probably even he could count and inspired many imitators – some of whom had his power and finesse, but many of whom were little more than power-hungry thugs. He was a trailblazer in what was possible in the world of criminality.

While he expanded his enterprises rapidly, what was more important was his vision and sense of what was possible. Some operators specialised in sly grog sales, others in the sex industry and other nefarious activities. Saffron saw that you didn't need to differentiate if the common aim was making money. And he also realised – like a good Monopoly player – that the key to it all was real estate. Own the property and you could do absolutely whatever you or others wanted within those walls, just so long as you didn't attract unwanted attention.

Individuals – not just in Sydney but around the country – would look at this Abe Saffron guy and think, 'Not only can I do that, but I also want some of what he has.' And Saffron did it with style, finesse – and muscle. He was understated but extremely powerful. Because he was so effective at what he did, he made it look almost easy to be the kingpin in this milieu. A lot of people, most of them not nearly as smart as Saffron, wanted in. The majority would find out that it wasn't easy but, in every nook and cranny in every back street of the country, there were individuals who figured their destiny was to do what Abe was doing. But no one could do it like Abe.

Saffron was not the first underworld figure to tap into the world of entertainment and he was certainly not the last. But few others had the acumen, nous and self-belief to build such a far-reaching empire as he did. Where did he get the gumption, the moxie, to become the King of Kings Cross? Let's find out …

PART ONE

ABE AND THE UNDERBELLY

CHAPTER 1

SAFFRON'S BUILDING BLOCKS

Abraham Gilbert Saffron came into the world on 6 October 1919 – a Libran, for those astrologically inclined. His lineage was Russian–Jewish and the inner-city suburb of Annandale was his home turf. It's increasingly hard to reconcile the Annandale of that era with the inner-west Sydney suburb of today, but you could probably say that for any urban landscape near an Australian city. These days Annandale boasts expensive real estate and the sort of people who expect to find themselves living in a gentrified, established area with renovated homes, some quite grand, but they still mingle with the dreamers and schemers and those simply down on their luck.

Time-travel back many decades and Annandale was predominantly known as a fairly typical enclave of lower middle-class and working-class folk. Not shabby at all but not exclusive either. Many of the families who traditionally lived in the area at that time weren't exactly on struggle street and their houses were substantial, many of them plonked in the middle of large blocks of land with impressive gardens.

But, as the years went by, many of these folk moved away for greener pastures. They'd go east, where they'd have even bigger houses, more substantial gardens and beaches and – if they were lucky – seriously good views of Sydney Harbour. When you've had a sniff of those sea breezes the summer heat of the inner west lost even more of its allure.

So change came. The big mansions were divided up and turned into cheap accommodation for the working-class people who moved into the area.

And those lovely gardens? You can't make money out of gardens. Bulldozers came in and ripped up the greenery, and neat and tidy little houses were built that could be rented. Owners could watch their bank balances grow faster than the trees and shrubs they'd destroyed.

Employment had been much higher in the 1920s but with a downward turn during the Great Depression there was less money around and more demand for cheaper accommodation. By the 1940s Annandale was on a noticeable slide in terms of its real estate and the socio-economic standing of its inhabitants. Not totally down and out, but not a patch on what it had been. However, it was a suburb still considered more desirable than many.

It wasn't dull. There was retail activity along Parramatta Road and a timber business. New industries were set up in the area, including building, plastering and stone masonry. It was also home to those making confectionery, jam, pianos and radios. A transition was underway. After being a predominantly residential area, Annandale was turning into an industrial area. This changing suburb was the Annandale young Abe Saffron grew up in.

The Saffron tribe was made up of father, Samuel, mother, Annie, and five children. Abe was the fourth of those five children after his two older brothers Philip and Henry, and sister Beryl. The arrival of his younger sister, Flora, was a blessing for Abe. He was no longer the youngest of the pack.

In his early years Saffron didn't range too far away from that area, attending primary school in Annandale and nearby Leichhardt before attending the 'destined for better things' Fort Street High School just down the road in Petersham.

As it does to this day, Fort Street prided itself on the pursuit and delivery of academic excellence. It is an institution that has educated the likes of Australia's first prime minister, Edmund Barton, former New South Wales premier Neville Wran, the Hon. Michael Kirby, former High Court justice, and famous explorer Douglas Mawson – all deemed to be fine and successful citizens. Abe would also be one of its most successful products but it's unlikely the school's brochures would trumpet this fact or could see the prescient aptness of the school motto *Faber est suae quisque fortunae*, 'Each person is the maker of their own fortune'. There has never been – and never will be – a promotional brochure for Fort Street saying, 'Want your children to follow in the footsteps of Abe Saffron? Fort Street is the school for them.'

Abe was a quick study and from an early age he was always looking for the main chance. As each year ended and pupils from the school moved on, Abe would make an offer on their schoolbooks, give them a bit of a clean and then re-sell them (with a tidy mark-up added) to the next intake of students. It was a seemingly small venture for a youngster but one that displayed the traits of opportunism and business that would carry Abe through life. It's all about the incremental growth.

In a way, that reminds me of the late music industry entrepreneur Michael Gudinski, who started his money-making life as a young kid by selling off parking spots in the vacant lot next to his family home in Melbourne's Caulfield on racing day to punters heading to the racecourse and needing somewhere to leave their cars.

Gudinski went on to form the Mushroom Records label, which would be home to everyone from Skyhooks and Paul Kelly to Jimmy Barnes and Kylie Minogue. His empire would expand to more than 50 companies involved with music publishing, concert promotion, films and event management and Gudinski himself would become the most powerful Australian music industry figure of the past half century. He became known as the Godfather of the Australian music industry. But he definitely wasn't a godfather in the Saffron mode. They were poles apart.

While it may possibly have happened, there is no evidence that Saffron and Gudinski ever met, despite the Melbourne-based Gudinski spending an enormous amount of time around Kings Cross and its nightlife. It's a question and a conversation I wish I had had with Michael. One imagines that they would have found much to talk about if the opportunity presented itself. Both were self-made men with a diverse array of business interests, a strong sense of deal-making, a take-no-prisoners approach to business, and demanding and earning incredible loyalty from those around them.

Both were powerful figures, confident in their abilities to rule their respective domains. Both were astute observers of people and when necessary played their cards very close to their chest. Both enjoyed the thrill of the chase in many aspects of their lives, and both made ridiculously huge amounts of money.

But that is where the comparison ends. Saffron was the prime mover in the organised crime world in Australia. He also changed the nature of entertainment and the pursuit of good times in this country but the other, Gudinski, made an empire and built an industry with good-hearted humanity that shaped and soundtracked a generation of Australian youth. There were no guns or enforcers, just business acumen. He knew the lines that should not be crossed. A high road, if you will, to Saffron's low route.

School may have given Saffron business ideas, but the sitting still and learning part wasn't his thing. Despite his mother Annie's hopes that he would become Doctor Abraham Saffron, Abe left school at 15 to work full time in the family drapery business, Saffron and Sons, in Pitt Street in Sydney's CBD. It wasn't that he was a bad student – not at all. He just wanted more than what school could offer. He was on a mission and running a business and making money were his calling from a very early age.

It seems drapery wasn't his bag for long, either. In 1938, Saffron was caught doing what a lot of young men at the time did as a sideline – he was a street-level worker for an SP bookmaker.

An SP bookmaker was someone who operated illegally in Australia when gambling was banned. This gave rise to these much-mythologised characters who could be found in pubs, around racetracks, in barber shops and anywhere else someone who wanted to make an illegal bet would frequent. SP stands for 'starting price', as that's what the illegal bookmaker calculated their offered odds on. As well as being able to make bets on horse races away from the track, many people liked the personalised nature of dealing with their own bookmaker – and in some cases the thrill of being involved in something illegal and risky.

The bookies used young, innocent-looking kids, fleet of foot, who were paid to collect betting slips from pubs and other locations and deliver them back to a bookmaker. They were not unlike street runners for bigger drug dealers in later decades: kids put on street corners to conduct drug deals for the bigger fish, kids who didn't look like they were up to no good and who were fast enough to make a run for it if the police came.

Abe obviously wasn't quite as fast as he needed to be. Dragged up before a magistrate, the almost 19-year-old Saffron didn't receive a significant punishment, as he was from a good family and he'd never been in trouble before. He received a stern talking-to and a fine of £5. But Saffron was now mixing with a broader group of mercantilists – the ones who possibly weren't quite as respectable as the established shopkeepers and proprietors his parents knew, but were every bit as ambitious and keen for a life that allowed power, comfort and status.

Saffron's next sideline during the late 1930s and very early into 1940 involved receiving and on-selling car radios that had been liberated from vehicles. Usually these radios were offloaded, for a decent margin, in local pubs. But by January 1940, the game was up. The young Abe was again before the magistrate, having been caught with six radios in his possession and charged with receiving and selling stolen goods. It was a charge and potential conviction that was a little more serious than the penalty he received for being a runner for a bookmaker. When he came before the court this time, the now 20-year-old was sentenced to six months in jail. Abe still had the support of his respectable family and luckily for him, the magistrate set the prison sentence aside and he was placed on a good behaviour bond.

Having come very close to being sent to prison, he appeared to get the message that this was not something he should continue with and possibly under order or promise, he returned to the family drapery business. While his father's business offered a sanctuary, a leg-up and a safety net, it wasn't Abe's destiny.

At the beginning of the 1940s World War II was escalating and intensifying globally. Months after Prime Minister Robert Menzies announced Australia's involvement in the conflict, he also announced compulsory military training with the Citizen Military Forces (CMF) or army reserve for men turning 21. Those conscripted with the CMF could not be forced to serve beyond Australia and its territories. Although it is said that Saffron enlisted in the Australian Army on 5 August 1940, which coincided with the end of his good behaviour bond, his records and discharge papers suggest he served in the CMF, which meant his participation did not go beyond Australian shores. Records indicate that when Saffron enlisted, he asked for an exemption from service (hardly the actions of a willing volunteer), arguing that his father's business depended on his presence. The exemption was granted until January 1942 when Saffron's service with the CMF commenced.

There is speculation as to what Saffron actually did during his time with the CMF, but he seemed to be involved in some type of administrative work both at Liverpool and in the city. It is likely he learned some basic bookkeeping, organisational and operational skills. He was promoted to the rank of corporal in 1943 and officially discharged in January 1944. He'd done his mandatory service and was now able to move on and make his way in the world.

Although some sources credit Abe as being the brains behind his father's business success, possibly more context should be given to the high demand for clothes and textiles during World War II and their scarcity, rather than the nascent business smarts of a teenage boy who was impatient with school and working nine to five for a minimum wage.

By many accounts, the young Saffron was self-disciplined and focused. He saw for himself a bright and lucrative future but while the drapery business was profitable, it was far too small for him. Being the boss of a family retail business isn't a dead-end job per se, but it felt like it to young Abraham. There were only so many suits you could measure up and make for other people. Abe didn't want to be doing the measuring up. This wasn't his calling. He wanted more – lots, lots more. But more of what? He wasn't totally sure – yet. But he knew he had to move on to utilise his growing desire for money and power.

Much is made of Saffron's time in the CMF. Usually a background in military service, especially during wartime in Australia, evokes many of the positive and heroic traits of the mythical Australian male. It's an accolade that is often synonymous with altruism, enormous self-sacrifice and good character, and it can also be used as evidence of redeeming qualities: 'See, he might have made a few bad decisions, but he's still really a good bloke.' But the war effort required lots of people power, and many people served. Not all of those people carried positive or heroic traits. Some of them were thugs and thieves. Although in later life an older Saffron might have made much of his military service, the discerning person might also suggest that Abe's bit for the war effort was, at the time, not something he did with enthusiasm. It seems the most that can be said about it was he made the most of it, learned how things worked and was even promoted.

The records are scant but it seems that after Saffron was discharged from military service in January 1944, he decided to do a stint in the merchant navy. For about six months he did basic administrative work, initially on the SS *Katoomba* and later the SS *Charon*. While on the SS *Charon* Saffron met up with Hilton Granville Kincaid, a friend he'd made while working at the drapery business. American-born Kincaid was a few years older than Saffron and had operated a cigarette kiosk next to the Saffron and Sons business on Pitt Street.

The shipping of cargo and people by the merchant navy is vital to a country both in wartime and in peace. Before the widespread use of aeroplane transportation, ships and ports were crucial to supply chains and the docks were a fertile ground for roughnecks and rogues. And perhaps another place of learning for Abe. They were also an important off-ramp for goods that found their way onto the black market, and with many goods in scarce supply, the black market was thriving in wartime Australia. Indeed, the black market was considered a problem so big that it resulted in the Commonwealth government passing legislation to curb it. The *Black Marketing Act* passed in 1942 came about to deter the profiteering of selling and supplying goods and services that were in short supply because of the war effort.

A lot of alcohol was already sold like contraband in Australia before World War II. In fact, the sly grog trade until then had been extremely lucrative. A combination of the temperance movement, the 1916 legislation to close pubs at 6 pm, resulting in the infamous six o'clock swill (which lasted until 1966 in New South Wales), and the limiting of licences led to a thriving criminal trade in alcohol. And there was even a beer shortage. The most in-demand times were every day after the pubs closed at 6 pm and on Sundays, when all pubs were closed for the Sabbath. You want alcohol at these times? Easy – find a sly grog seller, some of whom operated from existing hotels, others from private premises, but all expected drinkers to pay a premium for the availability of liquor. And the drinkers paid. If you make an in-demand product difficult to find or restrict its sale then guess what – enterprising figures are going to find a way to solve the problem.

The sly grog trade didn't end with the outbreak of World War II. Shipping disruptions and delays further limited supplies. There was, however, nothing complicated about this business. It was the selling of alcohol to fulfil a demand. It was the purchase and sale of alcohol whether you had a licence or not.

Saffron's mate Kincaid was always on the lookout for an opportunity to make a little extra. His family had a background in running licensed premises, so he wasn't naive about the value of alcohol. On the SS *Charon* he'd been caught with 60 bottles of whiskey, earning him a three-month suspension from duty. What was he doing with such a large quantity of alcohol? It certainly wasn't for personal consumption. Saffron the emerging entrepreneur observed his friend on-selling alcohol for a sizeable profit. The die was cast: there's money in them there bottles of booze.

Both Saffron and Kincaid said goodbye to the merchant navy in mid-1944, making it a very short tenure for Abe. It's not hard to imagine that Kincaid's indiscretion had put him and his associates under an unwelcome spotlight, which would have limited any money-making schemes Kincaid may have been dreaming up while still in the merchant navy. What better way to reset than to get out of Sydney, return to home territory and invite your friend along?

Very soon another chance to bring in some extra cash presented itself to Abe. This time it was all above board. Well, mostly. Initially Saffron spent a short period of time as a bookmaker, a legitimate one, operating at the Newcastle Jockey Club, before, thanks to Kincaid, a new career in hospitality and hotels beckoned.

Hilton Kincaid's mother was the licensee of the Station Hotel, a pub in Kurri Kurri, near the port town of Newcastle.

After the war, she needed someone to run the hotel and asked her son. He declined – partly because he wasn't keen on the long hours and partly because his suspension from the merchant navy for the stolen whiskey meant he was deemed an unsuitable person to hold a hotelier's licence.

Kincaid had an idea – why not get his mate Abe to run the pub while he helped out in the background. A silent partner, if you will. His mum must have agreed it was a good idea and it turned out Saffron and Kincaid were good at what they did. The Station Hotel was in a thirsty area. Alcohol sales and distribution continued to be heavily regulated and policed when the war ended, so early hotel closing times saw the sale of sly grog continue to flourish. Kincaid and Saffron prospered. After a year they sold up: get in, make the money quickly and move on.

It was now time to expand. The intrepid duo found another pub in Newcastle – the three-storey Hotel Newcastle. They bought the licence and this venue also did well.

There might have been some money to be made in bookmaking, but pubs were where the big cash was – a better punt – and where Abe Saffron saw his future. In 1946, less than two years after his move to Newcastle, Saffron had enough money to take over the lease on the West End Hotel in the then working-class suburb of Balmain. But he didn't think it necessary to tell anyone, including the police and licensing bodies, that Kincaid was his business partner. In those days it was one licence per person. No one seemed to care. In fact, their main supplier of beer, Tooth and Co. brewery, provided them with finance for the set-up and never said a word. Those were the days.

Soon after acquiring the Balmain licence, Saffron transferred it to his eldest brother, Philip, and immediately took over the Gladstone Hotel, at the time a rundown, working-class pub on the corner of Palmer and William streets in Darlinghurst.

Darlinghurst today is almost unrecognisable from the gritty, often violent place it was in Saffron's era, when it was also home to a tough underclass and prostitution was the only source of income for many of the women who lived there.

Saffron was edging closer and closer to the area that would become his domain for decades to come.

CHAPTER 2

KINGS CROSS BECKONS

A decade into the 20th century and into the 1960s, Darlinghurst and East Sydney were still dominated by tiny houses, many of which were operating as brothels. Legal and illegal alcohol flowed. It was an area of sometimes brutal indifference – spawned by the effects of the poverty, tough masculinity, misogyny and alcohol and not for the faint-hearted. The area had been ruled by the likes of Tilly Devine and Kate Leigh.

Before World War II, Devine and Leigh were known as the ice queens of the area around East Sydney, just down the road from Kings Cross. They dealt in – well, you name it – illegal booze and drugs, prostitution, gambling and an occasional sideline in extortion. If there was money in it, these two women and their loyal male associates and lackeys were almost certainly at the centre of whatever was going on. How did they maintain their crime empire? Guns, of course, but they were illegal and hard to come by. Knives weren't easy to conceal, but razors, very sharp razors, were the small and effective weapons of choice. And they used them often and with great gusto to the point that nearby Darlinghurst was more commonly known as Razorhurst. *Get in their way and they will cut ya – cut ya and maim ya and might even kill ya.*

The first American servicemen had arrived in Sydney on R&R (rest and recreation) visits during the war in 1942. They wanted booze, food, sex and entertainment – and a lot of all of it. And they had lots of cash. After months and months of having nothing to spend their wages on, they were loaded and ready to spend it on anything that made their lives more exciting. After docking nearby, they flooded into Darlinghurst, Potts Point and Woolloomooloo and up the road to Kings Cross.

As Larry Writer observes in his book *Razor*, 'the 1940s saw old warhorses like [Leigh and Devine] challenged by a new generation of younger, hungrier outlaws, including Dulcie Markham's occasional lover Donald "Duck" Day, Leonard Arthur (Lenny) McPherson, Dick Reilly and old razor-man Sid Kelly'. Then came Abraham Saffron.

* * *

After the war, Abraham Saffron arrived as part of the new generation of men who would rule not only Darlinghurst but also nearby Kings Cross. For a while after Saffron and Kincaid bought the Gladstone, they lived upstairs, right in the thick of the action. Saffron was just getting started and had some experience now about how the world worked, what he could get from it and what he needed to do to keep it. Saffron was the right person at the right time. He was a shrewd operator, and his rise coincided with the arrival of the nightclub era and the postwar generation of young adults who wanted to dance.

Even after the US servicemen had departed, the area continued to be a popular destination for those with money to spend who were looking for a good time. The reputation of Kings Cross was well and truly established. In the minds of potential and frequent visitors to the area, the message was loud and clear – come walk on the wild side. Finding a sly grog seller was easy. *Hold on to your head and wallet – you're in for a memorable night.* The world was changing again, as it always does, and Saffron was in the Australian Wild West at exactly the right time.

What was Abe Saffron like? Would you recognise him if you saw him walking the streets of the Cross? He was most definitely not a big man; his discharge papers have him at five foot eight inches, while later accounts record him only standing five foot six inches. With dark complexion and hair reflecting his Russian–Jewish descent, he had eyes that writer and Kings Cross chronicler Louis Nowra described as 'reptilian'.

Saffron kept quietly adding to his pub empire, confiding only in those closest to him. The law of the day stated very clearly that ownership of multiple pubs was not on. One hotel licence per person was the way it was supposed to be played out. And Mr Saffron, an upstanding and play-by-the-rules licensee, was involved with only one hotel, Your Honour – and that establishment was the Gladstone Hotel at the corner of William and Palmer streets in Darlinghurst.

Other hotel interests? No other hotel interests, Your Honour. Wink, wink.

Apart from the Gladstone and the West End hotels, Saffron did, in fact, take an interest in other establishments, often with partners. These included the Cumberland Hotel in the Western Sydney suburb of Bankstown, the Mortdale in Southern Sydney, the Albert Hotel on the corner of Mount and Walker streets in North Sydney, the Phillip in King Street and the beautiful art deco Civic Hotel in the Sydney CBD, which in the 1970s and '80s would become one of the most important rock'n'roll venues in the city, with an upstairs room where bands like Midnight Oil, The Saints, Mental As Anything, Cold Chisel, INXS and countless others would perform.

CHAPTER 3

THE ROOSEVELT

In the aftermath of World War II, the world felt once again buoyant and there was a sense of renewal and opportunity in the air. Saffron was already making the most of every opportunity and was poised to make his latest acquisition, a real step up. He had his eyes on a classy joint with more potential than any venture he'd previously been involved in, not just a rundown pub for boozy low-lifes but a certified nightclub. We're talking the Roosevelt, situated at 32 Orwell Street, Potts Point.

The Roosevelt was opened in 1943 by businessman Bernie Roth, who'd made his money in the clothes and fashion industry. It was then taken over by Sammy Lee, a confident, flamboyant performer and entrepreneur, described as a hard Colonel Parker–type character with a real feel for the world of entertainment. Sammy figured out that the key to a successful venue of this nature was dancing girls – preferably clothed in as little as was legally permissible at the time – coupled with visiting international artists. This was where stylish people hung out – drinking, eating and rubbing shoulders with other sophisticated people. Many of them had business interests in common. Some of those businesses were legal and others were very much not.

Over the years the Roosevelt became a home away from home for officers from the American military when they were visiting Sydney. They could feel relaxed and comfortable meeting local girls there, and local girls felt comfortable there too. It was that sort of place.

Entertainment in Sydney in this era was broken down on class and rank divides. The more senior officers hung at the Roosevelt while their subordinates tended to gather at the Manzil Room at 15 Springfield Avenue, Kings Cross.

Lee ran the Roosevelt until 1946, when he sold it to a Reginald Frederic Boom. Reg was from Melbourne, he liked his horse racing and baccarat, and ran the place for a year before moving it on to a trio of likely lads – Saffron, his mate Kincaid and a Saffron family friend, Mendel Brunen. The three partners set up Orwell Enterprises Pty Ltd and away they went.

By this stage Saffron, now aged 28, was romantically involved with hairdresser Doreen Krantz. The two had fallen in love and shared passions for the big revues and musicals at the Tivoli Theatre, the popular vaudeville venue on Castlereagh Street in Sydney's CBD, and going to the movies to see the latest that Hollywood had to deliver.

Saffron and Krantz attended the Roosevelt frequently where Saffron splashed his money around. One night Krantz told Saffron how much she loved the nightclub. So what's a guy trying to impress a girl going to do? Buy it, of course.

What a great early wedding present, the keys to one of the most upmarket nightclubs in Sydney. Saffron didn't do things by half. Doreen and Abe were married on 23 November 1947. If Doreen thought Abe was a one-woman man, though, sadly she was going to find out he wasn't.

Saffron's purchase of the Roosevelt coincided with another golden era in Kings Cross. It offered high life and good times with just the right amount of edginess to meet the bright lights – bohemians lived there; cafes were everywhere. There were art galleries and bookshops and a plethora of restaurants offering a vast array of food. Shady men and colourful women lived there. People with lots of money lived there. It was a hub for the gay community, although it was still extremely clandestine back then. Artists and actors called it home. Migrants ran fruit shops. Chic houses and apartments were nestled alongside low-cost boarding houses with rooms to rent.

Kings Cross had everything. It was the centre of glamour that attracted legions of folk from the suburbs who wanted to live it up, to put some glitz in their lives. In New York the people from the outer boroughs who flooded into Manhattan at weekends were known as the 'bridge and tunnel' crowd, as that's how they made their way into the metropolis. In Sydney people drove their cars to Kings Cross, leaving the quiet, dull and unimaginative suburbs behind.

Just down the road from the Cross was the Sydney Stadium in Rushcutters Bay. There was prize-fighting on Monday nights and a spectacular and impressive line-up of visiting international artists would perform there during the rest of the week.

The Stadium was built in 1908 and was leased by boxing promoter Hugh Donald McIntosh for sporting events, particularly boxing. Initially it had been constructed as a temporary open-air stadium to host the world heavyweight boxing championship title fight on 24 August 1908 between the Canadian world heavyweight champion Tommy Burns who was pitted against the Australian champion Bill 'Boshter' Squires. The fight was won by Burns with a knockout in the 13th round.

It was also the site of the then biggest-ever sporting event held in Australia in December 1908 when over 20,000 people were crammed into the venue to see Tommy Burns fight Jack Johnson, the first African–American to compete for the world heavyweight championship. Johnson won the title. His fame was such that he later inspired an album by musician Miles Davis.

Later, extra seating and a roof were added so that the venue could hold 12,000 people and it became the principal venue at which major international music stars could perform.

Who performed at the Stadium? Who didn't, is probably a shorter list. You'll read about some of the visitors soon, but suffice to say that Little Richard, Frank Sinatra, Ella Fitzgerald, Buddy Holly, Judy Garland, Chuck Berry, and Peter, Paul and Mary all performed there – along with Australian artists such as Johnny O'Keefe and Col Joye and the Joy Boys.

The Stadium was also where the Beatles performed on their one and only tour of Australia – that's probably all you need to know about its significance as an entertainment location in Sydney. And, while we are on the Beatles, they stayed at the Sheraton Hotel in Macleay Street, which is technically Potts Point but about 17 steps away from what is most definitely Kings Cross.

The Stadium also hosted wrestling and roller derby events. It was simply the premier venue for large-scale entertainment in the city – despite the fact that it was built for boxing and wasn't exactly renowned for its sound quality for singers and rock'n'roll groups. But you could pack 'em in and that was a promoter's dream.

The most prominent promoter of shows at the Stadium was Lee Gordon; and it seemed that Gordon and Saffron were almost destined to meet. But we'll get to that.

In that era a good night out was a show at the Stadium followed by carousing in the Cross. It was a short walk, albeit up a steep hill, from the Stadium to the Cross. Ten minutes tops for a young Sydneysider on the tear and determined to find good times. Who knew what the night might bring?

The Roosevelt still operates to this day at 32 Orwell Street. Close enough to Kings Cross to not even matter, unless you worked in zoning for the council.

Saffron was obsessed by the Roosevelt. He wanted it to be the best, top-rated club not just in Sydney but on the entire planet. He hired the sort of people who could deliver that for him, including a Las Vegas talent coordinator in Ernie Barron, whose job – his mission, thank you – was to find, book and nurture the best available talent in the city. And from the Tivoli came Sheila Cruz, who was charged with whipping the chorus line of fabulous-looking women into world-class shape.

Entry to the Roosevelt wasn't obvious; it was for people in the know who knew where they were going. Upon reaching their destination, a patron's first encounter was with a doorman placed there to make sure you knew where you were going – or ensuring that the threshold wasn't crossed by any riffraff. This was a fancy establishment, thank you very much. There was a stylish potted palm tree outside reminding you that you were entering another world. An aspirational world, a world very different from the egalitarian ethos of the other Australia. In many ways, Saffron was ahead of his time, presenting an experience that he hoped no one would forget – and his fingers were on every aspect of it. More than some of those involved might have liked.

In Saffron's care, the Roosevelt flourished. The food was always fabulous, the entertainment the same. And Saffron kept pushing boundaries. He introduced topless showgirls to the entertainment. The laws of the time allowed topless women to be on the stage, but they had to remain totally still. The chorus line – with more clothing on – were permitted to dance around them, but those with exposed breasts could not move at all. Any movement and you were under arrest for obscene behaviour and the nightclub's licence to trade would be under threat.

Looking back, this seems a totally bizarre situation, but it was only just over half a century ago. Having never experienced the show, I'm left with all sorts of questions – did they walk onto the stage with their breasts covered so that patrons weren't exposed to any movement? I imagine so. Maybe under huge feathery plumes. But what in fact was deemed to be movement? Was a stifled cough and the consequential ripple causing 'movement' considered boundary pushing?

Saffron, no doubt with a smile on his face, once quipped that the police kept a very close eye on the topless dancers – just in case they moved.

Not surprisingly, the Roosevelt became a target for criminal activity, like moths to a light. There were robberies and an arson attempt. The suggestion was that other club owners in the Cross wanted to remove some important competition. At this time Saffron bought a pistol from a contact, but it wasn't licensed and Saffron was found with it and charged. No conviction was recorded. Carrying a gun in a postwar world wasn't considered such a big deal and Abe's defence in court was that it was a souvenir from the war. Right, of course it was.

Given Saffron's previous activities, it was interesting that the magistrate who heard the matter took into consideration the gun-toting Abe's apparent good character when deciding not to convict him. Was the application not to impose a more severe penalty supported by the police prosecution? Was this an example of money changing hands to make a potentially serious matter go away? How did he get caught with the gun in the first place? Was it a tip-off? Did the police orchestrate the event to put Saffron back in his place? Too much time has passed to ever really know. Racism might also have had something to do with it. He wasn't a tall, broad-shouldered, fair-skinned Australian male. He had a European look about him.

Saffron was definitely learning quickly about what was required to survive and prosper in the world that he had chosen. Despite his previous brushes with the law in his youth, he was now considered someone who had standing in the community, but he had to work hard to maintain that position.

As the years went by he would become a master of knowing how to control people who might hinder his progress, and comparatively early in his career, he started assembling knowledge about those around him, including competitors and the law. He was in a position to see who came to the Roosevelt and with whom. Often these hopefully discreet visits were not with the person that the other party would be expected to be seen with.

Later, Saffron would become much more overt with his blackmail tactics but he was already compiling mental dossiers on those who might cause him grief. The perception of Saffron in those days was still comparatively good – smart operator, cool customer, an on-the-move kinda guy but with that demeanour that said Do Not Mess With Me. And he was already operating in a cutthroat world of nightclubs, showbusiness and money. Of course, there were people who were jealous of him. Of course, there were people who'd have been happy if he wasn't around – on both the wrong and right sides of the law. Of course, many of them carried weapons. Saffron might have been selling a fantasy, but he was doing it in the real world. A real world that dealt not in dreams but in cold, hard toughness, a toughness that required a lot of smarts, money and power.

* * *

Abe and Doreen Saffron spent the early days of their marriage in the manager's quarters of the Gladstone Hotel. Either these lodgings were penthouse-like or Saffron was still not rolling in cash. Or, more likely, Saffron was pouring all of his cash into clubs, pubs and entertainment to the point where his own living situation was of secondary consideration. Let's face it, when you're an on-the-rise mover and shaker in nightclubs in Kings Cross, how much time are you spending at home?

A few months later Saffron and Kincaid – under the guise of a business named Poate Investments – bought a block of flats in the street of that name in nearby Centennial Park. Mr and Mrs Saffron and son were soon living in one apartment, Kincaid in another.

However Abe was starting to come under the spotlight – and that was not something he wanted. What followed was a series of brushes with the law. Questions were asked about the allegedly illegal sale of alcohol at the Roosevelt. It wasn't just at Saffron's place that this was happening. Other Kings Cross nightclubs such as the Kit Kat, the Rubayat and the Pirate's Cave were also selling alcohol until daybreak and the hounds were sniffing around and starting to howl. Word was also leaking out that Saffron had interests in more than one hotel.

The Royal Commission into Liquor Laws was held in 1951. Saffron, then aged 29 according to his testimony, was called before the commission, which was fronted by Justice AV Maxwell. Saffron turned up at the Supreme Court of New South Wales where he stated that his occupation was hotel keeper and company director.

A young future prime minister, Gough Whitlam, was one of those appearing for the Crown, while Saffron had Sir Garfield Barwick QC in his corner. Barwick was a formidable figure, who would go on to be a minister in the Menzies-led Liberal Party government and later one of the longest-serving Chief Justices of the High Court.

Despite all the attention, the probing, the questions and investigations, the Roosevelt kept on trading. Drinks were served, singers sang and dancers danced. Night after night.

Giving Saffron the third degree was Bill Dovey, whose daughter, Margaret, was married to the young Gough Whitlam. When asked these questions, it was not that Saffron would try to hide matters of business – of course he wouldn't – but those involved with the commission, well, they kinda had a bit of a suspicion that Saffron was behind those hotels and their licences. They just had an inkling, that funny feeling you get when you see the names of people on hotel licences and go, 'Nahhhhh, something doesn't smell right here.'

Saffron was a smart guy but he wasn't going out of his way to put people totally off the scent. Adding two and two together with the names on the hotel licences was always going to add up to four – and Saffron. Let's take a look: Saffron's sister Beryl had signed on for the Mortdale Hotel. Now, the West End over in Balmain, that looks a lot like Philip … Philip Saffron … on that one.

Slightly more disguised, just, was the licence for the Cumberland, which was under the name Eddie Kornhauser. But hang on, a quick ask around the traps would tell you that Abe and Eddie were pals.

On top of these three enterprises, there was now a fourth venture associated with Team Saffron – this joint in Potts Point called the Roosevelt. To help that place get off the ground under its new owner, Justice Maxwell, who had clearly missed his calling in the world of advertising, gave Saffron the best possible advertising blurb when he described the Roosevelt as 'the most notorious and disreputable nightclub in the city'.

The fact that Saffron wasn't stupid, nor had he ever displayed an inclination towards stand-up comedy, means that he was extremely confident and not in the business of messing around when he was questioned. He had good advice and knew what he was doing.

Asked why he hadn't told the truth Saffron stared down his inquisitor and said, without a hint of a smile, that he had told the truth – as he knew it.

It transpired that Saffron hadn't even told the truth about his age. Nope. Not at all. As reported in the *Sydney Morning Herald*, the following exchange took place in court.

Mr Dovey: 'Do you remember quite early in your examination I was asking you about your name and occupation and I asked you what was your age?'

Saffron: 'Yes.'

Mr Dovey: 'Do you remember what your answer was?'

Saffron: 'Yes, 29.'

Mr Dovey: 'Why did you say that?'

Saffron: 'I always say 29.'

Mr Dovey: 'Although it is not true?'

Saffron: 'It is the age I have been using for years.'

Commissioner: 'Is there some magic in 29? Let us into the secret.'

Saffron: 'I do not know; I just like the age.'

Mr Dovey: 'How long have you been 29?'

Saffron: 'I suppose about four, five years.'

One thing is for sure – Saffron had a sense of humour and wasn't above playing free and easy with even the most basic details. The man who in his later years could easily be labelled Teflon Saffron was in his element in front of the royal commission. They charged him with giving a false testimony, but the publican was cleared of that charge.

The downside was that Saffron and his family were officially banned from holding liquor licences, but this didn't seem to faze Saffron. It was a trifling inconvenience that would just require more behind-the-scenes manoeuvring, but heck, that's not the end of the world.

Then, on 15 January 1953, the Supreme Court of New South Wales declared that the Roosevelt was not a Kings Cross entertainment jewel but a 'disorderly house'. Abe could live with that because a lot of this had to do with the club's flouting of the liquor laws. That flouting was making him a lot of money.

Nothing really changed at the nightclub, but Saffron decided to distance himself from the venue. A new management company was put in charge and, while Saffron was a shareholder in this venture, he stated that he'd no longer be involved in a decision-making capacity.

For a brief period he headed out of town. Right out of town to Perth, where he purchased the art deco Raffles Hotel in the southern part of that city, which was said to later be a favourite hangout of AC/DC singer Bon Scott. Here Saffron was a comparative unknown. There was still good money to be made but he was on the other side of the country, seemingly a long way from the prying eyes of the New South Wales Police Force. A relocated Sydney businessman simply going about his business.

And if the west coast wasn't far enough from the heat of Kings Cross, Saffron became proprietor of a mine in Noumea. It was a short-lived venture before he moved back to what he knew best – real estate, and entertainment within that real estate.

Despite his increased business activity he still had lessons to learn about discretion and keeping control of his personal activities and profile. His loose lifestyle hit the headlines in 1956 after a bloke's weekend away at Palm Beach, on the northern beaches of Sydney, a suburb far away from the glitz and neon lights of Kings Cross. A bunch of upwardly mobile, fun-loving blokes decide to party at what was then a comparatively sleepy, out-of-the-way enclave about an hour's drive from their usual turf.

On the excursion were Saffron, Hilton Kincaid and Wayne Martin. They were meeting up with hotel booker Max Murrell, who owned a home at 367 Whale Beach Road. The trio from the Cross arrived with four girls, beer, oysters, champagne and whatever other items might come in handy for a raunchy time away.

What followed was your typical run-of-the-mill orgy. Just another night in Palm Beach. One of the female participants was a woman named Jean, who apparently looked like a mild-mannered country girl but who boasted of her activities around Kings Cross and claimed to have had 32 men in one night. Without casting aspersions on Jean's memory or ability to count, one doesn't want to think too long and hard about the circumstances surrounding such activities.

So, by comparison, if this claim was even remotely correct, the time in Palm Beach must have seemed like a quiet night in for Jean. According to eyewitness reports, Saffron encouraged the women to kiss each other, and while they did, he took photographs. This would become one of Saffron's additional skills – photographing others in sexually compromised activities. By the time he died he had amassed a significant collection of such images.

On that weekend, just to spice things up, Saffron started using a fur-covered whip he'd decided to bring along to the soiree. Just a regular night out with a few friends, some oysters, champagne and a fur-covered whip.

At the end of the Palm Beach part of the activities everyone headed back to the city. Jean and one of her pals had a rest before heading to Saffron's office at 44 Macleay Street to rendezvous with Abe's brother Henry, Wayne Martin and Abe 'The Whip' Saffron himself. More fun and games were had.

That could have been the end of it. But no. While it's unknown what the catalyst was, a few months later Jean decided to get in touch with the New South Wales Police Vice Squad and tell them in very specific detail about the Palm Beach shenanigans. Was Jean after money? Was it a shakedown? Blackmail?

No matter what sparked the report, this was something that had to be taken seriously and on 25 October 1956, the legendary Bumper Farrell, a notorious take-no-prisoners cop who ruled Kings Cross in the 1960s and '70s, and his troops from the vice squad hammered on the door of 44 Macleay Street. Even though the Roosevelt had closed by then, Abe maintained his office upstairs. The 'office' also contained a bedroom just in case Abe wanted to spend a little time with someone at least temporarily special.

At the time of the raid Abe wasn't in residence but Bumper and the other cops went through the joint very thoroughly, watched by Henry Saffron. They found a cache of interesting items. Six books that the censor had deemed unsuitable for consumption by readers in this country, including *The 120 Days of Sodom* by the Marquis de Sade. They found a carved figurine – a penis-like fertility symbol – that had been gifted to Saffron on his buck's night, a vibrator, a camera (presumably the camera used at Palm Beach) and the whip. Yes, they found the whip.

Abe arrived back during the search and when asked about the whip, he drew attention to the fur attached to it, explaining to the cops that it was a feather duster. This was going to make news. There was no way the media were going to let this one slide.

Wayne Martin subsequently earned the nickname 'Morals Martin' on account of a tabloid headline when he was arrested with Saffron after the Palm Beach orgy. That report was in the *Sydney Morning Herald* on 27 October 1956: 'Moral Case: Nine Men, Girl Charged'. About 24 at the time, Martin was described as a steward. Saffron, then 37, was described as a taxi driver. All were charged with scandalous conduct.

The vice squad rubbed their hands together at this arrest and they wanted to know more, particularly about their nemesis Saffron and his activities. They found what they were after when another woman put him in for what was stated as committing an 'unnatural act'. The act in question was sodomy, which in those less enlightened times was an offence under the *Crimes Act 1900*.

As reported in the *Herald*, 'Such was the interest in the case that a large crowd gathered outside the court and police were called to keep traffic moving along Sydney's Liverpool Street.'

Ultimately the case collapsed, though. Jean was discredited, the other women involved delivered contradictory evidence, and Bumper Farrell blew the whole thing apart in court when he claimed under oath to have been at the Palm Beach house at the time of the alleged behaviour. Bumper reckoned he was outside the house and saw an open window, which he peered through and managed to see everything going on inside. Now Bumper was not a tall man and photos of the windows in question provided by the defence showed conclusively that he could not have reached the windows, let alone been high enough to see in. Case dismissed.

It has been suggested that bribery and the intimidation of witnesses were involved to get the women to change their stories but whatever the means all the charges were dropped. The only one that stuck was for possession of obscene publications, for which Saffron was fined £10. He appealed and won.

And what about Jean and her friends? Never heard of again. While it would be easy and dramatic to think that they met an unsavoury end, the chances are that they were taken to the nearest bus or train station by the police, given a swag of cash and told to never come within a couple of hundred miles of Kings Cross or Abe Saffron again.

Abe's long-suffering wife, Doreen, had momentarily had enough of the tabloid headlines and headed to Switzerland with young Alan in tow until things quietened down. It's fair to say that Abe didn't in any way curtail his activities with his wife out of town. Maybe, as with other aspects of his life, he learned a few lessons and was a little more careful about who he bedded and where. The fate of the fur-covered whip remains unknown.

After his encounters with the law, Saffron was a bit on the nose as the 1950s ended. His name was tarnished and closely associated with the illegal sale of alcohol. At one point he applied for a licence for the Napoli restaurant in the Cross. The assessment? Saffron was a person of 'low morality'.

Saffron and Kincaid ended their business association not long after. Saffron went back to buying and selling real estate but kept a low profile, as he would continue to do. No flamboyant displays anymore. The Roosevelt in particular was an ostentatious venture that had attracted a lot of attention and not all of it good. It made Saffron a target for envious figures wanting to make their names in this world and Saffron didn't like being a target. He was about money and power. He didn't need to win Entrepreneur of the Year awards.

Saffron had become smarter and more astute regarding how to go about his business without drawing attention to himself. There was nothing in his make-up that enjoyed answering questions in front of royal commissions or going to bed wondering if he was going to be woken by loud knocks on the door accompanied by subpoenas or worse. He'd learned his lessons and from then on, he buried his business dealings in complicated company structures, ones that would become even more labyrinthine as the years went by.

CHAPTER 4

THE TIMES THEY ARE A-CHANGIN'

As the 1960s approached, Kings Cross was changing. It was the dawn of the rock'n'roll era and the youth of Sydney gravitated to clubs in suburbs around the city centre – Darlinghurst, Surry Hills and Kings Cross.

More artists moved into the area. Art critic Robert Hughes and sculptor Robert Klippel hung out at Terry Clune's gallery at 59 Macleay Street, Potts Point, which in the heady 1970s would become the Yellow House where Martin Sharp and Brett Whiteley were central figures.

Jazz was flourishing at joints like the El Rocco in Brougham Street which opened in 1955. There's no evidence to suggest that Saffron was a big fan of jazz, but there are tangential signs. In the superb history of Australian jazz in the postwar era, *Bodgie Dada & the Cult of Cool: Australian Jazz since 1945*, author John Clare (who also wrote under the name Gail Brennan) writes of the influence of Charlie

Parker and Dizzy Gillespie on the Australian jazz world via band leader Wally Norman, who was given tapes of these two musicians while he was working at Saffron's Roosevelt.

Jazz clubs in Australia, just as they were overseas, were a favourite of local underworld figures. Gill Falson, a dancer, told John Clare while he was researching his book that around the jazz scene there were, 'a lot of black-market money, gamblers, bookies and underground characters. There were many Perce Galeas and Hollywood Georges.'

Singer Norman Erskine knew who these cats were, but he didn't have a problem with them. He was very defensive when their character and interests were raised by Clare: 'Okay, Joe Taylor who owned The Celebrity and The Corinthian – so he had Thommo's two-up school! ... Sammy Lee: he was a hustler, but a kind bloke in many ways. Denis Wong, who had Chequers, was a great man, and the Wongs a great family. Abe Saffron was a fantastic man to work for. All Abe ever wanted was to have a good time.' In Clare's book Erskine went on to declare, 'But most of them – if they were gangsters, I'm a fucking gangster ... Illegal gambling. Baccarat and two-up. You tell me what harm they did. They all paid their taxes. I grew up in Australia in the greatest era the earth has ever known. There [were] no drugs. People had work in the clubs and illegal casinos. Musicians were treated like kings in the nightclubs.'

* * *

Although Saffron was keeping a low profile, his wealth and power grew as he expanded his restaurant and hotel businesses, taking profits from these to buy more real estate and new ventures involving what could loosely be called entertainment. He had bought a three-storey building in Orwell Street right near the Roosevelt in 1959, where he opened Australia's first strip club, the Staccato Club. It would be followed not long afterwards in striptease lore by the more infamous Pink Pussycat.

The front guys for the Staccato Club included close Saffron associate the legendary 'Sir' Wayne Martin.

Martin was a face of the club because Saffron trusted him. A man like Saffron, labelled a man with apparent low morals, couldn't be seen to be fronting such a venture, and he was happy to be in the background. The money was the same whether you collected it at the front door or the back. Low visibility was where it was at. Saffron was confident that his two anointed public faces of Saffron Incorporated could be trusted to not skim on the takings and not make moves to undermine him and take over.

Like the Roosevelt, the Staccato Club was stylish, as stylish as a strip club could be. Certainly classy enough that a young Alan Saffron had birthday parties there. The strippers were given the day off and the kids' entertainment was provided by the likes of nightclub singer Sammy Gaha and other musicians and singers who were part of Abe's world.

While Saffron's main eye was for the dancers at his club much to Doreen's dismay, he had a good ear for singers, too, and the young Gaha's voice caught his attention. He quickly became a favourite, to the point where Saffron gave him a leg-up whenever he possibly could. Sammy would become part of Team Saffron.

While not overtly involved with Gaha's career, Saffron being his fan would have been a positive for an aspiring showbiz artist. Whenever Saffron took a shine to an artist, he did what anyone in his position would and gave them as many breaks and opportunities as he could. In return he expected loyalty. Being cast asunder from Team Saffron was not something that any aspiring artist wanted to experience – down on the end of lonely street was exactly where those ungrateful artists would find themselves in this highly competitive nightclub world.

Not surprisingly, the Staccato Club was a winner. Women taking off most of their clothes onstage in Australia in 1960. Which bit of licence to print money was confusing here?

'My father was again right in his element, surrounded by beautiful women,' wrote Alan of family man Abe in his 2009 book *Gentle Satan*.

'Shortly after, he opened the Pink Pussycat and began a period which would lead to his absolute control of Kings Cross. In the sixties, no one dared open any form of entertainment, nightclub or bar without his permission. The Cross was deemed my father's territory by the police and licensing authorities, and they made it extremely hard to open a strip club, bar or nightclub without going through him first. The rare club licences granted to others required a consideration paid to my father.'

That's the best summation of Saffron's role in Kings Cross during this era – and while there may not have been too many 'considerations' required you can bet they were large and paid regularly.

Saffron built a team around him – and loyalty was key. He trusted Martin, who along with another close associate, would continue their business links with Saffron when he had them run the Pink Pussycat club.

Martin was born in New Zealand and was orphaned at the age of three when both his parents were killed in a car accident. He was raised in an orphanage until he was 16, after which he went to the docks and with the help of a merchant seaman, he stowed away on a ship that delivered him to Woolloomooloo in Sydney, which became a central part of his turf.

For the first seven years of his time in Australia, Martin worked at sea, with Sydney as his base. He left the merchant navy in 1956 and started working for Lee Gordon, where his principal activity was chauffeuring big-name stars around Sydney. During this period Martin also befriended the young Billy Thorpe, a kid hanging around and playing in Kings Cross. The two remained friends for the rest of Thorpe's life.

While at sea Martin had got to know the infamous American mobster Benjamin 'Bugsy' Siegel, giving the young man an entrée into the club scene on the Las Vegas Strip. The infamous Siegel had a well-deserved reputation as one of the most feared gangsters of the era and was a significant figure in the development of the Strip.

Upon his return to Australia, Martin was all fired up with ideas gained from seeing what was happening overseas. He went to see Abe Saffron, as you did, who was then the proprietor of the Roosevelt among his other hotel venues.

Martin and his associate had the idea to open a strip club. Abe could see the benefit in having them around, so they fronted the Staccato before Abe backed the Pink Pussycat which opened not long after the Staccato. Money for the Pink Pussycat venture was coming from the purse of Abe. Then over the next couple of decades he continued to add to his strip club empire.

Alan Saffron viewed this business activity as an example of his father's 'poor judgement in character'. Establishments opened included the Pink Panther, the Bastille, which was an all-night bar he opened with Peter Farrugia. Farrugia was another notorious figure around the Cross who, having tried and failed to gain a strip club licence, partnered with Wayne Martin, who then hooked him up with Abe Saffron. The Pink Panther was the result.

While Farrugia was known for owning a gun, violence against women and drugs in his clubs, the Pink Pussycat was Martin's baby and had a different decorum. In an interview with *Time Out Sydney* in 2007, Martin said: '[My associate] and I would open up the Pussycat at 7pm and look in on the girls in the first show. Then we'd stroll down Darlo Road and the shop owners would load us with champers and ham and oysters for the girls in return for a few palmed tickets.'

Martin was involved with the Pink Pussycat for twelve years and an estimated 39,000 shows.

CHAPTER 5

SAFFRON, SINATRA AND LEE GORDON

In the 1950s, as aeroplanes replaced ships as the more common mode of international transport, it became easier and faster to transport international performing artists to and from Australia. Saffron embraced this at the time because he believed where stars performed, crowds turned up and the money followed.

It would take a little while before Saffron would realise how precarious the life of a fledgling promoter could be. Working with Australian singers and strippers was one thing but importing and paying for international talent was another. Like so many would-be promoters, Saffron swallowed the proverbial bait big time. Find some form of entertainment that was drawing big crowds overseas, stick them on a plane (no waiting for months for a boat to arrive), organise a bunch of shows, take the money and send the performers back home. How hard could it be? While it never appeared on posters or in advertising, the era of Saffron Incorporated Presents began.

For someone like Abe, the worst thing that can happen is when your initial ventures are super successful. You suddenly start thinking you're a genius. Infallible. You're wondering why everyone isn't in on this caper. You might be – like Saffron still needed to be – low key about your involvement as there was a lot of red tape to be sorted out and people of so-called low standing received more scrutiny than others, but Saffron managed to sort out people to do what needed to be done, and he started with a big win.

First up in the move to Saffron Incorporated Presents was the September 1955 tour with the Canadian Hell Drivers, precision drivers who performed all sorts of stunts in their vehicles. They were a big hit and drew incredible crowds to the Sydney Showground (now the Entertainment Quarter, Moore Park). Saffron made sure it was filmed for later screening for those people who couldn't make it to the venue.

Again, this was far ahead of the existing game. Television was on the horizon, and Saffron was a very early content provider. This was cutting-edge entrepreneurism and a very smart move, not to mention suitably lucrative. You can bet the television station wasn't getting this sort of action for free.

Already well acquainted with the concept of why pay when you can get someone else to, Saffron had pulled in a sponsorship deal with Ford and the Goodyear tyre company. Their financial input took care of the majority of the costs – and hell yeah, Ford threw in a half a dozen cars to be used in the shows and Goodyear of course supplied the tyres.

And then after the Sydney extravaganza, Saffron and the drivers went on a broader tour. They did shows up and down the east coast of Australia and also ventured to Broken Hill. Saffron wasn't the greatest driver but he loved cars and the thrills and spills involved. Like an old-school impresario, he was on the road with the talent. Of course there was a financial imperative to his travels. He collected the cash after each event.

It was around this time that Lee Gordon entered Abe Saffron's world. Gordon became a regular at the Roosevelt and struck up a friendship with Saffron, one that endured until Gordon's death in 1963.

* * *

Born in America, Lee Gordon arrived in Sydney in 1953 after a chance meeting with an unknown Australian used-car salesman in a second-hand car yard in Toronto, Canada. A mysterious figure, 'Lee Gordon' wasn't his real name. He was born Leon Lazar Gevorshner in March 1923. Or was it 1917? Like Abe, he could be tricky with his age.

Gordon had been involved in a wide variety of potential money-making ventures – exporting Cuban roses and Havana cigars to New York were a couple of them. There had been an early showbiz venture involving a jazz concert at an ice rink in Muskegon, Michigan.

He may have booked acts for the Tropicana, Havana's legendary open-air, Mafia-run nightclub. There was talk that he'd been involved in a travelling circus in Peru. Then he became an electrical goods salesman using all sorts of gimmicks to lure customers, some of which brought him to the attention of the US Electrical Retailers Association, who lodged an appeal with the US Senate which was upheld.

Gordon headed north with a view to promoting shows in Canada where he met the Australian car salesman, who filled him in on this land of opportunity called Australia. Discovering that very few of the major American entertainers had made their way to this country, Gordon decided to check it out for possibilities. Soon afterwards, he boarded flight PA 182 in Los Angeles for a flight to Sydney via Honolulu, Nadi and Auckland.

From the moment he arrived in Australia, Gordon honed his already well-developed skills as a great con artist. He funded his early excursions into concert tours with the proceeds from scams he ran at Sydney's Royal Art Furnishing shop in Castlereagh Street. It was owned by businessman Ralph Rosenblum and his family. Gordon negotiated to take over and run the ground-floor showroom in exchange for a percentage of the business's existing turnover.

Gordon's ways of increasing trade were many and varied. For instance, he would ring housewives and offer them a cheque if they could answer a simple question, like: 'What colour is a red door?'

It was one of those competitions where everyone was a winner. But of course, there was a catch. The cheques were in fact discounts that were only redeemable at – guess where? Gordon's furniture shop.

After making a lot of money from that furniture scheme, Gordon hired an accountant and decided to bring Ella Fitzgerald, Artie Shaw, Buddy Rich and Jerry Colonna to Australia, where he booked them into the Sydney Stadium in Rushcutters Bay. The tour was announced on 16 July 1954 – with the first dates at the Stadium commencing on the 23rd – of that month. No waiting, no delay. Lee Gordon was at the helm.

And yes, you read that right – there were only seven days between tickets going on sale at the first concert of a tour that would also take in performances in Melbourne and Brisbane. Gordon had gone from flogging furniture straight to international concert promoting in one fell swoop. No thinking. No pontificating. Just do it. Gordon was that kinda guy. He loved the devil-may-care nature of promoting, selling and hustling, well, just about anything – cigars and roses, anyone? And he had the financial resources as the furniture caper was doing so well that he was staring down the barrel of some serious taxation issues.

Then there was the guy in the used car lot who'd told him that Australians didn't get the opportunity to see many international entertainers – and had made the point that while a few came from the UK, hardly any Americans visited.

Even though Shaw, Fitzgerald et al weren't exactly raucous noise merchants, the Stadium quickly became the mecca for this new-fangled thing called rock'n'roll. Gordon bankrolled his first forays into the promotion of live music shows at exactly the right time. Rock'n'roll was really taking off with the kids. And the kids had money. Gordon didn't care if the money came from the kids themselves or their parents, he just wanted it.

If the Stadium was going to be the centre of the teen entertainment universe in Sydney, then Gordon was to be its self-styled messiah. He was a cool cat, and he was neat'n'tidy, intensely caring about his appearance.

While not a tall man, he had a presence. If there was a new fashion trend then he was an early embracer. He was a guy who exuded being totally in the moment, living life to the full. Those who knew him unanimously described him as a man who loved life and embraced everything that was on offer. Others probably had additional descriptions – crazy, overenthusiastic, hustler, impetuous, flamboyant and completely unpredictable. He was also a heavy gambler, and it would later be surmised he only felt comfortable when he was hovering on the brink of financial ruin.

Gordon billed his events as Big Shows, and things started off really well. There was no competition, so he quickly became the pre-eminent concert promoter of his time. He toured a lot of artists both by the standards of his time and today. He was popular with travel agents as he frantically scheduled, rescheduled, promoted and publicised visits by almost 500 artists.

Pretty much every major American star of the era came to Australia thanks to Gordon. Who are we talking about? Frank Sinatra, of course, but also rocking artists like Eddie Cochran, Duane Eddy, Jerry Lee Lewis, Del Shannon, Johnny Burnette, Ricky Nelson and Gene Vincent.

There were the smoother pop stars of the era such as the Bobbies – Vee and Rydell – and the greats of jazz, Nat King Cole, Louis Armstrong, Ella Fitzgerald. Then there was Bill Haley, the Everly Brothers, Harry Belafonte and legions of others. What sort of genre did Gordon personally like? That's easy. His favourite genre was … money.

In this era Lee Gordon was *the* guy. He toured all these artists between 1956 and 1962. This was the era of multi-bill tours where up to five or six of these artists would appear on the same night, usually with a token Australian artist opening the proceedings. Everyone played short sets.

One musician around at the time has recalled that Gordon once had twelve different American artists touring in Australia in various combinations at the one time. Initially Gordon made an absolute fortune but then lost almost all of it after a number of disastrous tours. The last straw was his fevered idea to bring roller derby to Australia. After that he still had the seat of his pants – just.

It's the life of the promoter – you're on a roll, feel invincible and then a couple of tours don't work, often through no fault of the promoter, and you're back at square one, or worse. It's gambling and everyone knows how that usually ends up.

Gordon was still in business, but only by the skin of his teeth. And there was always another idea. Of course there was. What could he do next? What artists could he bring to Australia? During that rough patch in 1957 the Gordon lightbulb went on. He headed back to America with a plan – to get Colonel Tom Parker to agree to Elvis Presley doing a tour of Australia. It obviously didn't wash with Team Presley as the King never toured Australia. Nice try, Lee.

If you can't get the King, go back to the Chairman of the Board – that Sinatra guy.

So Gordon turned his 1957 around. No Elvis, but a Sinatra tour, his second, was put in place. Then came a problem. The notoriously grumpy Sinatra threw a tantrum and told anyone within earshot that he was not – no sirree – getting on the plane in Honolulu for the leg to Australia. Why? *Goddamn it, Lee, there's not the sleeping booths for my guys on this plane that you promised. Screw you and your tour.*

When Frank was grumpy, he was very grumpy and there was no changing his mind. The tour had to be aborted; Gordon lost another £100,000.

However, Sinatra offered Gordon some compensation, the chance to promote a swag of Sinatra appearances in the US. After that, Gordon headed back to Australia, launching his own record label Leedon (a combination of his own names) in 1958. He began managing Johnny O'Keefe. Gordon even did a stint as a recording artist, most notably on the faux beatnik tune 'She's the Ginchiest'.

Gordon was known for his strange – some may say inspired – business tactics. One ruse in particular was a simple one, especially for someone who loved gambling, Las Vegas and stardom. Gordon mooched around Vegas casinos, watching for big-name celebrities to come in to settle down for a night of blackjack, poker or roulette. Hanging nearby, he'd be on the lookout for any star doing their dough – dropping all the money they'd made from recent performances and tours. He'd spot one.

There's Sammy Davis Jr., looks like he's had a really bad night at the table. 'Poor Sammy,' thinks Gordon, who wanders over to the hapless singer to offer salvation. 'Sammy, baby, let's make it all better, I'm your saviour, I reckon a quick trip to Australia's the way to go. You in, Sammy?' Gordon's modus operandi seemed to work. Not just once, but frequently. Financial problem solver Lee Gordon strikes again.

He would zip back to Australia, head to his office in Rushcutters Bay, a brief stroll away from his venue of choice, the Stadium, and get to work organising the latest Lee Gordon Presents tour.

His activities weren't just with touring overseas artists. He loved that, but he loved money most of all, so he'd go wherever there was a potential earn – which in his case often turned into a loss. For all the initial business brilliance there was also a recklessness that was self-destructive.

Attracted to the fast-paced glitter and glitz, there were Lee Gordon–owned nightclubs and cabaret venues in and around Kings Cross. And like most entrepreneurs of the era, Gordon swung a bit free and easy with what was and wasn't allowable. The police kept an eye on him as they did everyone else but nothing serious happened. He'd been given sage advice on how to keep the forces of law calm, contained and frequently suffering from sight and hearing problems when it came to him flaunting the law.

Some would call Gordon an entertainment visionary. He was certainly an opportunist with an eye to giving the people what they very clearly wanted which as far as he was concerned, like Saffron, was attractive women with as few clothes on as was legally permissible. To that end, Gordon opened the Primitif in Bayswater Road in Kings Cross. What was it? A strip club. Then came the Birdcage, which was a nightclub featuring women dancing in … you guessed it, not much at all.

Some have suggested that the Birdcage marked the first business collaboration between Saffron and Gordon, which would soon become more intertwined. The idea was pretty simple, and typical of Saffron. Look at a piece of real estate and imagine what you could do with it to make money. Here we had a building that had housed a cinema. Nothing wrong with that, but there was clearly more money in catering to the burgeoning youth culture who wanted to dance, watch music and have a good time – and hey, throw in a few dancers in cages, which was in vogue at the time. This idea they almost certainly pinched from discotheques in America.

The Birdcage was an immediate success and continued for years as such albeit under another name and operator. After Lee headed back to America the enterprising John Harrigan took it over, splashed a bit of paint around and did some other renovations and opened it under the name Surf City. There is no suggestion that Harrigan was at any time aware of or involved in any illegal activity or organised or drug-related crime. He just knew how to entertain well.

It was the right venue at exactly the right time. Surf City became one of *the* most influential and popular venues of the era in Sydney, riding the wave of the pop music Beatles-inspired Beat boom in the first half of the 1960s. It became very much associated with the early days of Billy Thorpe & The Aztecs.

Once they started rolling there was no stopping the entertainment juggernaut of Gordon and Saffron. Team Make Money also opened the first drag club in Australia. They named it the Jewel Box Revue Club and the Darlinghurst nightspot was responsible for launching the stellar career of the now iconic drag queen Carlotta. Later, under the management of Sammy Lee, it would be renamed Les Girls, which sounds a lot better than the Jewel Box Revue Club.

What hadn't our intrepid duo of Saffron and Gordon investigated as a money-making activity? Ah ha – well, food! Why not? Who knows which of the pair suggested it, but my gut tells me it was Lee who had the idea and Abe put up the money. Everything they touched made money, so a restaurant caper seemed worth the gamble, and before you could say *bon appétit*, they opened Sydney's first American-style drive-in fast-food restaurant, the Big Boy hamburger bar on Parramatta Road in the inner west. Unfortunately, this was one caper that didn't take off.

In 1959 Gordon also opened Lee's, an upmarket adult cabaret venue in Woollahra that featured exotic entertainers such as Parisian transgender performer Coccinelle, who modelled herself on the blonde bombshells of the day such as Marilyn Monroe and Brigitte Bardot. Gordon reportedly developed a fixation with the beauty, but Lee's was another short-lived venture.

The Primitif followed closely behind Saffron's two similar ventures, the Roosevelt with its 'don't move your breasts or you'll be arrested' topless showgirls and the Staccato with more overt strippers, both set up in 1959.

The idea for the Primitif was suggested to Lee by his close associate Alan Heffernan in September 1960. In a slight snubbing of Saffron's other ventures, Heffernan figured that what would set his and Gordon's venture apart from the Roosevelt and the Staccato was that theirs would be 'high class'. Gordon was initially reluctant to pursue this venture. As far as he was concerned, in the States strip tease was already passe so why get involved here.

Gordon obviously thought about this for another 57 seconds and decided, 'Why not, bring it on, baby!' The next morning, he was on the phone to a contact in Detroit to book three top-class strippers and get them to Sydney as fast as possible.

Heffernan leased the premises and three weeks later the doors opened. Gordon and Heffernan figured that there was a strong chance the police would show up. To circumvent what might occur, Gordon had Heffernan read a speech from the stage prior to each night's performance informing the patrons that they were about to witness an art performance which they should not consider pornographic in any way.

That was all well and good but then a family who lived next door to the Primitif started complaining about the noise and succeeded in gaining an injunction. Initially Gordon paid them off with several thousand pounds and the tenants agreed to the injunction being lifted. It wasn't long before the family had their hands out for more cashola but this time Gordon had had enough and said no. After just six months he closed the Primitif.

It was Gordon's first venture into the nightclub world, which he'd been itching to immerse himself in since he first observed the Roosevelt. He'd talked often with Heffernan about opening a nightclub and had scouted for locations.

Heffernan reminded Gordon that running nightclubs wasn't all beer and skittles. The hours were long, the competition fierce, the hiring and managing of staff time-consuming – and the failure rate was high.

The list of Sydney nightclub casualties was long. The Ginger Bar, the Palms, the Colony Club, Ziegfeld's, Joe

Taylor's Celebrity Club and others had all gone out of business. There were success stories of course, but there were fewer of these. There was Denis Wong at Chequers, Sammy Lee and Reg Boom running the Latin Quarter nightclub, and Jim Callaghan trying to stay afloat with Andre's.

Heffernan also pointed out that Gordon trying his luck interstate was almost certainly a recipe for disaster. The other capital cities just couldn't sustain stand-alone nightclubs like Chequers and the Latin Quarter at the time.

The majority of nightlife venues were housed in major hotels such as the Savoy Plaza in Spencer Street in central Melbourne and the Chevron at beachside St Kilda. In Brisbane there was the Lands Office Hotel, but that wasn't in the same league as the Sydney counterparts.

By this stage Gordon was knee-deep in partnership with Abe Saffron. Of course he was. How did Gordon get so heavily involved with Saffron? How did the power dynamic in the relationship shift so dramatically in Saffron's favour? A few joint ventures were one thing, but such financial dependence was another matter. That's an easy one to explain. It happened the same way it did for many other people who found themselves in Saffron's orbit. If you needed money, call Abe.

The relationship between Gordon and Saffron had really cemented big time in October 1960 when Gordon had promoted a jazz festival which had been a financial disaster. He'd billed it as the 1st Annual Australian International Jazz Festival with the intention that it would become the Antipodean version of the famous Newport Jazz Festival in America. In theory it was a good idea. Sarah Vaughan,

Dizzy Gillespie and a number of other international artists were booked to appear.

Once again, Gordon was both ambitious and ahead of his time. Attendances at shows in Sydney, Melbourne, Brisbane and Adelaide were poorly attended. Very poorly attended. Gordon claimed he lost £70,000 whereas his financial guy Alan Heffernan put the figure at £200,000. Whatever the precise figure, Gordon was in big financial trouble. This was a big hole he couldn't dig himself out of alone.

Need cash to bail yourself out from potential crippling debt, don't call Saul. No, call Abe. Saffron could solve problems involving Gordon's finances, but there were other aspects of his behaviour that were out of Abe's control, chiefly Gordon's obsessive smoking of marijuana, which he was not about to give up.

As Damian Kringas points out in his excellent book on Lenny Bruce's 1962 tour of Australia, *Lenny Bruce: 13 Days in Sydney*, Saffron was the guy who offered cash to those who needed it when more traditional options weren't available.

By that time Saffron was already strongly rumoured to have underworld connections, but he also stayed in business via more traditional methods. According to Kringas, Saffron had a 'good relationship' with his Kings Cross bank manager. Saffron would borrow money from the bank and then re-loan it at double the interest rate to those who didn't have the same relationships with their own bank manager.

Via this method, Saffron was an investor in a lot of businesses whose owners may not be inclined to call the cops if things weren't going well. And if Saffron's loans weren't repaid in a timely and appropriate fashion, he would take over the business.

There would be an initial option to pay whatever premium percentage had been added to the loan, and maybe a couple of warnings, but after that things could and frequently did get a little more serious. The television series *The Sopranos* was based on reality and these ways of doing business were very real in Kings Cross in this era.

Simple really. If someone couldn't pay their bills, the way to avoid anything more unpleasant happening – and trust me, Abe no doubt would say, something more unpleasant could easily happen – was for the individual who owed money to get out of the way and let a real professional take over the running of the enterprise. Did Abe owe money to other people? No, he did not. That's because he knew how to run a business. So on your way now and we'll forget the matter.

Saffron and Gordon complemented each other perfectly. Saffron was reclusive and reserved but tough as nails and a highly organised businessman. Gordon was loud, flamboyant, erratic and completely hopeless with money.

The two had first worked together on the 1959 Frank Sinatra tour of Australia. Gordon had first brought Sinatra to Australia in 1955 under his own financial steam before Frank canned the second trip and cost Lee money, as mentioned earlier. But four years later while Sinatra's price had risen significantly, he was open to touring again. This time Gordon was looking for some financial insurance, as he was in one of his many downward financial spirals. Saffron was rolling in dough at the time and up for anything that presented as an opportunity for him to make more cash.

Gordon and Saffron headed to Mascot, hopped on a plane together and headed for Las Vegas where Sinatra was doing a residency at the Sands.

At this stage, Sinatra was the king of the known and unknown universe. Everything operated on Frank time. Gordon and Saffron followed him around like lost dogs, waiting for the Chairman of the Board to find the time (and the inclination) for an audience with them.

When the meeting did happen Gordon explained his current financial predicament to Sinatra, who wasn't impressed. 'You're a fucking idiot. You make money and then you lose it,' is how Duncan McNab describes the encounter in his excellent Saffron biography, *The Usual Suspect*.

Sinatra looked at Gordon and said, 'But I might just do you a favour.'

Saffron spoke up and asked Sinatra about a contract for the mooted but now highly probable tour of Australia. Sinatra looked at Saffron in a way that Saffron was not used to being looked at – like he was a dead mouse dragged through the door by a stray cat.

'No fucking contract,' said Sinatra.

This was not the way Saffron was used to doing business, but this was Frank fucking Sinatra and what he said was what happened. The 1959 Frank Sinatra tour of Australia – promoted by Lee Gordon and Abe Saffron (but with just 'Lee Gordon Presents' on all the advertising) – was sealed with a handshake. Nothing more. Sinatra's word was solid.

For his end of the deal Saffron ponied up money for Sinatra to bring his entourage, which included someone to prepare his meals and a number of assistants who, as McNab puts it, came with 'snappy suits, sharp features, bad attitudes and masticated vowels'.

Saffron also suggested that Sinatra perform some shows in Melbourne as well as Sydney. However, Sinatra's former wife, Ava Gardner, was in Melbourne at the time filming *On the Beach*. Sinatra wasn't taken with the idea. He looked Saffron in the eye and made his position clear.

'No fucking way I'll be in the same city as her.'

Sinatra obviously gave way – or Gardner was out of town for a few days – as he played two shows at the West Melbourne Stadium on 31 March and 1 April, followed by three shows at the Sydney Stadium on 2, 3 and 4 April before heading home. Short and sweet. In and out of Australia in a week.

The two Melbourne shows were recorded and released as an album, with the majority of the performances being from the second show, and some from the first. *Frank Sinatra with The Red Norvo Quintet: Live in Australia, 1959* was finally released by Blue Note Records in 1997.

In those days there was barely any need to advertise big tours – the announcement itself was headline news in all the media so you received blanket national advertising for free. This was a time well before ticket agencies and credit cards. Ticket sales were predominantly in cash and at the actual venue. Easy to manipulate. Easy to under-report. Easy to launder.

On this tour Sinatra and his significant entourage stayed at the Chevron in Kings Cross, selling out three shows at the 10,000-capacity Stadium, and selling out the two shows in Melbourne.

Wayne Martin, Saffron's man from the Pink Pussycat, drove Sinatra on all of his 1950s and early 1960s tours of Australia. During the second tour, Martin received his 'knighthood' and became known around the traps as Sir Wayne Martin. The story goes that Sinatra asked Martin if he was interested in such a title; Sinatra was serious. As reported in the *Sydney Morning Herald*, he allegedly said to Martin: 'I'm buying a couple for some jokers here in the States and can bump up their price to buy another one for you if you want one.'

Martin thought this sounded like a mighty fine idea and soon afterwards he received everything – a diplomatic passport, medals and letterheads. How did Sinatra manage this? As is well known – it was Sinatra's world, we mere mortals just lived in it.

Martin (or should we say Sir Wayne) lived in the eastern suburbs of Sydney, in upmarket Paddington where his terrace became a well-known party spot notorious for hosting visiting stars, strippers and underworld figures.

As Martin told *Time Out*: 'One night I bring Frank [Sinatra] the mail that Ray Charles has just been pinched for drugs in America. Frank was just outta the shower with a towel around him and he sits down on the lounge and leans back. Well, my jaw dropped. His valet says: "Now you know why they call him the King."'

According to Alan Saffron, Abe Saffron was concerned about Sinatra's excessive spending and the huge phone bills he was running up so he went to see Sinatra – who Abe described as 'the man' – hoping to negotiate a better share of the concert gross sales to offset some of the expenses.

As Alan writes: 'This was one of the very few times where my father was laughed at and told to get lost, in a few choice words to the effect of "Fuck you, Abie baby". Dad was startled as he never used profanity and only my mother ever called him "Abie".'

The tour was a success. Of course it was. It was Frank Sinatra. In 1959. In Australia. It made Gordon and Saffron a crazy amount of cash. And for just five shows in one week. In his book *Big Shows: The Lee Gordon Years*, Alan Heffernan told an illuminating story about the relationship between Saffron and Gordon. On the final night of the Sinatra tour, Gordon approached Heffernan (who was in charge of Gordon's accounting and general manager of his promotions company) to meet with Saffron. This was a surprise to Heffernan as their discussions were rarely so formally organised.

Gordon produced a copy of the contract between Heffernan and their company Big Shows Pty Ltd, and it became immediately clear to the accountant that Gordon had changes, big changes, in mind. Heffernan recounts in detail in his book the way the meeting went down. Gordon said: 'As you are aware Alan, our company owes Abe 30,000 pounds. The profits from the Sinatra performances has placed finances in a position to repay immediately Abe's account together with 2000 pounds being interest for one month. You have the cheque book handy there Al, and I would like you to pay Abe 32,000 pounds to bring him up to date.'

Gordon wasn't finished. He looked at Heffernan and told him that he wanted him to resign as general manager and sell his interest in the company to Saffron. This was not the first time the two had clashed and Heffernan had handed in his resignation on a number of occasions. More often than not, the two calmed down after a day or two and it was back to business as usual. But this was different. Gordon was not in great mental shape and prior to this tour had spent time convalescing in both Beverly Hills and Hollywood.

According to Heffernan, he realised that Gordon would be better off with Saffron as a formal partner and agreed to a proposal whereby he would receive the television rights to a Sinatra performance that had been filmed by Channel 9. This was a figure of £3000. Saffron agreed to pay an additional £3000 directly from his own funds and that was made available to Heffernan via his George Street bank the following Monday morning.

In exchange for this remuneration Heffernan would enter into a new agreement with Gordon and Saffron whereby he agreed to assist the two partners in any and all future promotions for a fee that would be no less than £3000 per venture. In other words, he had been reduced to operating on a fee-per-tour basis and had no financial interest in the profits (or otherwise) of Gordon's and Saffron's enterprises together.

There was no time to dillydally. Gordon and Saffron were well advanced in planning for a Chubby Checker tour and wanted the new agreement in place before that began. The twist was the dance craze of the moment and the tour promised to be suitably lucrative.

Gordon was undoubtedly pleased with his new business partnership and a week later organised for Saffron to be delivered a brand-new (of course) white Ford Galaxy, which was sent direct from the showroom and came bearing the number plate ABE 1.

According to Heffernan, 'Lee admired Abe's deliberate style of expansion, which was the complete opposite to his own attitude of not wanting ownership of even a typewriter … he was always ready to fold his tent and disappear into the desert. Lee always needed freedom.'

Word is that every night after the show, Sinatra's entourage – Gordon, Saffron and whoever else Sinatra had in tow – would head to the Chelsea restaurant in Macleay Street, which was near the Roosevelt.

Duncan McNab quotes Christine Knight, one of Gordon's many girlfriends, saying Sinatra behaved very badly. At one point she became disgusted at his manners and put her cigarette out in what was left of the Chairman's meal. The table gasped. Sinatra stared at her.

'No broad has ever done anything like that and got away with it,' he said to Knight, who spent the next few days looking over her shoulder. Between Saffron, Gordon and Sinatra – well, they knew people.

Knight would later name her dogs after members of the Hollywood Rat Pack: Sinatra, Dean Martin and Sammy Davis Jr. Perhaps now she could continually order Sinatra around.

* * *

By this stage Saffron was bitten by the promoting bug. This tends to happen to people if they have big wins with their early ventures. In the wake of their clean-up on the Sinatra tour, Saffron and Gordon formed Perrin Productions Pty Ltd for their concert-promoting ventures.

The way they conducted their business was pretty straightforward. Saffron provided the financial backing and controlled the accounts and Gordon booked the artists and supervised the tours.

In the opinion of Alan Saffron, concert promotion held great appeal for his father as it bolstered his ego and enabled him to associate with big-name celebrities. Together Gordon and Saffron brought more than 100 international artists to Australia.

As Alan recalls: 'I have great memories of many of the tours. In my teens I went with a few friends to see Sammy Davis Jr. on my birthday, and to my surprise Lee had arranged for Sammy to sing "Happy Birthday" to me, bringing me onto the stage in front of 10,000 people … By the time I was nineteen I was helping out in all areas of concert promotion, and I was assigned to Bobby Rydell for a "Legends of Rock and Roll" tour with Dion and Chubby Checker. I got dance instructions on how to do "the Twist" from Chubby Checker himself …'

For Gordon, his connection with Saffron brought him into contact with what could be considered as the elite of Sydney's more colourful patrons. It was good for his business.

Whether Saffron provided anything other than a financial contribution to Gordon's tours is uncertain. It's hard to imagine Saffron wandering into a meeting with Gordon and going, 'Lee, baby, I can't stop listening to Eddie Cochran – we oughta bring him out.'

But it might have happened.

* * *

By the early 1960s, as well as his marijuana obsession, Gordon had developed a significant drinking habit. Towards the end of his life, only a short time later, he would admit that he was an alcoholic. He was also no stranger to all manner of drugs. To add to the mix, Gordon was travelling between Australia and the States on a very regular basis. Here-today, gone-tomorrow Gordon.

As Alan Saffron outlined in his memoir, Gordon's gambling and partying lifestyle meant he never saved any money and would regularly front up to Abe to borrow more. 'Dad had no objection and charged no interest to his partner, and Lee paid back the debt on the following tour every time.'

In 1961, Gordon announced his engagement to an American stripper who called herself Lee Sharron. Nothing too unusual about that until you dug a little deeper and discovered that Gordon had already married and divorced her twice previously in the United States. Third time lucky?

It wasn't to be. Lee and Lee never made it to the altar for the trifecta. Why? Gordon had always exhibited signs and behaviour that suggested that all was not always correctly wired in his psyche and in this instance that manifested in a significant episode that necessitated him spending an extended period in a psychiatric hospital in New York.

Gordon may have been mentally unwell, and increasingly so, but he wasn't a quitter. Not in the slightest. He was 'one more time' Gordon who never entertained the notion that he wouldn't return to the heights of favour and fortune that he so craved. He was never going to be a Marlon Brando-like figure sitting quietly in a bar muttering about how he could have been a contender. No sir, he was Lee fucking Gordon.

To get himself back in the big league – well, there was no slow rebuild for the likes of Gordon. GO BIG. GO NOW. That was how it worked. Lee hit the phones. 'Frank, baby. It's Lee here. Listen, have I got a deal for you. Frank – stay on the line baby. It's Lee.'

So, yes, Gordon snared Frank Sinatra for yet another sojourn in Australia. No doubt one criteria was more sleeping booths on the plane for the boys in the entourage. And he had made sure no exes were shooting films during the tour. What Sinatra wanted Sinatra got. Lee understood that. He was the Chairman.

The tour was another massive success even though it was shorter than Sinatra's previous visits, with just four shows, all of them at the Stadium in Sydney, in late November and early December 1961.

Whatever you may think of Gordon he clearly had an allure, and Sinatra dug him, big time. Otherwise, why would Sinatra fly all this way for just four shows and then – wait for this – waive his fee so that the unwell Gordon could get back on his feet. *That* does not happen often in showbiz.

Pretty soon things were back on track again for Gordon. And he was once again in love. That's l-o-v-e with a dancer from Queensland, Arlene Topfer, who became the sixth Mrs Gordon when they married in Acapulco in 1962.

And you're not going to guess who Lee's best man was. Not Saffron, who didn't actually attend, but Frank bloody Sinatra. Oh yeah. Now, how many people had Sinatra as their best man? Not many. Would it otherwise have been Saffron? Probably not, as things were just a little strained between them at this stage – Gordon owed Abe a significant amount of money, which Abe was keener to get his hands on than Gordon was to give it to him.

In reality things between the two were unravelling at a rapid rate. While out of hospital and back in the game, Gordon was still exhibiting increasingly erratic behavioural signs and Saffron was really starting to question whether he could deliver the goods and was as visionary as he'd initially believed.

Gordon kept the ideas coming, even if they were usually ideas he'd picked up from what others had already done and figured they could easily be transposed to Australia. Enter the twist – a big dance craze at the time originating in a New York club called the Peppermint Lounge.

There was a Gordon lightbulb moment. He went and rented a joint in Goulburn Street in Sydney's CBD. There was no agonising about what to call it. Not at all. He called it the Peppermint Lounge. Simple. Then Gordon hit the phone again and did a deal with a group from the New York club and quickly Diane Hilton and the Peppermints were flying to Australia.

Typically, Gordon was thinking big and then bigger. In addition to appearances at his new club, he put on shows at the Sydney Stadium and in Brisbane and Adelaide. Meanwhile the Sydney Peppermint Lounge failed to take off and was another expensive failure.

When they were in Sydney, many of the international artists stayed at Saffron's apartments on Poate Road, Centennial Park. By this time he'd moved his family out. Another way to trim costs. This building was managed by Abe's mate Wayne Martin, who made well and truly sure that everything the artists needed was provided and that discretion was maintained at all times.

As mentioned, in later years, hotels like the Sebel Townhouse in Elizabeth Bay would pretty much turn a blind eye to any activity within its walls so long as no one was hurt and the damage bill wasn't going to be too high – but back in the 1960s things had to be much more clandestine.

By the time Saffron did his last tour as an overt promoter, things were much more lenient. As an example, Big Top Beauties (the showbiz name for a group of women with extremely large, often surgically enhanced, breasts) who would tour in the early 1970s did not receive nearly the same scrutiny as they would have only a few years earlier.

Despite the allure of being associated with glamorous and high-profile international artists things started to sour for Saffron. As far as he was concerned at this stage, working with and around Gordon was more trouble than it was worth, and it was undoubtedly dawning on him that international concert promoting, with or without a stable partner, was a precarious business in which it was possible to lose a lot of money very quickly.

That was not Saffron's style. He preferred slow and steady income which ideally was as risk free as possible. Money from clubs and real estate came in absolutely each and every week, 52 weeks a year. A misstep with an international tour promoted by him and Gordon could set him back months and months, if not years, of income in a matter of days or a week or two. There was no mileage in this long term. Abe was out. There were to be no more potentially costly Lee Gordon tours with him in the background.

It seemed Saffron pulled the plug at the right time for him. Things began to increasingly spiral downwards for Gordon – he'd ridden that showbusiness rollercoaster like no other, with some observers estimating that he'd made and then lost around £3 million. A lot of money now – an unimaginably huge amount in those days.

Gordon did manage to get American comedian and social commentator Lenny Bruce to Australia in 1962, but that tour didn't go so well. Presented at the Wintergarden Theatre in Rose Bay, it was an almost last-ditch attempt by Gordon to pull his finances back together, by now without the financial backing of Saffron.

Bruce came onstage and before too long told the assembled fine citizens in Rose Bay, 'You're a fucking great audience.' They may well have been, but you did not say that word onstage in Australia back then. The police, who were aware of Bruce's reputation and were waiting in the audience, pounced immediately. Within a few days he was deported back to America.

Saffron would have been glad to have positioned himself at some distance from that carry-on. Promoting international artists was risky enough without having the cops sniffing around. There was enough of that already without Gordon bringing extra heat to the party.

It all came crashing down when Gordon appeared in the bankruptcy court in April 1963. His representatives listed his assets as 'his ability and his name'.

* * *

Lee Gordon was a strange operator. It has been suggested that he never had a bank account, never owned a home and rented the majority of his possessions. A strange way to live, but then again there were few people like him.

In quick succession events unfolded that brought the Lee Gordon story to a close. An arrest in Kings Cross in July 1963 after he attempted to buy the opioid pain medication pethidine, which required a prescription. Gordon didn't have such a document. Released on bail and given a court date, he hightailed it to the airport and bought a ticket for an Alitalia flight bound for Rome.

Given he'd fled the country, there was a warrant for his arrest if he returned, which clearly he had no intention of doing.

The documented short version of the end is that he was subsequently discovered in an apartment in Waikiki. He was in bad shape. He then moved to London with his wife and baby daughter and tried to find work. He died four months after he did a runner from Australia, on 7 November 1963. His cause of death was listed as coronary occlusion. He was just 40 years old.

The death of Lee Gordon was the line under Abe Saffron's stint as a tour promoter, but not the end of his entertainment interests. There was too much money to be made in that game to walk away completely. If nothing else, his association with Gordon had taught him a lot. In the future his deals would be tougher and more loss-proof.

CHAPTER 6

NIGHTCLUBS, SLEAZE AND AN IRON FIST

The 1960s were a golden era for entertainment in Australia, and Sydney was flourishing. International artists came and went on what seemed like a weekly basis. This was also a boom period for Australian entertainers. Appearing on these shows were the likes of Col Joye, Johnny O'Keefe, Sammy Gaha and Norman Erskine. They'd play the Stadium or, if they weren't quite in that league, they'd appear at clubs owned by Saffron or other figures in the Sydney nightclub world.

There was Denis Wong and his Chequers club in the CBD, and Sammy Lee and Reg Boom at the Latin Quarter nightclub at 250 Pitt Street. This club was across the road from what would become the Hilton Hotel.

The Latin Quarter would become infamous as the location of Lennie McPherson's shooting of Ray 'Ducky' O'Connor on 28 May 1967. This apparently happened within sight of not only many patrons, but also two detectives who were clearly having vision problems on this particular evening.

Meanwhile up on Saffron turf there was the Silver Spade Room at the Chevron Hotel. The crowds who frequented all these venues were huge and monied. Even the less well-heeled patrons shelled out big bucks. This might be their one night out for the next few months, so bills be damned, honey. We're going for it. Let's party.

Saffron made money and he hung onto it. His venues and his friends' clubs made money. Abe went where the money might be.

Being an astute businessperson and a quick learner, with each experience he became more adept at assessing potential ventures and those requesting his involvement. He had more and more money and therefore had the power in these relationships. The people who came to him for possible investment needed him more than he needed them. If he didn't like the smell of a deal or the people involved, he moved on. There was no shortage of people for Abe Saffron to work with.

No doubt he had paid close attention to the profit and loss statements on his ventures with Gordon and others. He was building both significant financial resources and growing his business acumen. Knowledge and (financial) power are both significant assets. Put them together and they're formidable. Saffron was becoming increasingly formidable.

As he had learned earlier, concert and event promoting is a precarious business at the best of times. But who always gets their money? The people who own the venues where these artists perform. And these sorts of clubs were emerging on what seemed like a weekly basis in and around Kings Cross.

Real estate. Saffron knew that's where it's at.

It wasn't just the locations where the shows happened; there was good money, really good money, in catering for the crowds who attended. They wanted to eat and drink before the show, which wasn't always an option at the venues, and once the performances were over, they wanted to kick on. Saffron and others provided the places for these people to spend their money. Much less risky than gambling on promoting the shows – and the income was steadier.

On a typical night in Sydney, those in search of fun and good times would meander between locations such as the Chelsea, where they'd have dinner before heading to a Saffron-owned venue or Tabou, Chequers or the Latin Quarter.

It seemed money was everywhere. It wasn't just coming from Sydney – the majority of international performers who visited Sydney would continue on to Melbourne, Brisbane, the Gold Coast and a crowd would follow.

Duncan McNab tells of an instance during the Diane Hilton and the Peppermints tour, which went on to Melbourne. Sammy Gaha wandered into the hotel where Saffron was staying to get a cash advance. He recalls walking into Abe's room to find a table in danger of collapsing from the weight of bank notes piled up on top of it. Saffron was obsessive about accounting. He knew where every last pound was.

If Saffron liked you, a lot of good things could and often would happen. Saffron liked Gaha and even provided the funds for him to attend the Seattle World's Fair in 1962.

Saffron ploughed his profits into more and more real estate to make more profits. A house in Kensington, the Raffles Private Hotel in Bondi, a huge pile in Vaucluse, the Woollahra Hotel, apartments in Paddington.

Then there was an old movie theatre in Oxford Street, Darlinghurst, that had been developed to combine retail shops on street level and a large open-plan loft-like area above them. There was only one door that allowed access to the first floor. This was just the right set-up for a casino – one that, you guessed it, was highly illegal and joined a number of others dotted around the area.

In 1962 Saffron also purchased what would become Saffron Headquarters – 44 New South Head Road in Edgecliff. Lodge 44, as it became known (it still stands), was perfectly located as it was a hop, skip and small jump from the Stadium, Kings Cross and the CBD, and only ten minutes from Bondi.

With Lodge 44 as the centre of his activities, Saffron continued adding, and adding, and adding, to his real estate portfolio.

Orwell Street, Potts Point had become a little too quiet and sedate, so Saffron shuttered the Staccato Club and focused on the strip of real estate that evolved into the iconic Dirty Half Mile. This hotbed of sleaze, food and girls stretched along a relatively short piece of Kings Cross real estate centred on Darlinghurst Road, but taking in the numerous alleys and side streets running off and criss-crossing it.

Starting at the Bayswater Road intersection, under the giant Coca-Cola sign, it extended in the Potts Point direction, effectively ending at Fitzroy Gardens and the El Alamein Fountain.

Then there was the wander down past the Gazebo Hotel, either turning right to the Sebel Townhouse or heading down Macleay Street to the Chevron, the Texas Tavern and Challis Avenue, which would later become home to Benny's nightclub, one of Sydney's most legendary and infamous late night rock'n'roll dens of iniquity in the 1980s.

By the mid to late 1960s it seemed that if anything was happening in Kings Cross, Saffron had a hand in it. Yet he managed to keep at several arm's-lengths from the law. His time at the Roosevelt and his appearance in front of the 1951 royal commission had taught him lessons about being cautious and keeping his head down. He didn't want another public grilling like that ever again. The less that people knew about his business ventures, the better. He wasn't running for electoral office. Invisibility was his friend.

Make no mistake about it, Saffron was smart and getting smarter. He'd buy clubs and lease them to other individuals. Many of them bought their alcohol from his Crown Street liquor warehouse in nearby Surry Hills. What happened inside those clubs and the manner in which the alcohol was sold had nothing to do with Saffron. None of his business. So he took the income from both the property leasing and booze sales but was comparatively untouchable as, well, he wasn't really doing anything wrong. Not legally, anyway. Or at least not anything that could be proven in a court of law.

* * *

On the surface everything was going along fine. Abe was a tough, smart businessman with his fingers in a whole lot of nightclubs and other ventures. He was a married man with a young family. Just a typical hard-working, trying-to-make-a-buck Australian guy, right?

Not so. Not by a long shot. Saffron ruled with an iron fist. He was subtle and stayed at a distance from anything truly nasty maybe, but he was the guy who gave the nod to the enforcers and when the word went out that Saffron wanted something – or someone – dealt with, then the job was done.

In his personal life Saffron was a very long way from being an angel. Husband of the Year was not an award he was ever likely to get nominated for, let alone win. His drive to accumulate wealth and grow his power was an aphrodisiac. His lust for sex and women, many women, was masked by his outward appearance of temperance.

Saffron and Doreen Krantz would celebrate many wedding anniversaries and remain married until the day Krantz died. Yes, on one hand that is a major achievement, but Saffron's 'until death do us part' didn't exclude other relationships or fast and furious sexual encounters. Marriage wasn't that type of a commitment for Saffron. Like so many men with money and power, he took full advantage of every temptation that came his way.

Saffron craved and loved sex with as many people as often as possible. Occasionally that may have happened in the matrimonial bedroom – but usually it was in apartments that he owned, the houses of others, the backrooms of his nightclubs, in hotel rooms. If there was sex to be had,

Saffron would have it. Now, right now. And with incredible frequency.

Some of those women whose names were not Doreen managed to attain more of Saffron's attention than the regular one-night (or morning or afternoon) dalliances. Hell, Abe had a romantic heart and from time to time he allowed it to beat for an extended period of time.

Saffron's attitude to Doreen might be considered today as a form of coercive control. He constantly humiliated her. It's been suggested that he spent at least half of every week with one or more of his mistresses. For the majority of his life he had three mistresses at a time, and he made no attempt to hide this fact from his wife or his family.

One time, Doreen had had enough and headed to the Roosevelt. When she arrived, she insisted that the cloakroom attendant hand her the mink coat belonging to the current mistress. Upon receiving it, Doreen threw it on the ground and repeatedly stomped on it.

More often than not she stayed at home looking after Alan and let Abe go about his life. What was the point in trying to stop or change his behaviour? That was never going to happen. Maybe she feared what leaving the marriage or divorcing would mean to her personally, socially and financially. Maybe Abe wouldn't let her go, anyway? He needed her to perform a function and he was the one who called the shots.

Those close to Doreen have stated that she loved Abe and was prepared to put up with any and all of his indiscretions to stay the only Mrs Saffron. None of the others could have that title. Abuse and love are sometimes hard to untangle when there is a power imbalance. One thing is for sure, it was complicated.

No further proof of his philandering is required beyond a quick look at how Saffron's fortunes were divided up after his death. Who scored the buckaroonies? Saffron's mistress – I mean secretary – Terry Tkaczyk scored big time. So did Melissa Hagenfelds, who is his daughter with an earlier mistress named Biruta 'Rita' Hagenfelds.

None of this pleased son, Alan, who estimated that Hagenfelds would get close to $4 million while he was given a comparatively paltry $500,000 – but we'll dig further into that later.

Melissa wasn't born until 1963 but that was kept hush-hush until her mother, who had worked as a dancer at the Tivoli, sued Saffron (unsuccessfully) for palimony in the early 1980s.

Saffron was clearly enamoured with Melissa to the point that in his will all three of her children were given $1 million each, the same figure that went to each of Alan's five kids.

* * *

Business dealings aside, Abe Saffron's behaviour towards and treatment of women seemed reflective of the attitudes of the day. As Anne Summers has said, women were considered either whores or Madonnas. Being a man of money and power allowed Saffron – usually – to get away with whatever he wanted to get away with. While Doreen and their child were at home, he not only made money from brothels, which were not known to be places that cared about women's welfare, but was making as many conquests as opportunity allowed.

The man was, not to put too fine a point on it, a bully and a dick. Speaking of the latter Louis Nowra writes in his biography of Kings Cross that Saffron was 'inordinately proud of his penis and as a party trick would whip it out and compare it favourably to those of his cronies'.

Saffron clearly had an incredible, insatiable and unstoppable sex drive – the stuff of legends and the envy of those around him. How Doreen managed to put up with the relationship remains an eternal mystery. It must have been extremely tough. Clearly it wore her down and impacted severely on her psyche to the point where her husband's brazen and seemingly endless extra-marital activities and psychological abuse resulted in her attempting suicide on a number of occasions. Did that prompt Saffron to consider modifying his behaviour to protect the woman he married? It would seem not.

Saffron continued to indulge in orgies and acts of sado-masochism, attending gatherings at numerous properties owned by friends and associates or hosting them himself at Lodge 44 or at his Appin private hotel in Springfield Avenue, Kings Cross.

This was a man who wanted to get his own way and a man who refused to curb his behaviour for anyone. Saffron did not like being crossed or not getting what he wanted. If things didn't go his way he could be very brutal – instigating retribution from others to get his message across. He was known to get a kick out of observing his hired muscle sending a very physical message to any male foolish or unaware enough to be seen in the company of one of his numerous mistresses.

Saffron once intimidated writer Roberta Sykes, who performed a snake act in the clubs on Darlinghurst Road. After she rejected an advance from Abe he turned nasty, big time nasty. There were intimations of a possible beating. She took the threat seriously. Anyone who didn't was a fool and was asking for trouble. You didn't mess with sex-crazed Saffron. You gave him what he wanted or removed yourself from his proximity and stayed removed. In fact, you didn't mess with Abe Saffron, full stop.

A more correct way to say that Saffron 'controlled prostitutes' would be to say that he owned and rented out numerous properties in and around Kings Cross that were knowingly used for sex work. Not only did he receive the rent for these properties, but he also received payments from people working more directly with the women who worked in these locations or sex workers who needed rooms on a short-term basis for entertaining their clients.

Abe was in no way deterred by the sex parties being revealed to the public via the 1956 trial. Not one iota. He had a bit of a think, did the maths and came to the conclusion that this was not only a way to make lots of money, but also – and this probably loomed larger in the Saffron brain – it added to the arsenal of blackmail material that might come in handy at a later date.

This is where it gets more than a little sordid. As Nowra writes, Saffron held many orgies and made arrangements for men who attended to indulge in pretty much whatever sexual acts and fantasies they desired. 'The parties were attended by gay men, S&M aficionados, and others with sexual kinks that would have outraged mainstream Australia. And in order to fulfil the dissolute tastes of some of his clientele, he brought in young children to service them.'

Make no mistake, reader, the suggestion of this is as abhorrent to me as it is to you.

Saffron's orgies were attended by prominent businessmen, politicians, judges and lawyers and he allegedly secretly had the sessions photographed through a two-way mirror. Perfect blackmail material.

These were cards Saffron held for decades and played a role in his ability to do business not just in the 1960s but through the next two decades and beyond.

Both Nowra and author Tony Reeves have cited Federal Court Justice Lionel Murphy, who had a weakness for young Filipinas – sourced by Saffron – as a very keen participant in the parties.

As a result of this, Saffron held some pretty formidable cards and the photographic evidence was placed in a safe and secure location and would only reappear if it became necessary to bring a judge, politician or prominent figure back into line – or encourage their compliance if a favour was required and they were displaying a reluctance to do what was asked of them.

These photos have never surfaced, and other observers of Saffron's world remain sceptical that they actually exist. Maybe all he needed was the suggestion that they existed to have these powerful figures ducking for cover and prepared to do his bidding. None of them wanted to find out if such photos did actually exist by seeing them on the front page of the newspapers or delivered to their wives.

He wanted to go about conducting his business without headlines and court appearances. Heck, he wasn't all that keen on doing any jail time either. The way to ensure this happened was to make certain that he had as much control over those who might seek to cause him problems. They were filed under P in his world – Police and Politicians.

Added to this was M for Muscle. Saffron wasn't big on inflicting physical reminders on people who were getting in his way or not doing what he wanted. It wasn't his style. It was uncouth. He liked to think he was above administering the encouragement that some people clearly needed to pay their bills or step out of the way if they dared think about becoming realistic competitors. There were people who thrived on that. They may not have been super bright, but he wasn't looking to hire Mensa members for this side of things. All Saffron was looking for were men with big fists, a knowledge of firearms and a lack of real interest in why they were being asked to do something but a willingness to do what they were told to do – in exchange for cash or favours.

Street-level annoyances were comparatively easy to deal with. It was the bigger fish who required more finesse. You couldn't just walk up to a cop or judge, punch them in the head and tell them to get out of the way. That was never going to work.

In the 1970s Police Commissioner Merv Wood was someone Saffron wanted and needed to have under control and on his side if required. How did you deal with people like this? Show them respect and if you didn't have any immediate dirt on them, make sure they were well and truly financially compensated for their bouts of temporary amnesia and blindness, and fulfil any other favours they might want.

Wood was known in Saffron's circles as the Sculler – not a nod to a drinking problem but a reference to Wood having previously been an Olympic rowing gold medallist. Saffron and Wood co-existed very well, thank you, usually via Saffron's solicitor and overall facilitator of things that needed fixing, Morgan Ryan.

There would have been a few smiles and raised eyebrows – not to mention nods of 'we got him' between Saffron, Ryan and others in that world when soon after he was appointed to his position in 1977, Wood stated that as far as he was concerned all this talk about organised crime in Australia was just that: talk. I mean, of course he'd act – and to the full extent that the law allowed and maybe beyond – but there was no need as there was no real problem. There were far more pressing matters for the police commissioner to be concerned with.

Those grins would have turned to outright laughter when in December 1977 good old Merv Wood stated that he had absolutely no plans to close the many illegal casinos operating in Sydney. At least Wood was acknowledging that such activity did occur but what's a guy gonna do – shut them down prior to Christmas and put all those poor workers out of jobs at a time when they needed income to buy presents for their families? Merv was not going to be responsible for disappointing children on Christmas Day.

This pronouncement was not because Merv had been nominated for a Humanitarian of the Year Award. Commissioner Merv had obviously been a very good boy and Santa had paid him an early visit, putting a significantly big envelope in the Santa sack hanging from his office desk.

Wood could usually be counted upon to do whatever he possibly could to help Abe Saffron and his mates. He eventually came unstuck and found himself on the other side of that line after being nabbed trying to sort out a little matter for one of Morgan Ryan's other clients. No, not a parking fine. This was a known drug trafficker who needed a little assistance, the sort of assistance Wood could usually provide. But crossing the line too many times means eventually your luck runs out. And Merv's sure did.

Then there was Attorney-General Lionel Murphy. Did Saffron have photos? Most probably. But even without 100 per cent certainty that evidence existed against him, Murphy was clearly an ally of Team Saffron.

At one point in 1975 Morgan Ryan had a little chat with Lionel and as a result of that confab, Lionel made a couple of calls to people in senior positions at the departments in charge of customs and immigration. He made sure that Saffron's bags were not the subject of an inspection on one of his frequent flights in and out of the country.

Who knows, Saffron might be bringing in a new exotic fur whip, some banned books, another vibrator or any manner of things that he didn't want either put on display in front of others at Sydney airport or confiscated, and he definitely didn't want to be charged for possessing prohibited items.

This move from Ryan on behalf of Saffron primarily came about because Abe had previously been searched coming into Australia and particular attention was paid to his address book, which had an eye-watering array of names and contact details, among them a New South Wales Supreme Court judge and other individuals who were undoubtedly of use to Saffron and on his payroll.

It became known that this judge was particularly helpful and accommodating. He was the guy who was called if an associate was about to go before the courts and all steps needed to be taken to make sure that this person appeared before a 'sympathetic' judge or magistrate. Sure, these things cost money. Often lots of money. But Saffron Incorporated had deep pockets.

Saffron didn't like spending any money that he didn't need to, but some things had to be taken care of. And you could be sure that those recipients of his influence were expected to make in-kind contributions either in cash or in whatever assistance they could provide Saffron.

Attorney-General Murphy actually went as far as to attempt to get federal police to have intelligence reports on Saffron go 'missing' or accidentally burned in a fire, but even Lionel couldn't get away with that one.

In another instance the cops arrested well-known drug runner Ramon Sala (not the hockey player Ramon Sala) as he was departing Saffron's Lodge 44 in Rushcutters Bay. Murphy intervened and ordered the police to hand back Sala's passport. What did Sala do? Headed straight to the airport, bought a one-way ticket and got out of town mighty fast.

Then there was Deputy Police Commissioner Bill Allen, who was just one of many senior police officers who had a very comfortable relationship with Saffron. Not one to challenge the upper echelons of an IQ test, Allen didn't see any issue with making his friendship with Saffron public to the point where he actually invited Abe to police headquarters for a yarn.

It's therefore no real surprise that Allen's position was scaled way down the chain due largely to his close association with Saffron. You didn't need to be a rocket scientist to think that what bonded the two of them was more about large quantities of bank notes than an interest in fly fishing or lawn bowls.

Allen's time came and he was jailed in the early 1990s for bribing a police officer working in the licensing division. At Saffron's behest? Maybe – it's a stretch to believe that Saffron was the only one ponying up piles of cash to allow the wheels of illegal commerce to continue, but he was clearly a man of wealth and influence. He was the right crook at the right time – and he rode the zeitgeist well.

Abe Saffron's desire for money and power meant he would ruthlessly exploit whatever and whoever he could to build more of both. As his empire grew so did his hold on Kings Cross – the seedier the business the more lucrative it seemed to be.

CHAPTER 7

KINGS CROSS BECOMES DANGEROUS

As the years went by, Kings Cross became a less and less attractive place to hang out. By the late 1960s, the Strip had become the flashy, trashy epicentre of Sydney. Humanity of every shape, size and economic stratum moved up and down it constantly, seemingly 24 hours a day. Suited spruikers promised to make your dreams come true – at a price. A large local European community meant that fruit and vegetable street stalls were everywhere alongside cafes and restaurants offering a wide variety of fare. Live music still dominated the clubs and venues and professional musicians if their band was in demand could earn a regular income playing repeat shows night after night into the early hours of the morning.

It was all a far cry from the Kings Cross of today, which is dominated by fast-food outlets unless one ventures to the more high-end restaurants in Potts Point. Booze was even more prevalent. Sure, the neon lights were bright and exciting but behind the façade was a seamy and often violent world. Good times could easily spill over into danger. It was not a safe place for women; in fact, it wasn't particularly safe for anyone who didn't keep their wits about them.

Money, girls, glitz – they're always going to attract an unsavoury element. People keen for a good time headed to Kings Cross but increasingly so did those intent on hustling, exploiting or intimidating others. Some people headed to the Cross in search of a quick buck, bringing a side hustle of any description. There were runaways and neglected kids. Some people went there to buy and sell drugs. Those on the financial downside or with extreme psychological issues headed to the Cross to disappear into the back alleys behind the glittering lights. Some slept on those streets, some picked pockets, some waited for an unwitting person to take a wrong turn into an area away from the crowds where they could be told to stop now and empty their pockets, perhaps with a gun-like object or an actual gun pushed against their back.

This was the Vietnam War era and an opportunity waiting to happen for the likes of Saffron. Abe had profited from the end of World War II so he knew what soldiers could bring – money and a desire to spend it. Kings Cross and its entertainment businesses were one of the real winners in that terrible and tragic war. From October 1967 legions of American soldiers, sailors and airmen headed to Sydney on R&R trips, leading to an incredible six days of whatever goes for each on their R&R.

They were cashed up, horny, thirsting for booze and hungry for something other than military rations. They were primed for what Kings Cross had to offer. And they changed the face of Sydney as they brought with them, as Duncan McNab says, 'a taste for heroin, marijuana, and pharmaceuticals such as Mandrax, Seconal, and what became the hit of the 1970s, LSD'.

Was Saffron involved in the supply, importation or distribution of drugs? He certainly would have been aware that drugs were being sold and consumed in and around his turf, but like with so many things he was very good at turning a blind eye just as long as it didn't impact on his core business of real estate or draw unwanted attention from the cops. And of course, just as long as his kickbacks arrived on time.

It has been claimed by some in the police force that Saffron was directly involved in the financing of drug importation but 'SAFFRON – THE DRUG KINGPIN' was never a newspaper banner headline, despite many thinking that was the case and wanting desperately for it to be true, whether it was or not. With all his other activities, how could Saffron not be involved with drugs?' people wanted to know. His nightclubs were rife with them. Kings Cross was always awash with one drug or another. It was illegal. There was big money to be made. Give us a break – are you really trying to tell us Saffron's hands are clean here?

It has certainly been claimed by some in the police force that Saffron was directly involved in the financing of drug importation. It just seemed so obvious that he would be. If in fact he was, how did that work?

Pretty much the same way as when he invested in any business venture, such as concert promoting. Saffron would front up whatever cash was required to get the illegal show on the road and with the full knowledge that this was a precarious thing to be involved in. Drug syndicates weren't and still aren't infallible. How easy would it be if they were? Saffron knew how to stay out of sight.

So, there is a fair chance that if he was involved, Saffron would have insisted on a safety net. In other words, if the syndicate went down Saffron would still be repaid his money, and if things went to plan his money would come back with an added 'usage fee' of, perhaps, at least 25 per cent.

In the case of large-scale drug importation, one imagines that Saffron would have put a lengthy and complex distance between himself and those on the ground. Drug importation charges were not something he wanted or needed in his life. He had created multiple other ways to make good money.

To that end I actually find it possible – despite the hearsay of others who were closer to the action than I ever was – that Saffron didn't finance drug importation. Of course, he was all about making money, but surely he was too smart to get involved in that world; the risks were too great and the penalties too severe if he was caught. Saffron didn't like jail and drug importation was one sure way to get an extended experience of what it was like.

Lending money to people who needed backing – that was something he would do. If that money was used for a drug operation, so be it. The man wasn't a saint and his hands weren't dirty. The money was.

Drugs aside, Saffron gave customers what they wanted, namely dreams, booze and girls. Escapism. As he prospered, he quickly added to his real estate and clubs with the Persian Room, Crazy Horse and the Venus Room.

* * *

The Venus Room was Saffron's attempt to re-create what he'd had at the Roosevelt. Initially it didn't work, as it was too upmarket for the majority of Kings Cross denizens.

In the second half of 1969, Saffron put James (Jim) McCartney Anderson in charge of the Venus Room with the brief to start attracting punters and lots of them. Give them what they wanted, not what Saffron hoped they'd want. If someone was needed to turn a venue downmarket, Anderson was your guy. He was also the guy who, as McNab says, 'would turn out to be the turd in Saffron's punchbowl'.

Originally from the UK, Anderson was a formidable-looking figure, a former traffic cop, bus driver and conductor in New Zealand where he'd moved after he'd dabbled in the nightclub scene in London – his dabbling being largely connected with the criminal element hanging around such places.

After moving to Sydney in 1959, Anderson had lived around Kings Cross, including taking a room at the Rex Hotel, which at the time was a popular bar whose fashionable clientele mixed with the occasional member of the underworld. It was also a popular and comparatively safe location for Sydney's gay community to mingle.

When I started to hang around the Cross a lot in the 1980s, the Rex was a very different proposition. It was a venue for rock'n'roll bands of the punk, new wave orientation and decidedly seedy. Many of the patrons looked like they were either about to go to jail or had been recently released. Drug deals seemed to be happening everywhere with people meeting quickly and heading to the bathrooms or out to the street.

I must have been oblivious to it but there was a Middle Bar known as the Bottoms Up Bar which, according to McNab and others, was frequented by trans and male sex workers and drag queens. I guess I only had eyes for the rock'n'roll. In fact the Bottoms Up Bar has been claimed to be Sydney's first gay bar.

Like Saffron, Jim Anderson also figured there was quick and easy money to be made in the world of entertainment, so he took over running the showbiz side of things at a city nightclub called Andre's, where he concentrated on bringing New Zealand artists to town. First up were the Māori Hi-Five, a seven-member rock'n'roll show band formed in Wellington in the late 1950s who specialised in traditional New Zealand dances and songs along with pop music of the time.

The Māori Hi-Five supported the Beatles at their concert in Hong Kong on 9 June 1964, just before the Fab Four (well, minus Ringo, who was ill with tonsillitis) arrived in Australia.

Soon afterwards, Anderson was approached about a gig as the director of entertainment for the Chevron Group in Queensland with an emphasis on their new property on the lucrative nightlife hub of Surfers Paradise.

Anderson spent half a decade in the employ of the Chevron folk as well as a similar role at the Rex group of hotels before moving to Sammy Lee's Latin Quarter nightclub in Pitt Street where he had a management role.

This was the era when the likes of Lennie McPherson, Stan 'The Man' Smith, George Freeman, Milan 'Iron Bar Miller' Petricevic and Arthur 'The Duke' Delaney were among the hard and tough men who reigned supreme in the Sydney underworld. On one occasion all of the above (minus Smith) entertained visiting American Mafia figure Joseph 'Dan' Testa at Chequers nightclub in the city.

Saffron wasn't part of the gathering that night.

Anderson then moved back to Kings Cross and became financially involved with a cafe called Showbiz, which was subsequently sold to Kentucky Fried Chicken who wanted a premises in the area. It was then that he came into contact with the likes of Lennie McPherson and Donny 'The Glove' Smith.

As reported in the *Sydney Morning Herald*, a ccording to Anderson, Smith 'used to wear a leather glove with lead lined all through it. And when he hit you with that, you stayed hit.'

For a period, the cashed-up Anderson thought about buying Saffron's Crazy Horse strip club. The only problem was that Saffron wasn't selling. But he offered Anderson the job of running the Venus Room instead.

* * *

By the early part of the 1970s things were spinning out of control on the streets and in the suburbs of Sydney. Violent retribution and struggles for control of the drug business but also other areas of crime were getting uglier, more dangerous and far too frequent. The underworld was breaching into the light.

During this era there was a message from figures in the police force who had a cosy relationship with the criminal world – stop making everything so public and messy, settle your scores with a little more subtlety please, we're just a tad sick of all the work and prying eyes.

The crims listened and, for a period, things in Sydney were handled a little more clandestinely. Those destined for an early grave were ambushed or kidnapped and taken away from the urban streets to meet their fate. Bodies weren't left to be easily found but disposed of in remote rural locations or in Sydney Harbour. Some went into the harbour as deceased individuals; others took a leisurely cruise while still alive before tumbling over the side – either with weights attached to chains around their still-breathing bodies or with a recent gunshot wound in their head.

Heroin and its dissemination was at the core of most of the activity – and at one centre was the Mr Asia organisation.

Fighting it out for control of the drug action – and the Sydney underworld in general – were three groups. None of them were part of the Abe Saffron group.

Lennie McPherson's and George Freeman's main activities were gambling (of the illegal variety) along with all sorts of money-making scams in nightclubs and brothels. These guys were – like Saffron – the remnants of the more traditional old-school crooks. Their associates included Stan 'The Man' Smith, Frederick 'Paddles' Anderson and, according to some, the notorious hitman Christopher Flannery.

Their rivals included the infamous Neddy Smith and Graham 'Abo' Henry, whose chief source of income was armed robberies (back before bulletproof glass and other deterrents appeared in banks) and – yep, drugs. Included in this corner were Warren 'Frenchie' Lanfranchi, Harvey

Jones and Barry 'Brain' Chubb. In their corner was also a certain Roger Rogerson, at the time in the employ of the New South Wales Police Force and anyone else who would pay him.

Barry McCann, whose main interest was drugs and the money that could be made from them, was part of another faction. It was inevitable that he would come head-to-head with Smith's gang and many shots would be fired.

It was in everyone's best interests if the violence was curtailed or ideally concluded. In 1972 the rival factions agreed to meet. In theory the plan was to carve up the available turf. Recent visiting American underworld figures had observed that the Australian set-ups were pretty chaotic, disorganised and lacking in cohesion. The biggest problem was that most of the serious money was now in drugs and everyone wanted a piece of that action.

Saffron didn't attend any of the organised sit-downs involving the core of Sydney's other underworld figures. Abe always tried to stay aloof and above this kind of stuff. Meeting with such people would suggest he was involved in criminal activity, wouldn't it? Abe wasn't involved in such ventures. He was a businessman working largely in the real estate world. Of course he was.

Saffron hated the innuendo and suggestions that he was an underworld figure and involved in criminal activity. He sued and he sued often if it was ever even insinuated – usually with success.

What particularly got up his nose was the description of him as Mr Sin. Any headline or story with those words and he was quickly on the phone to his lawyers. He sued *The Age* in 1975 after the Melbourne newspaper put the two words in print. The matter was settled out of court.

Much later, in 2003, Saffron went after the *Sydney Morning Herald* on grounds of defamation, but he lost that one. He did prevail against the authors, publishers and distributors of the book *Tough: 101 Australian Gangsters* by Andrew Rule and John Silvester, and again in a case against the *Gold Coast Bulletin* after they published a crossword with the clue, 'Sydney underworld figure, nicknamed Mr Sin'. The answer was 'Saffron'. Abe didn't like that. And the publication couldn't prove his underworld connection as a defence.

Even the notorious Lennie McPherson – known as Mr Big – had nothing but nice things to say about Abe. When asked in a 1974 radio interview if he'd ever met Saffron, McPherson replied: 'Well, I have met this man they claim to be Mr Sin on about six or seven occasions in my life. You couldn't get a softer-spoken man than him. He is the loveliest person you could meet and regards to saying any man is "Mr Sin" I can only say that any man who is behind drugs would be classed as Mr Sin and there are many Mr Sins, so you can just nominate a man and say this is Mr Sin.'

As befitting such a lovely man, Saffron kept away from the limelight. He didn't like publicity one bit and in fact only gave two media interviews in his life.

Writer Peter Rees comments: '[Abe] never mixed with staff, instead walking around very quietly, rarely talking. Staff called him "the ghost". Even people who worked in the clubs on his premises … would have no idea who he was. He would just sit down, pay for his meal or his drink and watch the show. This was his way of checking up on things at his clubs …'

If you knew who he was and moved in his circles, he was *the* guy. If you didn't, he was just another guy in the audience. You weren't to know that he owned most of the locales he stepped into. Money was being made hand over fist. Did he care what his premises were being used for? Probably not much. Did he know that many were being used as illegal brothels or for drug dealing? Of course he did.

Regardless of his financial standing, Saffron was described by those close to him as a modest man. In a superb piece published in the *Sydney Morning Herald* in 2021, Kate McClymont described him as 'a workaholic who derived little pleasure from his wealth'. McClymont quotes his niece, Anne Buckingham, as saying: 'He never flashed money around. He didn't live extravagantly. He drank Great Western champagne as opposed to French.'

Buckingham said that Saffron was also not a gambler: 'He didn't follow the horses or football, not even soccer, which is a Jewish thing.'

McClymont says that the police and others who watched and listened to recordings of his phone conversations agreed that he didn't have many interests beyond his business activities. One source told her: 'Power and the exercising of it – that was his narcotic.'

While Abe's wife, Doreen, had a significant art collection, Saffron instead chose to cover his office walls with photos of American gangsters. In the wake of Abe's death, his son, Alan, claims his mother's art collection 'disappeared'. No one wanted Abe's photos.

Saffron spent his days and nights going about his business. The Cross and environs ran on booze, food – and by the hour, sex was plied in places like the Lido in Roslyn Street in Kings Cross and dozens of tiny street-front terraces around the area and down in East Sydney. St Peters Lane, which runs parallel to William Street leading up to the Cross, also saw its fair share of quick sex for money activity, as did William Street locations such as the Barrel Inn and the Jewel Box, both in William Street, which attracted the gay community.

Abe might have been one of the main men, but it was a competitive business. Lennie McPherson was a big mover in the illegal sex business, as was Joe Borg – known as the King of Palmer Street – who was said to own 17 houses in the East Sydney area that were used as brothels. You get the idea that competition wasn't always wanted. Joe's reign came to an end when he turned the key in his car on 28 May 1968, causing a bomb under the seat to detonate. See ya, Joe.

Despite all these and many other characters running around conducting their cash-only and less-than-classy business ventures, it was Abe Saffron who was consistently referred to in the media as 'Mr Sin'. To those who didn't know, it seemed there was only one operator in the sex and sleaze business in Sydney – Abe Baby.

Abe might have fought against that moniker but the facts indicate there was truth in the nickname. Saffron was a mover and shaker. He made incredible amounts of money from exploiting women directly or owning premises where this occurred, selling alcohol and at the very least turning a blind eye to drug dealing and the nefarious actions in his premises. He kept increasing his real estate interests but somehow managed to stay clear of any clashes with the law, for the most part. He was stylish. He was smooth. And, perhaps most importantly of all to stay above the fray, he knew how to delegate.

CHAPTER 8

THE SEVENTIES AND SEXUAL FREEDOM

As the 1960s came to a close, Harry M Miller, then a young impresario from New Zealand, opened an Australian production of rock musical *Hair* at the Metro Theatre on Orwell Street in the Cross. The main thing everyone knew about this musical was that at a certain point the whole cast got well and truly nude. Full-frontal nude. And the cops didn't arrest anyone. The times were definitely changing in Kings Cross and Sydney. Things that had been taboo in the previous decade were no longer so.

While Lee Gordon had opened the first drag show revue in Sydney, Lee's of Woollahra, back in 1959, it was Saffron who took it over and transformed the show. If anyone epitomised glamour, good times and the classic era of Kings Cross it was Carlotta who was, from 1963, the undisputed Queen of Kings Cross as the principal figure at Les Girls, a cabaret drag show.

In Carlotta's memoir, *He Did it Her Way*, James Cockington wrote in his Introduction about life in the Cross at the time: '… it started at midnight while the rest of us slept. … [The] rules that governed the suburbs ceased to exist. Prostitutes lined the streets, offering their services as openly as newspaper sellers. Any taxi driver in town would be able to take you to the nearest illegal casino where, if you were dressed well enough to impress the bouncer, you would be able to rub shoulders with radio and television personalities, barristers and off-duty policemen.' Drugs were common on the streets, as were drag queens and kings. All part of the scene.

We know Saffron made his early fortune supplying women, places to gamble and booze but as Cockington says, 'the glittering mile suddenly began to fade. By the end of the decade, the Cross had become a human sewer, and it was no longer safe for a decent girl, even one who had been born a boy, to walk the streets alone.'

Carlotta's career really began when she was a trainee window dresser at Mark Foy's in Sydney. She happened to be very good at dancing the twist, the dance of the day. One of the fashion co-ordinators at Mark Foy's got her onstage to dance during fashion parades.

Lee Gordon was at Foy's for one of these fashion parades. By this time he had opened the Peppermint Lounge and Carlotta got a gig there teaching patrons how to dance. She also told Gordon that she liked dressing up in drag.

'Lee Gordon was fascinated by drag queens,' she writes. 'A few months before he brought out … Coccinelle who caused a riot when she appeared at a club called the Golden

Horseshoe near Centennial Park. Coccinelle caused a huge fuss by pretending to perform oral sex on her high-heel shoe. In the early 1960s this was outrageous, and the police ended up stopping the show, but it made Lee Gordon think that there must be something in this drag stuff.'

Not long after this, Gordon came up with the idea of putting on an all-male revue in Sydney. He'd been inspired by a cabaret show he'd seen called The Carrousel de Paris while visiting Europe.

Gradually things changed and attitudes towards drag shows in Sydney relaxed a little. Carlotta writes that for a time the biggest threat was Bumper Farrell, the cop I mentioned before who ruled Kings Cross in the 1960s and 1970s. She says he was known as 'the great drag queen hunter' and recalls him walking into bars and dragging people out onto the streets. For some reason Farrell left Carlotta alone and eventually the attitude of the police in general became more broad-minded.

After Lee Gordon died in 1963, the role of running the Peppermint Lounge had been turned over to Sammy Lee, who Carlotta describes as: 'A showman, flamboyant, but a hard taskmaster and he insisted on tits and arse, even for us boys.'

Sammy Lee was a tough guy who took no shit from anyone. Carlotta and her crew soon learned that Sammy pretty much owned them, and they were not to think about challenging that situation. She recalls a time when two of the girls, Simone and Monique, announced that they were leaving Les Girls with the intention of starting their own club. Sammy wasn't having a bar of that. On what was to be their last night, Sammy told the whole crew they needed to stay back when the show was finished. This was non-negotiable. After the show, Lee's minder, a big guy called Lurch (after the butler in *The Addams Family*), took Simone and Monique up on the stage. He then savagely beat them with a bar stool. Everyone was informed that if they decided to leave the club, that would be their fate as well.

So Carlotta stayed. The consequences were too horrible to think about.

But there were constant upsides. Les Girls was famous, a showbiz mecca in Sydney – for both local paying patrons and celebrities.

Carlotta tells of when Led Zeppelin toured Australia in 1972 they used to come regularly to Les Girls. As she says, it was one of the few places in Sydney they could go to and not be worried about being mobbed by screaming, semi-crazed teenage girls. Not that Led Zeppelin appeared to really have a moral issue with screaming, semi-crazed teenage girls.

She recalls Robert Plant only came to one show but drummer John Bonham and guitarist Jimmy Page were there every night they could be. Why? Apparently Page had fallen head over heels in love with one of the girls and Bonham was besotted by Carlotta.

The majority of Sydney gangsters of the era seemed to love a drag show and were frequent visitors at Les Girls. Carlotta says the most notorious 'used to scare the shit out of all of us', and one individual would insist that all the girls sit at a table with him – they didn't dare refuse as he always carried a gun. He had a speech inflection that Carlotta thought was the result of him being shot in the mouth.

Other underworld figures who came to Les Girls were George Freeman and Lennie McPherson, but neither made a big deal of who they were. 'They weren't frightening at all. They always came across as gentlemen, at least to me.'

And of course Abe Saffron was in Carlotta's orbit. He was in everyone's orbit around the Cross, plus he owned the club. But Carlotta is at pains in her memoir to dispel persistent rumours and speculation that she and Saffron were close. He came to Les Girls often, but that was it. She is adamant that she had nothing else to do with him and that there was no other connection between her and him and the club. Just business. Saffron had a club. She worked there. Nothing else to see here.

Carlotta is a Saffron defender. She writes that both Abe and Doreen had always been good to her; she'd even been to their home for Christmas celebrations. The performers there were told they were big crime bosses but Carlotta 'never felt uncomfortable with most of them. They were just patrons who liked to come into the club … and if you like that was one of the unwritten laws of the Cross, to judge people by how you found them, not by their reputations … No one can ever convince me that Abe Saffron is a shady character because to me he was always a gentleman.'

Sammy Lee getting Lurch to bash some of the girls working at the club with a bar stool was not what I'd call gentlemanly, but the question is, did Abe know these violent tactics were used in his clubs? My hunch is, of course he did. The next question is whether he knew before or after the event. I'm guessing it was after. But who knows?

* * *

Sometimes, just hanging out with someone connected to the game and the world in the shadows could come with a heavy price tag in the Cross. Romantic entanglements in particular could be deadly. The hint that someone was trying to muscle in on someone's gal could have dire consequences. I have been told numerous times about the death of Mike Furber and the whispers are very different from the official story.

Mike was a good-looking, charismatic English-born singer who moved to Australia with his family at the age of ten. In 1966, Furber and his band the Bowery Boys had a number of hits, and following that, Furber was one of the Top 5 in the Male Vocalist category in the *Go-Set* magazine's 'Pop Poll'. That was probably the height of his fame – there was a schism when he was conscripted for National Service during the Vietnam War. He served 18 months and was discharged in 1969, enough time to go from top of the pops to yesterday's hero.

Mike was talented and had real appeal. There was no question about continuing his music vocation and he went on to try out a solo career, securing a record deal with EMI Columbia, touring with the band Doug Parkinson In Focus, recording with Albert Productions and appearing in the musical *Godspell* in the early 1970s. Within his circle, however, Furber was known to be struggling with his mental health. His fragility wasn't aided by his time in Vietnam – those who knew him say that he was 'traumatised' by the national service experience. And of course he was a long way from being alone there.

On 10 May 1973, Mike Furber was found dead in the garage of his home. A police investigation determined that he had taken his own life, and it was suggested that he was in the depths of a major depression. Not long before his death, he had been fired from the musical *Nuclear*, which was enough of a justification for some. But others insist Furber was murdered, and still do.

This is, however, where there are no readily demonstrable facts, just lots of speculation. The rumours are that Furber had befriended either a Kings Cross prostitute with connections to an underworld figure, or that he had become involved with the girlfriend of an underworld identity who was none too happy about the liaison.

The gossip swirled and while writing this book, one well-known music industry figure who wishes to remain anonymous wrote to me, saying that Furber had been 'living in the Cross and had upset the wrong sort of people'. This person also said: 'There's also the fact that the length of his "suicide" rope was longer than the drop. There did seem to be something very fishy about the death.'

I am not saying the police are wrong, that this anonymous figure is right and the rumours are true. But there is doubt and conjecture. Unless there's a deathbed confession – and there's not the slightest reason to suggest that there will be – the death of Mike Furber will remain officially ruled a suicide.

Furber's sad death and the speculation around it is just one of the tawdry stories in the entertainment world behind the flickering neon lights.

* * *

Despite his experiences with Lee Gordon during the 1950s and the first years of the '60s, during the mid '70s – while extremely cautious – Abe couldn't quite pass on business opportunities in the international touring world. No doubt armed with the increased knowledge about the risks involved, he entered into business arrangements with other promoters such as John Harrigan to promote tours by Ike and Tina Turner and the folky British Bob Dylan wannabe, Donovan.

Saffron had learned from his past dealings. As the years passed he was more careful about who he worked with and made sure that he was not as financially exposed as he had been. Backing promoters for a specific sum of money and taking an override on what was effectively a loan was a far safer way to use his money than footing the bills himself. Plus, he became a little more cautious about who he got into a financial bed with, looking for more astute and business-orientated individuals to work with. There was only one Lee Gordon and Saffron had well and truly learned from that experience.

Alan Saffron, then in his mid-20s, remembers the Tina Turner tour: 'I was also heavily involved in the Ike and Tina Turner tour … I had never seen anyone treat a lady like Tina was treated by Ike. Dad would often say that after a bad fight between them, he would console Tina and ask her why she stayed with him. It bothered him that he couldn't stop Ike from hitting her, no matter how hard he tried.'

Alan also writes about how his father had become involved in promoting wrestling a few years earlier.

American wrestling promoter Jim Barnett was in Sydney and, having heard of Saffron's huge success in the concert business, met with Abe. Plans were hatched to hold World Wrestling Championship matches in Australia, with Saffron financing the first tour. Immediate success followed, with all arenas sold out.

Alan recalls, 'Of course, the wrestlers knew who was going to win – it was showmanship and hence right up my father's alley.'

* * *

Change is the constant in everyone's world. The gay liberation movement was finding its voice in Sydney. The dramatic change in the acceptance of non-heterosexual sexuality in the Kings Cross clubs was driven by Roger-Claude Teyssedre and Dawn O'Donnell. They were, as Duncan McNab observed, 'The double act that, through the 1970s and 1980s, would come to dominate the pubs, clubs and restaurants that catered to Sydney's gay community.'

The two did exactly what Saffron had done during the 1940s and '50s – work out what the public wanted and then give it to them as quickly and efficiently as possible. And in the process get their money. As much of it as possible as quickly as possible.

Together and individually Teyssedre and O'Donnell would operate a huge number of clubs and bars. Flo's Palace and Ruby Red's were two clubs catering to lesbians and operating above what was then the Crown Street Wholesale Liquor Supply. Catering to the gay clientele were Patches Disco, where the 33 Club Casino had previously operated, and the Exchange Hotel, plus sex shops catering to that market like the Toolshed, and a gay sauna at 253 Oxford Street.

And guess what? Many of these businesses were set up in properties that were owned or leased by Saffron or one of his increasingly complicated business entities. The man was a money-making genius. No risk for Abe. Just collect the rent.

Considered to be potentially the classiest of all the newer places was Jools nightclub on Crown Street, which would later become a Hard Rock Cafe. And yes, that property was owned by a Saffron entity. The building was spectacularly renovated inside and out by a previous tenant, who had intended for it to become a casino. But gaming laws didn't change the way they'd been expected to and the venture floundered and eventually failed. Abe had a building to die for but no tenant.

In waltzed Teyssedre and O'Donnell and things took off. Aiming to attract the gay community, Jools featured drag shows, cabaret and lounge acts combined with a discreet upstairs area where all manner of activities took place.

Abe Saffron was happy. And he could see a new wave happening, so he increased his holdings in the real estate area aimed at the gay community, having taken over the property on the corner of Roslyn Street and Darlinghurst Road in Kings Cross, which featured the drag show revue Les Girls led by Carlotta.

The establishment was soon re-named the Carousel Club and after the first gay Mardi Gras parade, which was held near the end of the decade on 24 June 1978 the place was packed. This club continued to be a major and iconic Kings Cross attraction for years to come.

While all this was happening, Saffron made another associate in Todor 'Tosha' Maksimovich. Saffron was a businessman, so he mixed with legitimate businessmen often. I am definitely not suggesting that Mr Maksimovic was involved in any organised crime or drug dealing. A builder by trade, Maksimovich was used to hard physical labour, but like a lot of people he might have hoped there was a faster and easier buck to be made. And he had an idea of what that could be.

This was the heyday of the disco boom and, really, how hard could it be? Find a big room where people could buy drinks, get a couple of mirror ball lights and hire someone to spin danceable records.

The fact that Maksimovich had no idea about music or the culture surrounding disco didn't matter. He just saw the opportunity to make lots of money. First up he revamped the African Queen disco in Chatswood, which became a hit.

Maksimovich wanted to expand. Where would you do that? Not in Chatswood, my friend. You'd head for the glitz and glamour of Kings Cross. And that meant a conversation with one Abe Saffron.

While on the hunt for a location, it was almost inevitable that he would deal with Saffron. If you wanted an entertainment venue in or around Kings Cross, chances were Abe or an associate would own it or control the lease.

Maksimovich first earned the trust of Saffron by reverting to what he knew much more about – looking after necessary repairs, and in some cases renovations, for Team Saffron's properties. Among these responsibilities were renovations for Dawn O'Donnell and her clubs. The way to Abe's cold, black heart was to be useful and make money for him.

* * *

While Saffron was going about his business, things were hotting up politically. Not directly for him, but all sorts of allegations of organised crime activity in New South Wales clubs were flying around. And most of these allegations were focused on the Cross.

The state government needed to be seen to be doing something about this and so a royal commission, presided over by New South Wales Supreme Court Judge Athol Moffitt, was convened in August 1973.

The government wanted the public to be relaxed about what was going on in their state. The *Sopranos* television series was decades away but the *Godfather* book and film were everywhere at this time and seeping into the collective consciousness, causing concern that Australia was about to be overrun by the American Mafia stereotype they read about and saw on their screens. This wasn't the Red Scare – it was the Mafia Dons Scare. What a way to deflect, even for a short while, the spotlight from the career criminals and their bad cop mates.

The nub of the commission was to look into allegations that the Bally poker machine company (now known as Bally Technologies), who had machines – lots of machines – in every licensed club in New South Wales, had links to the American Mafia and that these shady types were intent on expanding into Australia.

What was likely to happen? Stand back, Mabel – those Mafia types are going to take over the country. Clearly organised crime and its tentacles were already in Australia and had been for some time but now it was hitting the headlines and the general public's fear button had been pushed. Careful everyone – it's only a matter of time before Vito Corleone is running the country.

But there was a more serious need for this, which led back to power structures in New South Wales. Both the police commissioner Norman 'Bill' Allan and premier Robert Askin were undergoing significant speculation that they were involved in organised crime. Both wasted a lot of breath denying that organised crime existed in their wonderful state and – how dare you even think it – there was absolutely no connection between these filthy criminals and the fine upstanding gentlemen of the police force and government officials.

Where there's smoke, however, there is, as we well know, a degree of smoke – and as far as the public was concerned this was starting to seem like a full-scale bushfire. There had been many goings-on that gave the public good cause to believe that their representatives might not have been completely straight up about what they knew and were doing.

The most publicised became known as the Arantz Affair. Here we had an early version of a computer expert and, what's more, they worked for the police. Philip Arantz was booted from the police force when it was discovered that he had been leaking information about crime in New South Wales to those horrible bastions of news reporters known as the media.

It seemed that the New South Wales Police Force had for a long time been under-reporting statistical information about crime in that state. What was revealed showed that things were much worse than the public had been led to believe.

Then there was the fear about the drug trade, that not only was it growing at a rapid rate but it was in danger of spiralling out of control. Heroin in particular was on everyone's mind. This was a drug that was impacting on the lives of Mr and Mrs Suburbia in ways that drugs hadn't before. Pot smokers and tripping LSD takers were comparatively harmless, but people dropped dead very quickly from heroin overdoses, and that was happening a lot, and the related visible presence of addicts stimulated public scrutiny. More impactful was that some of these heroin addicts experienced cravings so intense that they smashed in windows and doors at your home, stole your family jewels, television sets, stereos and anything else that could be quickly fenced for cash. And terribly, the really desperate would knock over little old ladies for their handbags, too. Violent crime associated with drug users of harder drugs was and is really terrifying.

The Moffitt Royal Commission opened for business on the morning of 16 November 1973 and the first attraction was Israel (Jack) Rooklyn, who ran Bally Australia.

Rooklyn was the main game in town but of course Abe Saffron's name came up. I mean, Abe's a guy involved – very involved in all sorts of largely unregulated areas of entertainment – in those things called nightclubs. Throw in a club's interaction with sex and alcohol and why wouldn't Abe and the Mafia be involved?

Rooklyn's life encompassed many activities. Born in the UK in 1908, he was four years old when his family migrated to Australia. His older brother was a magician, and this was Jack's entrée into vaudeville. He would have a stint in the US and this introduced him to coin-operated amusement machines and in 1952 he became the Asian agent for the Bally Manufacturing Company of Chicago, which he distributed in Australia via his Electronic Amusements company. He promoted vaudeville and when poker machines became legal in New South Wales clubs in 1956 he was right there, ready to capitalise on other people's weaknesses. He would become a significant figure in the criminal world.

And yes – hold the headlines – Rooklyn and Saffron had known each other for over two decades. Slam dunk, you'd have thought. Also, look at this – Saffron and Rooklyn had purchased a development site in the West Beach area of Adelaide. They subsequently sold it for a tidy profit but hey, they had been in business together – for many people, two and two was adding up to four.

Rooklyn was immediately interrogated about his relationship with Saffron. Had they met up in Jakarta? Yes. Had they discussed Saffron setting up a series of restaurants and nightclubs in Indonesia? Yes. What about moving into the brothel business in that country? Never.

Then it was time for Abe to front his second royal commission. The probing about Indonesia didn't get much joy and was clearly not going to yield anything of substance. Two businessmen meet in a foreign country and discuss business. Anything to see here? Nope, as far as their lawyers were concerned at least.

Saffron was pressed on his company structures and those of which he was a director. He was asked about the Pink Pussycat strip club and his involvement with Peter Farrugia and others.

Then came the question that was bound to set Abe Saffron's blood a-boiling: Was he the person commonly referred to in the press as 'Mr Sin'? Saffron kept his cool and stated that he was aware of the reference and that, until that question no, he was not aware that it might refer to him. It was also later suggested in the hearing that there was another figure who was 'Mr Sin' and not Saffron. Would the real Mr Sin please stand up and be identified?

On it went. Pushing, probing, alleging, inferring, trying to join dots that were separated by several country miles.

Even Moffitt got in on the action by trying to suggest that there was a connection between Saffron and high-profile Mafia dude Joseph 'Dan' Testa. Saffron had heard that but had nothing to add, but even the fact that the two were mentioned together was enough for many people to make assumptions that could in no way be proved. But never let the facts stand in the way of some good rumour-mongering.

Justice Moffitt handed down his findings in 1974. He found that there was a danger that organised crime would infiltrate Australia from overseas. While recognising that this was not an easy area to investigate, he recommended the establishment of a specific squad of police to deal with these matters.

For Saffron it was the most publicly stated alleged link between his activities and organised crime. It would be fair to say that at this point Abraham Saffron had – in the minds of the public at least – ascended to a position where he was considered the Australian equivalent of a Mafia don. It was not where he wanted to be.

Saffron was also having a spot of bother in Adelaide. As with Sydney, Saffron had a highly impressive real estate portfolio in the city. There was the Brighton Hotel and the Elephant and Castle – but also the Castle Motor Inn, the West End Restaurant, La Belle Cabaret, the Belair Hotel and the West End Casino (a venue for cabaret not, as the name suggests, for gambling).

The cops thought Saffron also owned a bunch of other pubs and a nice collection of sex shops such as the chain of Lovecraft shops, Ecstasy and the city's Adult Movie Club. In reality these were owned by Peter Farrugia; another example of Saffron appearing not to be running businesses of this nature. But he was and the money from them was ending up in his pockets.

Despite stories that Saffron organised orgies at his properties in Adelaide – ones that allegedly involved judges wearing nothing other than their wigs – not everyone was happy about his activities in the City of Churches. The most prominent of his critics was then Attorney-General Peter Duncan who, in the South Australian Parliament, described Saffron as 'one of the principal characters in organised crime in Australia'. Saffron was furious. In a rare move, he called a press conference where he denied the claims and challenged Duncan to repeat his accusations outside of parliamentary privilege.

Suddenly there were media reports – well, in fact, suggestions – that Saffron was involved in drug trafficking through these venues. There was an article in one of the Adelaide Sunday papers claiming that an unnamed Sydney businessman was in control of the drug trade in Adelaide. There were more suggestions and innuendo in parliament. Saffron was without question the person behind the moral disintegration in Adelaide. He and he alone had decided to cease the supply of soft drugs into the City of Churches because everyone knows that if there's no pot around, the next move is to jab a needle in your arm and get hammered on heroin.

Clearly those South Australian politicians weren't all that across what was happening with the hard drug trade in Australia. There were a lot of other players whose names weren't Abe Saffron. And there had been truckloads of heroin – quite possibly arriving there via the Mr Asia syndicate and other outfits that remained undetected for many years. Heroin hadn't just become a thing in Adelaide. Not by a long shot.

Clearly the ongoing suggestions that he was involved in drugs rankled Saffron more than usual and really got under his skin. He responded to these accusations saying they were 'an appalling lie'. Such was his anger that he did something he hardly ever did – spoke to the media. His usual form was to remain completely silent, as if to engage in speculation was both beneath him and also might add credence to whatever smears and innuendo were being slung in his direction. But Saffron wasn't going to take this lying down.

At Lodge 44 in Edgecliff, accompanied by son, Alan, he let fly, stating: 'These statements are completely without truth and entirely false. I deny with all the strength at my command each and every allegation made against me. I am appalled that such allegations should be made under parliamentary privilege, and which have caused my family distress and anguish.'

Saffron was asked about the 'Mr Sin' allegation and the Moffitt Royal Commission, to which he replied: 'Even though a police witness told the same hearing that "Mr Sin" was someone else and not me, I have been called that name again in Adelaide recently. Apparently, I have corrupted the NSW Drug Squad … but I have never had any contact with the Drug Squad and I don't know any of its officers.'

And on he went: 'People have said all sorts of things about me for a very long time. I have been asked many times to give press interviews, but for 25 years I have declined. On this occasion the accusation that I am involved in drugs is so vile to me that I am compelled to deny it as vigorously as I can through the press. I regard drugs as totally evil, even soft drugs like marijuana, because I believe they can lead on to hard drugs. My business interests are all perfectly legitimate. I have discotheques, hotels and motels in Sydney, Adelaide and elsewhere in Australia. In Adelaide, I own or am associated with four hotels, restaurants and a cabaret. I would not in any way permit or condone any form of drug activity on the premises with which I am associated.'

Son, Alan, who clearly has a unique insider's knowledge and by the nature of his troubled relationship with his father a certain opinion, weighed in as well at the gathering: 'Anybody who knows my father would also know that he would not be associated with drug trafficking. But soon after this story was published last week, my wife got a call from the headmistress of the kindergarten our four-year-old son attends. She apparently wanted some confirmation that the stories that were flying around were not true. Even though they are not true, my son missed out on three of the four birthday parties he would have normally been invited to.'

These drug suggestions had completely messed with Abe's family's social calendar. Alan's reasons for various family problems later in life can quite possibly be traced back to the Great Birthday Party Snub of '76.

Despite the speculation and rumour-mongering, no one was able to pin anything on him. They were watching and waiting for him to slip up.

Saffron rarely made a false move. Maybe not a false move, but a slight and revealing hiccup, was the time when he was searched by a customs officer in Perth in 1973. During that encounter, his address book was found. It contained 105 names, a number of them judges and police.

There is no law against having the phone numbers of judges and police. People can have friends – and it's none of your damn business what they do for a living. Saffron then took steps to make sure that in future his address book was kept well away from such prying eyes.

There appeared to be virtually no end to Abraham Saffron's business interests. And some of them, at least superficially, were quite unlikely ventures. But that adds to the fact that Saffron was in business to make money and he didn't particularly care what caper it was, as long as it turned a significant profit. Maybe he drew the line at drugs. Or maybe – despite his public protestations – he didn't.

At the end of the decade, Saffron branched out again and became a significant retailer of recorded music in the country. He already owned the Record Shack shops in Newtown, Pitt Street and Kings Cross, and now he bought into the Sydney CBD – Peaches record shop that was run on a day-to-day basis by Morgan Ryan's son Peter and Abe's own son, Alan. He also for a period of time owned Edels, the shop started by Geoffrey Edelsten, hence its name.

Abe had very little to do with the running of Peaches but one former employee tells me that Saffron would frequently use the back room for business meetings – the type that required one of his henchmen to stand guard over the closed door to make sure there were no interruptions. Whether these meetings were with a woman or had a more capitalist bent, I am not sure. Bit of both, I'd say.

Looking at Abe's foray into the world of record sales, it turned out Saffron Inc didn't like too much competition in that branch of retail. In 1979 Brian Bell, owner of successful New Zealand chain Chelsea Records, opened an Australian outlet near Central railway station. Things worked well and within months he'd opened a second shop in Bondi.

Soon after the Bondi outlet opened, Bell received a visit from two gentlemen who were both polite and yet exuded a sense of unstated menace. They informed him that their boss wanted to have a chat. The boss was apparently Saffron Snr (but sources suggest a visit like this was more in the style of Saffron Jnr) who came on with the 'friendly but not to be messed with' routine, explaining that he was a fair man, but that Bell couldn't have two shops in Sydney. It was his call which one stayed open. Bell decided to cut his losses, closed both shops and concentrated on his New Zealand business.

Saffron may not have been mad keen on the concert-promoting business after his dalliance with it, but if there was a way to put real estate and music together, you had Abe's attention and he'd give it a crack.

CHAPTER 9

BOURBON, BEEFSTEAK AND BERNIE

Aside from Saffron, others were selling these dreams of booze'n'girls, such as the proprietors of similar establishments like the Bourbon and Beefsteak bar and restaurant. The Bourbon and Beefsteak, while not a Saffron entity, was a significant Kings Cross bar from the 1960s onwards. Situated on the main drag of the Cross, it was established by a fascinating individual named Maurice Bernard Houghton – known to everyone as Bernie.

Houghton was an American businessman with alleged links to the US intelligence community, including the CIA-connected Nugan Hand Bank in the 1970s. The Nugan Hand Bank was an Australian merchant bank suspected of being involved in all manner of things that banks don't usually involve themselves with – stuff like drug smuggling, funding arms deals and getting involved with the CIA.

Not the usual day-to-day business of the ANZ or Commonwealth banks. In fact, most banks go out of their way – or at least they should – to make sure that funds are handled in a very legitimate and above-board way. The Nugan Hand Bank set the standards for dodgy banking very, very high, such that no Australian financial institution since has come close to matching them and probably never will.

After serving in the American military in World War II, Houghton spent the next two decades working in various jobs. From 1964 until 1967 he found himself in South-East Asia involved in any and all business ventures he could find – many of which presented themselves during the Vietnam War. Those activities apparently included trading in slot machines and opium.

After the investigations into the Nugan Hand Bank, Australia's Joint Task Force investigating the bank and its activities stated that Houghton was 'part of the intelligence community' during his time in Asia. In other words, he was reporting back to American interests and no doubt enjoyed a degree of protection in exchange for this.

These investigations happened between 1983 and 1985 and were conducted by the Commonwealth–New South Wales Joint Task Force on Drug Trafficking, and the Royal Commission of Inquiry into the Activities of the Nugan Hand Group – both of which were bodies created specifically to look into the bank and its activities. The Corporate Affairs Commission of New South Wales also became involved through digging into what went on.

I am only guessing, but for someone like Abe a focus on someone else meant he could carry on as normal.

And maybe competition from Houghton wasn't an issue for him.

As Kings Cross took off with the influx of American soldiers on R&R, Houghton moved to Sydney and opened several bars. At the time, the American soldiers enjoying their R&R in Sydney were plying a staggering $9 million a month into the local booze'n'girls-based entertainment economy. Everyone wanted a piece of that pie.

Of all Houghton's ventures, the Bourbon and Beefsteak was the best known and most successful. It opened in October 1967, a mere month before the first thirsty'n'randy troops docked and made their way up through Potts Point to Kings Cross.

In his landmark 1972 book (updated in 1991), *The Politics of Heroin: CIA Complicity in the Drug Trade*, Alfred W McCoy claimed that New South Wales premier Robert Askin and our mate Abe Saffron were often guests in Houghton's private area at the bar. Also known to have visited was John D Walker, the CIA's Australian station chief from 1973 to 1975.

No one knows for sure exactly what Houghton's connections with the CIA were – that stuff doesn't usually crop up on anyone's CV – but we can be sure they were significant and reached the upper echelons of power and influence in this country. Evidence of this includes Houghton's flight back to Australia in 1972 without a visa after a trip overseas. For most other people this would be a significant impediment to being allowed back into the country. Not for Bernie. He asked to use a phone at Sydney airport's customs and immigration department, called the state director of the

Australian Security Intelligence Organisation (ASIO), whose name and direct phone number he just happened to have with him, and Mr State Director vouched that Bernie was kosher and fine to come back into Australia.

This wasn't the first time Houghton had called in favours – back in 1969 he'd also obtained a security clearance through ASIO. Houghton was pals with and from time to time during the 1970s would entertain Major General Richard V Secord, a US Air Force officer who was known to work in covert operations. Secord was involved in the Iran-Contra affair and made over US$2 million in the arms transactions. He was nabbed for that and soon after moved into the private sector. Yes, Houghton had connections.

Owning and running the incredibly popular and profitable Bourbon and Beefsteak would be enough for most people but, like Saffron, Houghton wanted lots of more. He left others to manage the bar and travelled overseas frequently.

In 1975, with Kings Cross continuing to be a lucrative area for anyone with a business on the Strip, Houghton headed to Washington, DC with two Nugan Hand Bank employees. Why? To help support Michael Jon Hand's plans to arrange arms deals supplying weapons to people in southern Africa. As you do. While in the States on this visit Houghton was in contact with Edwin P Wilson, who was then working for the Office of Naval Intelligence. He also worked with Wilson to supply Iran with a high-tech spy ship. He flew to Iran in March 1975 with a US Army colonel.

Heavy-duty stuff for a Kings Cross bar owner. This was wayyy out of Abe Saffron's league of wheeling and dealing.

In 1976 Houghton took even more interest in the Nugan Hand Bank, as his bar business in Sydney had gone into bankruptcy with debts of over $1 million.

Houghton's ongoing wheeling and dealing continued through until the very early 1980s. There were serious amounts of money involved, including $5 million in cash deposits collected from US expatriates via the Nugan Hand Bank. That all went missing when the bank collapsed in 1980. Things got too hot for Houghton and he left Australia in the mid-1980s.

In a slightly bizarre twist, after Houghton died in 2000, a statue was erected in his honour in Fitzroy Gardens in Sydney. The justification? Partly to recognise Houghton's approximate $1.5 million of charitable donations. The statue was approved by South Sydney Council, whose then mayor said that it was due to Houghton that the Kings Cross community was 'vibrant, alive, and so diverse'.

There are no similar statues of Abe Saffron, Lee Gordon or others of their ilk. Clearly, they weren't considered to have donated enough to charities – despite Saffron's well-known philanthropic generosity.

CHAPTER 10

THE LINGERING JUANITA LEGACY

That matter of the disappearance and presumed murder of heiress, urban conservationist, and newspaper founder and writer Juanita Nielsen on 4 July 1975 highlights the cruel brutality of the decade and dispels any glib perception of cartoonish robbers and cops. Tens of thousands of words have been written, several books published, and films and documentaries made about the disappearance, yet the mystery continues to this day. Her body has never been found, and her last known whereabouts was … Abe Saffron's Carousel Club.

Nielsen had been very vocal about proposed developments in Victoria Street, Kings Cross, which was initially driven by another former clothes maker, in particular lingerie-cum-property-developer Frank Theeman under the business name Victoria Point Pty Ltd. The intention was to redevelop the terraces along Victoria Street. 'Redevelop' was very thinly disguised code for getting rid of the people who lived in these terraces, knock 'em down and build something new and more profitable.

The plan was for three 45-storey apartment buildings and a 15-storey office block. They were significant-sized structures even by today's standards and mind-blowingly large for 1972, especially in the sedate area behind the craziness of the main drag of the Cross.

While writing this book I took a walk around the area with writer Duncan McNab just to reinforce in my mind how gigantic these structures would have been, how they would have dominated the landscape and destroyed all the charm and gentility that in fact still remains given that those homes were not bulldozed.

Thank goodness for community action in the street and surrounding areas, because had the developers got their way even the rapidly changing landscape of Kings Cross would have been dramatically different and significantly lacking in some of the charm that still exists along Victoria Street.

Residents and those sympathetic to their plight banded together to fight against the developers who used increasingly threatening, violent and confrontational methods to get them to move. Early assistance came from the Builders Labourers Federation (BLF), led by the outspoken Jack Mundey. They slapped what were known as 'green bans' on the site in 1972, refusing to do the work. This added considerable weight to the grassroots efforts of residents.

So where did Juanita Nielsen come in? Why was she to become the name most associated with the Victoria Street struggles? For starters she lived in one of the houses planned for demolition. And she had an albeit fairly rudimentary vehicle to aid the campaign in the form of *NOW*, a local newspaper that was published fortnightly.

From her home at 202 Victoria Street, Juanita published the newspaper which had been purchased for her by her father. What could it do against the might of the developers? Maybe in reality not a lot beyond galvanising the community. It was their voice, their outlet to get their message to a slightly wider audience.

By doing so Nielsen came to be central to the campaign. To outsiders she and *NOW* were considered the focal point of the resistance, one that became nastier by the week as the developers and their hired muscle used any method they could think of to terrify residents into moving. This was pitched-battle warfare in the streets of Kings Cross.

As an indication of the extent that the developers and their associates would go to, look no further than what befell resident Arthur King in July 1973. Kidnapped by two men, King was shoved into a car, driven to a suburban motel and held there for three days. This was playing-for-keeps stuff. At the end of his ordeal King was released not far from the Venus Room. Draw your own conclusions about that. Was Jim Anderson involved? Later evidence suggested that he may well have been and the drop-off point for King is a little suspicious.

No one was moving. Galvanised as a community and with Juanita Nielsen and her newspaper as a mouthpiece, they were there to stay. 'Bring it on' was their attitude, despite many clearly being terrified of the violence and intimidation.

Theeman and his associates appeared to be increasingly desperate for a resolution. Time is money in real estate as it is in many other areas and this caper was costing big time. Among the muscle dragged in to help break the deadlock was a certain Fred Krahe, who had previously been a detective sergeant in the New South Wales Police Force. But like so many coppers of the day, Krahe had a reputation for mixing with characters on the other side of the law. He was also suspected of murdering prostitute Shirley Brifman. What had Brifman done to end up murdered? Well, she'd accused Krahe of corruption, hadn't she? Of course, that and her death may have been a coincidence and there may have been other reasons for her demise.

So, if you're (allegedly) capable of murder, scaring the living daylights out of the residents of a quiet semi-suburban street would be a walk in the park. But despite all the muscle involved, the result Theeman wanted was considered a long way off.

And there were all sorts of behind-the-scenes activities. The BLF changed leadership and withdrew their ban – apparently after significant figures were offered as bribes. The Federated Engine Drivers' and Firemen's Association of Australasia moved in to take their place as did the Water Board Union.

The delays in the project were reportedly costing Theeman $16,800 every week in interest as he'd borrowed money for this development, which was currently going nowhere.

Abe Saffron knew about money and property but he and Theeman weren't particularly close, suggesting Saffron had no skin in this game – the money hadn't been borrowed directly from him. Or had it?

For an indication that the relationship might have been otherwise, we once again have to look at Alan Saffron's chronicling of his father's life – and he makes it clear that Theeman was someone to whom his father had lent a significant amount of money. For this development or something else? That's not made clear.

The murkiness continues. Jim Anderson, one of Saffron's deputies, was subsequently found to have owed Theeman $260,000. Certainly, the suggestion that Anderson attended to a couple of bits of 'business' for Theeman in return for a reduction in his debt could be a big motivating factor.

It is known that on 13 June 1975, Anderson invited Juanita Nielsen to an event at the Carousel Club and when she didn't attend – and why would she – Anderson was reportedly mightily pissed off. Not giving up, a fortnight later the Carousel's PR manager, Lloyd Marshall, invited Nielsen to another meeting, this time at the Camperdown Travelodge, allegedly to discuss an advertising campaign. Now, several rats could be smelled here. Why in heaven's name would a meeting like this need to be held at a Travelodge in the inner west of Sydney when everyone involved either worked or lived in Kings Cross? Hello! Nielsen was a smart person who no doubt would have been spooked and suspicious about this invitation, and declined to attend.

Something was definitely up. Two attempts down. They tried a third time. Cut to 30 June. It was the end of the financial year so perhaps time that finances needed to be in order. Edward Frederick 'Eddie' Trigg and Shayne Martin-Simmonds, both of whom were employed at the Carousel, arrived at Nielsen's home. It was the old 'we want to chat about an advertising campaign in *NOW*' ruse.

It would later be revealed that they intended to grab Nielsen and take her with them. Things didn't work out as Nielsen's partner and boyfriend, David Farrell, was visiting at the time. Not surprisingly, Nielsen and Farrell were now seriously concerned for Nielsen's wellbeing

Yet another meeting was called by Trigg and Simmonds for 4 July, this time at the Carousel Club. We can only speculate on why Nielsen decided to attend this one – alone. Perhaps she thought that any physical threat at such a public location would be farfetched and being on home turf, she could manage any overt intimidation. Who knows, but ultimately, a grave underestimation – she was never seen again.

Was Saffron involved? Certainly, he owned the Carousel Club in the Cross where Nielsen was last seen, and Anderson was the manager of the club. Anderson had a reputation as a hard man who wasn't afraid to shoot a rival dead. The man eventually convicted of conspiring to kidnap Nielsen, Eddie Trigg, was employed as the night manager at the Carousel. So, it was all a bit close to home for Abe. Throw in his alleged financial links with property mover and shaker Frank Theeman, whose development Nielsen was vocally campaigning against, and you can see why people wondered if Saffron was knee-deep in it all.

Nothing ever went beyond innuendo, but I think Saffron knew exactly what happened and who was responsible. People like Saffron made it their business to know what happened in the Cross. Did he order it? Probably not. Was he happy that Nielsen was out of the picture? Who knows. But maybe not, particularly if in fact Saffron still stood to get his money back and then some, even if the Theeman venture never got off the ground. That's what experienced businessmen do. There does not seem to be any evidence that Saffron was a front- or back-end investor in Theeman's venture. He lent Theeman money just like Tooth and Co. had given him a loan when he was starting out. A loan that required repayment with interest, a loan that was collectable whether the business venture succeeded or failed.

In Alan Saffron's memoir he states that his father was approached by Frank Theeman, who explained that he was having a few problems with a property development in Victoria Street. The chief problem was Juanita Nielsen, who just wouldn't go away or let up with her campaign.

Theeman's logic – and it was pretty good – was that Saffron appeared to control most of what happened in Kings Cross and therefore was the obvious Mr Fix-It to approach her. The two met and Theeman hinted that maybe Abe could sort the matter out. But, as Alan writes, 'my father would never condone extreme violence and murder', so the discussion went nowhere.

We must of course remember that despite their sometimes-tempestuous relationship, Alan was a strong defender of his father, so his opinion on what his father may or may not have been capable of or condone should probably be taken with several grains of salt. Or maybe what Alan observed – that Abe drew a line against physical violence against a certain class of women – should be given credence. There is nothing to suggest that he ever touched Doreen or his mistresses, and as mentioned earlier he was truly appalled at Ike's abuse of Tina Turner according to his son. Psychological intimidation may have been one thing but raising a fist or worst just wasn't on. When it came to women Saffron considered himself a lover not a fighter. If you're looking for the truth as to what happened to Nielsen and who was behind it, maybe Alan Saffron's account is a better place to start than first thought.

Alan reckons that Theeman then went directly to Jim Anderson. Maybe Saffron directed Theeman to Anderson, who he knew would dish out the type of psychological intimidation Theeman was after. Or maybe Anderson's reputation was known and after Saffron said 'sorry, no can do', Theeman approached Anderson independently, or Anderson presented his services independent of Saffron and without Saffron knowing the full extent or any of Theeman's brief.

What we do know is that to sort this pesky Nielsen business, a part payment of $50,000 was put into Anderson's bank account and it was game on.

Alan Saffron's version of what went down was that Eddie Trigg and Shayne took Nielsen by force to a North Sydney motel, where Anderson, Theeman and a police friend of Anderson's were waiting. Theeman offered Nielsen a large amount of money to stop carrying on about the development.

This version seems just a little doubtful – that Nielsen, who was already independently wealthy (remember the heiress bit) – could be bought. Unless the likes of Anderson, his backer and henchmen were so dark of heart and narrow of intelligence that they couldn't conceive the notion of a truly independent and intelligent woman with an unwavering moral rectitude.

Juanita was the great-granddaughter of Mark Foy, and her father was a major shareholder in Mark Foy's Ltd retail business. That's code for 'not short of money'. She was educated, had ideals and considered, broad social values. She believed that there was a right way and a wrong way to go about things.

Her campaigning was so determined, focused and passionate that it seems highly unlikely that those who kidnapped her thought that a big chunk of cash was going to make her either quietly go away or become a vigorous campaigner for urban development – unless they lacked the intelligence to see that. No – buying Nielsen's silence or support was almost certainly never going to succeed.

If this was something known to Anderson, his backer or the men who did their legwork, then something more was definitely on the agenda that day.

In Alan's account, and remember he wasn't actually there, Nielsen was (understandably) furious about being kidnapped and screamed loudly. Anderson got angry and hit her – hard – and she fell down, hit her head on a glass coffee table and died. Theeman and the cop made themselves scarce quickly.

Alan reckons Big Jim bundled Nielsen's body into the boot of his car, drove to a remote location, cut her into pieces and placed the body parts in sealed plastic bags with weights. Later that night Anderson went boating on Sydney Harbour and dropped the bags over the side.

After Nielsen's disappearance there were unsubstantiated suggestions that she had been blackmailing Saffron because she'd been in possession of a document that could be damning for Saffron and a number of his associates if it was made public. This document, which Nielsen allegedly carried with her at all times, could connect Saffron with property developments in Victoria Street.

Saffron was questioned by police about Nielsen's disappearance but stated that he'd never even met her and denied any suggestion that she had been blackmailing him. According to Saffron, he first heard of Nielsen's disappearance when he read about it in the newspapers and had insufficient interest in the matter to make further inquiries.

An inquest into Nielsen's disappearance was held in 1983 and concluded that Nielsen had died, according to the inquest documents, 'on or shortly after 4 July 1975'. It was also stated that there was 'evidence to show that the police inquiries were inhibited by an atmosphere of corruption, real or imagined, that existed at the time'.

In the subsequent decades, seemingly endless new theories and speculation have emerged. Marilyn King, a former girlfriend of Eddie Trigg, told a newspaper journalist that Eddie came home with blood on his clothes the day Nielsen disappeared and – she said – a bloodstained receipt signed by Nielsen apparently for advertising money. File this one under Highly Unlikely. And impossible to substantiate as King said Trigg had thrown out the shirt and paper.

Loretta Crawford, who was at the time of the incident a receptionist at the Carousel Club, told so many different versions of events that even she was probably having trouble keeping up. In 2000 she reckoned that Jim Anderson was not in Surfers Paradise as he'd claimed, but at home in Vaucluse.

Originally Crawford, along with Trigg, had said that after meeting Nielsen at the Carousel she left very much alive, and alone. Then Crawford said that Nielsen and Trigg departed together. A Kings Cross real estate agent claimed to have observed the goings-on and told police that Nielsen got into a yellow car parked outside the club and that there were two men in the vehicle.

Back in 2004, Crawford told ABCTV's *7.30 Report* that everything she'd previously said was wrong and that she had simply been trying to protect Anderson. Given that Anderson had recently died, she was able to finally tell the truth.

Version 875 from Crawford was that Nielsen had been murdered in the basement of the Carousel and that Trigg and Martin-Simmonds were there. She'd been shot once and a third unidentified man was standing over the body, holding a pistol.

Coupla things here. Why didn't Crawford identify the third man? And was it usual for a receptionist to wander down to a nightclub basement and happen to walk in just as a murder was committed? And if this did happen, why hadn't the three men taken steps to make sure that this witness kept her mouth shut? You've just shot one woman, why stop there? Who needs a witness who can't necessarily be trusted?

Also doing the rounds was the theory that while no one was thrilled about Nielsen's campaign against the developments in Victoria Street, there was another reason –

maybe connected, maybe not – that caused people to want her out of the way.

John Glebe, Juanita's friend and the General Secretary of the Water and Sewerage Employees' Union who were supporting the cause, testified at the 1983 inquest that Nielsen had received many telephone threats in the lead-up to her disappearance and also that she had carried cassette tapes with her at all times – tapes that could, in his words, 'blow the top off' something she was working on.

Then in a 2005 story in *The Bulletin*, journalist Barry Ward stated that Nielsen had dossiers on what Ward called prominent Sydney identities – which is thinly disguised code for people in high places. Ward said Nielsen had been given this information by a private detective named Allan Honeysett. The article suggested that the material related to figures in the gambling industry in Sydney.

And so it goes on. The reward for information about Nielsen's disappearance currently stands at $1 million. It was doubled to that figure in June 2021 by the New South Wales Police Force. Homicide Squad Commander Detective Superintendent Danny Doherty said at the time it was still hoped that someone in the community might have additional information about her disappearance or the location of her remains.

Will we ever know precisely what occurred? Probably not. There are too many variables and too many of those alleged to have been involved have died. As for Abe Saffron, there will almost certainly always be speculation and innuendo about his involvement, which is unlikely to ever be put to rest.

In reality, arguably the largest amount of money Saffron ever made in one transaction happened just up the road from the proposed Victoria Street developments and on the other side of the street. And it happened legally.

With the building of the Kings Cross railway station in the late 1970s it was necessary for the then New South Wales government led by Neville Wran to purchase the land where the station currently sits. Within that complex of buildings at the time were two substantial holdings of Saffron's. One was used as a brothel, the other as an illegal casino. Not that Abe knew anything about this. He just owned the properties.

The government needed that real estate badly. Saffron knew this and the price was high. It was a big payday for Saffron, and a legitimate one. Thank you, Neville Wran.

* * *

As the 1970s ended, despite his attempts to appear as though he was a respectable businessman, Abe was starting to attract the wrong kind of public attention. The Nielsen disappearance was just the start of rumours beginning to stick to him a little more.

It was all, or mostly at least, just rumours, but those rumours were starting to gain some traction – and in the eyes of many people, hey, they must be true. People were hearing and reading about the speculation so often that they were beginning to treat it as fact. If it was in the daily papers it must be true. They wouldn't allude to things if they weren't true just to sell papers, would they? Of course not.

Abe may have just been another Sydney man going about his business but his name was increasingly cropping up in the wrong contexts and with each instance there was more momentum to the rumour mill and it was harder and harder for him to enjoy anything close to the anonymity he desired.

The next bit of unwanted attention Abe attracted came from the 1985 publication about organised crime in Australia, *The Prince and the Premier* by journalist David Hickie. There was a lot about Abe Saffron in this thoroughly researched and damning book, which centred around the belief that former New South Wales premier Robert Askin was extremely corrupt and that he and then police commissioners Norman 'Bill' Allan and Fred Hanson were the recipients of massive bribes from those involved in the illegal gaming industry. This trio effectively either turned a blind eye to, or actively assisted, the expansion of organised crime in New South Wales.

Hickie relied on material that was then in the public domain: evidence tendered at and to royal commissions and the many allegations by politicians using parliamentary privilege. Not surprisingly, Saffron featured prominently in the book as someone who had benefited enormously from the support of these powerful figures.

Hickie used evidence from the 1954 Maxwell Royal Commission investigating the liquor trade in New South Wales. The outcome of this royal commission had been the determination that Saffron had actively established a covert controlling interest in many New South Wales pubs to enable the supply of his sly grog outlets, and in doing so he'd made false statements to the commission and sworn false oaths in front of the New South Wales Licensing Court.

Added to statements in *The Prince and the Premier* was the publication of a second edition of *The Politics of Heroin in Southeast Asia: CIA Complicity in the Global Drug Trade* by Alfred W McCoy. In this book's chapter on the Nugan Hand Bank, McCoy claims that Premier Askin and Saffron regularly dined together at the Bourbon and Beefsteak restaurant in the Cross.

On the surface there's nothing wrong with that. A compromised premier eating with a prominent Sydney businessman – who just happens to be an alleged key figure in the world of organised crime. But there was still nothing to prove Saffron's power and influence when it came to the police and government. Nothing to prove that he engaged in anything other than buying property and using the majority of that to entertain you and me, the public, who definitely needed and wanted entertainment.

Mr Sin? The biggest mover in the world of Australian organised crime? That's the story the media constantly circulated and embellished. Abe Saffron was a bad, bad man. So why wasn't he in jail?

The New South Wales Police Force spent almost four decades trying to nab Saffron on all matter of charges and allegations, but nothing stuck. Questions remain as to how hard they tried, or whether it was a case of some elements of the police working hard to get Saffron, and other factions working equally tenaciously to make their investigations difficult and protect the man.

It's well established that the New South Wales Police Force was a fairly corrupt organisation in this era. There were a lot of bent coppers and many with things to hide. Saffron knew this and undoubtedly had a significant dirt file on many of them. Photos of them up to no good at Lodge 44, for instance – or playing up in any of his nightclubs. That sort of stuff.

For the ones who didn't have a dirt file of significance, there was good old-fashioned cash, and lots of it if required. Saffron knew who the power players were and his longevity relied on keeping them under control.

It has been suggested that Saffron paid $750 per week per club to local police and up to $5000 a week to senior police to have the required eyes blinded to what may have been going on at his various enterprises. If true, that's a significant amount of money going out each week, therefore showing just how much money must have been generated by these clubs.

It seems there were two distinct elements on the New South Wales Police Force: those who wanted Saffron and many others reined in and charged with what they believed to be illegal activities, and those who were terrified of this happening or had their mortgage repayments dependent on the largesse flowing from Saffron and other prominent Sydney businessmen.

So people continued to speculate and still nothing stuck. It evolved to the point where if there was any mention of organised crime in this country, tongues started wagging and muttering the name Abe Saffron. But none of the mud slung around amounted to anything concrete. The man was truly made of Teflon – or so it seemed.

CHAPTER 11

ANDERSON'S FIREWORKS

Jim Anderson was not the smartest guy in town, but he was ambitious and power hungry. That's always a dangerous combination. He'd worked his way up to become a very significant and trusted player in Saffron's world.

Described as 'a cunning, callous and vindictive liar – the Iago of Kings Cross' by writer Louis Nowra, Anderson knew how to handle himself, which he'd proved when he managed the Latin Quarter nightclub. The story goes that Anderson allegedly killed Donny 'The Glove' Smith when Smith took a swing at Anderson and connected with him big time, knocking him off his feet and breaking Anderson's jaw in the process. Not a smart move.

Smith was clearly not aware or smart enough to realise that Anderson was armed. Anderson figured enough was enough. This guy had crossed the line. He reached for his gun and fired. While some reports said it was two shots to the back, Anderson reckons it was one to the front into the heart and two to the back. The one to the heart was the initially planned shot but then Smith got up – obviously running away.

Anderson argued that it was self-defence and reckoned that The Glove was coming at him with a gun. So, he was initially charged with murder, which was then downgraded to manslaughter – and eventually the charges were dropped.

Why? It would be a tough one to fight in court, you'd think, but someone had to have had a chat to someone else and the matter was no-billed by the Askin government, even after Anderson had been committed for trial.

Not too long after, Anderson and Saffron formed a business connection and Anderson was soon managing several of Saffron's business interests in the area of bars, nightclubs and strip joints, including Les Girls, the Carousel Club and the Venus Room.

Once Anderson was asked if the women who were renting apartments above the Venus Room were involved in prostitution. 'I don't think they were playing Scrabble,' he famously retorted. He may not have been too smart, but he could be funny.

Wherever Anderson was, trouble was never too far away. In 1973 he was badly burned after being just a tad too close to a petrol bomb that exploded in a nightclub. Late in the 1980s he would be shot. He survived.

Anderson was rarely out and about without his weapon of choice – a .32-calibre Browning pistol. When you moved in the sorts of circles Anderson did, you were wise to be armed and potentially dangerous at any given time.

Anderson was a tough, nasty piece of work, short on subtlety and with the physical ability to back up any verbal threats. When he wasn't doing the enforcing himself, he was delegating it to other toughs; anyone who got in his way or underestimated him was simply asking for trouble. And he was Team Saffron all the way.

After Anderson died in 2003, the *Sydney Morning Herald* didn't hold back, stating that 'the many activities the pair were suspected of being involved in, but never proven, according to the parliamentary joint committee of the NCA [National Crime Authority] in 1994, were bribing police, illegal drugs, arson, prostitution, brothels, massage parlours, liquor offences, blackmail and extortion'.

Nothing else. Just those things.

Relations were ostensibly rosy between Saffron and Anderson for a significant period, particularly from during the 1970s. They both had their skill sets and for a long time that was the way it worked. Abe was the boss and the owner; Anderson worked for Abe and made sure things ran the way Abe wanted them run.

That was until Anderson decided he wanted more. He began to get tickets on himself. Big tickets. He was planning to move on from Team Saffron. Alan Saffron describes Anderson as 'one of my father's more questionable associates' and observes that it was during Anderson's time in control of the clubs that drugs were starting to be extremely prevalent – something his allegedly staunchly anti-drugs father was completely against. Of course he was.

While there is complete conjecture about Saffron's position on drugs and whether or not he was involved in their importation, distribution and sale, it would be fair to say that this was an area he most wanted to keep a distance from.

So if – and only if – Saffron was involved in any aspect of this business, he wanted it on the QT. And if drugs were increasingly creeping into his clubs, he wouldn't have been at all happy about it.

Alan confirms that Anderson was incredibly jealous of Saffron and 'always wanted a larger piece of the action for himself', and says that he stole regularly from Saffron's clubs.

Saffron's trouble with Jim Anderson was starting to eat at him. Abe was the Boss. An associate undermining him was just not on. Something had to give.

One night Saffron drove to an eastern suburbs nightclub, at the time one of the fanciest and must-be-seen-at discos in Sydney. It was operated by Saffron's son, Alan, and an associate.

Alan Saffron wasn't in charge of operations that night. While Alan was meant to be the club kingpin, things took a turn when he fell in love with a woman from America, divorced his current wife and caught the next plane out of town. Abe was obviously a little overwhelmed at this turn of events, because he poured out his concerns to a friend about his son and about Anderson, and the friend had a pretty simple suggestion. Saffron was all ears. The way this mate saw it, Anderson's sidekicks were big, tough fuckers who didn't scare easily – but his guys were bigger, tougher fuckers.

So in a very short period of time, those bigger, tougher motherfuckers removed and replaced all of Anderson's muscle from their positions in any business owned or controlled by Abe. Anderson was pretty much finished and it didn't take long for the word to get around.

With son, Alan, gone, Saffron offered Anderson the opportunity to take over the lease on the club, which was soon to temporarily close for renovations. But Anderson wasn't taking this sitting down. No, sir. Abe usually knew most of what was going on with his associates but every so often something slipped past him – like the fact that his former second-in-command-cum-enforcer had decided to become an informant for the state and federal police.

Things started to heat up. Literally. In the early 1980s, six properties connected with Saffron managed to catch fire. That's an incredible run of bad wiring.

Word had it that kerosene could be smelled at some of the locations. Who would do such a thing? Anderson had a word to the people interested in the answer to that question and – hey, Abe, here's looking at you, babe. Arson? Insurance?

It was Anderson who had a history with fire. Way back in November 1973 there had been an explosion and fire at the Staccato Club, which was operating at the time as a strip club. (By the way, this was another Staccato Club at 101 Darlinghurst Road – not the one connected with Saffron.)

This bit of enhanced fireworks happened when the strippers of the Cross were out on strike. Clothes on and staying on, chaps. They reckoned their conditions were shite and that $75 a week was an insulting wage, especially as they were expected to use some of it for their stage gear. Backed by Actor's Equity, the strippers staged a march to El Alamein Fountain and picketed the venues over a number of weeks. It was said that strike breakers, rumoured to be employees of Saffron's, were brought in from Adelaide to work the clubs during the strike. Word on the street was either that the explosion at the Staccato was intended to frighten them into abandoning the strike, or provide an out for its operator as business was declining.

This was the event during which Anderson was badly burned, even though he allegedly had nothing to do with the club. He reckoned the owner was a buddy and he was driving past that night when he saw a couple of dudes acting suspiciously. You'd have to be acting *very* suspiciously to stand out in the Cross in that era – especially to someone in a moving vehicle.

But big Jim decided to take a look. He parked, found a door partially opened, walked in, cigarette in his mouth. He reckoned he tripped over, got up and BOOM. Anderson drove himself to hospital where it was discovered that his shoes had traces of petrol on them. Shit happens.

No charges were laid and, all those years later, no one seemed to consider he may have had something to do with the six Saffron-related fires. Despite Anderson trying to finger Saffron, no one thought Abe would be so careless as to do something that would draw attention to himself in such a dramatic way. That wasn't Saffron's style. Only an idiot would torch six of their properties in quick succession. Saffron may have been a lot of things, but he certainly wasn't an idiot. Maybe if it was expedient, he'd get someone to torch one building – but not six.

Now, to make things interesting – and remember that at this stage no one knew Anderson was playing buddies with the law – in May 1980 Anderson and one of Saffron's associates met at a large nightclub in Bondi. This place wasn't owned by Saffron but it was leased on a long-term basis to one of his companies.

There'd been big plans for the club. The publicity word was that it was Australia's biggest nightclub. They reckoned 150 people could fit on the dancefloor and the overall capacity was 1400 – legally. They'd squeeze a few hundred more in if no one was looking. The joint had everything. There was a restaurant and a bar, the latter fitted out to resemble a space station.

For a club like this you needed a world-class artist on opening night. Who ya gonna get? At that time the absolute zenith of glitz, glamour, showbiz and disco was Donna Summer. Team Saffron was going to bring Hot Stuff Summer to Australia for their club.

But outside of discos and Donna there was tension in the air. One day Jim Anderson went to the club for a little chat with the owner. At one stage, Big Jim looked out the window and pointed to a house on a headland overlooking the ocean. He inquired – although he obviously already knew the answer – if that was the guy's new home.

Not long after the meeting, the house caught fire and was completely destroyed. The night after this fire, a building (owned by Saffron) that had been renovated before it became a new classy upmarket brothel also caught fire.

There were a lot of unexplained fires in Sydney around this time. On 30 June, nicely timed for the end of the financial year, a nightclub in Bondi Junction that attracted a lesbian clientele called Peak (the lease for this one could be traced back to Saffron too) had a fire.

There was a brief respite before – yep, a big fancy club caught fire.

The cops were starting to put two and two together and drawing certain conclusions about what was going on. On average there are only a number of serious property fires in Sydney every year and when a number of them are connected to a certain Abe Saffron (and associates), a man alleged to be involved in some dodgy activities – well, even the slowest member of the New South Wales Police Force could start making a few assumptions.

There were other theories at the time: one was that the gay bar and nightclub owners were having a highly inflammable spat. That might explain the Peak fire and the subsequent fire at Capriccio's, another well-known gay venue on Oxford Street in Darlinghurst that wasn't owned by Saffron, but not the other properties.

It was all a bit weird. Then came a fire at Alan Saffron's Fonzies Fantasyland, an amusement arcade stocked with all the games of the moment.

Taking the tally to six was a small fire at the Venus Room, which by that stage had closed.

The investigators looked closely at Alan Saffron. All these entertainment venues catching fire. Did insurance have something to do with it? The conclusion was that the owners and/or licensees of the properties were highly unlikely to have started or organised for the fires to be lit.

There was no tangible reason for them to do so that anyone could establish – and in fact to the contrary, it meant a significant loss of income at all these establishments. This wasn't like Victoria Street and no one was hoping to build

45-storey residential towers on the real estate. No, this was clearly destruction as a warning.

But a coroner's inquiry took place, initially into the first four fires and then the other two were added as they occurred during the hearing. Things at the inquiry became sticky for Saffron when big Jim Anderson took the stand and testified that he had personally heard Saffron and an associate having a little natter about fires and insurance claims. Anderson went on to suggest that things of value had been removed from the properties before the fires.

Just before the coroner made a finding against Saffron, his legal representative got the matter kicked upstairs to the Supreme Court. Eventually it was decided not to pursue further investigations.

Anderson had thrown his weight around and almost landed a few serious and damning blows. Saffron didn't realise that his former deputy was just getting started. Anderson wanted Saffron taken down and he wanted it with a passion.

Things became so tense that at one stage Anderson approached a former Saffron employee, Con (just Con), with a proposal. Con had previously been the manager of the Pink Panther and a trusted employee of Saffron's until he was caught helping himself to the till and got fired.

Anderson's proposal was simple: he wanted Con to kill Saffron. Not a beating or a couple of broken legs. Abe was to be dead. Very dead. Not coming back to the Cross dead.

The payment offered was a share of the Venus Room plus $25,000 in cash, apparently the going rate for a hit at that time. Anderson told Con that the gig was his if he wanted it, but if not then some experts from America would be flown in to do the deed. Con might not have been smart enough to avoid nicking cash from his place of work, but he was smart enough to know where the power in the Anderson–Saffron relationship lay. And it wasn't with Big Jim.

Con told Saffron about the plot. And Abe told the cops.

All this was happening as Kings Cross entered its downward spiral. It was increasingly grubby and dangerous. The only respite came very early in the morning as the sun came up.

I saw this on a few too many occasions as I stumbled out of places like the Manzil Room or Benny's and tried to navigate my way home. The street sweepers worked their way up and down Macleay Street as other stragglers went about their business. It was strangely quiet and often I found it rather poignantly beautiful. The comparative calm was all the more profound considering what had come before, and what would start again in a few hours. It was a brief moment of quiet every day.

Anderson wasn't Saffron's only headache. The 1980s wasn't an easy time for him: a new breed of criminal was entering the scene, many of whom were fuelled by drugs that frequently made people violent and irrational. Saffron was growing older and the almost gentlemanly way, at least compared to these times, that business was done in previous eras was changing. There were more and bigger firearms around and people were less discerning about how, why and where they used them.

And people knew about Saffron. Whether they knew about him in person or just through the media, they were aware of his reputation and with it came the assumption that he was a very wealthy man. It was an assumption that was correct.

The new breed of Kings Cross crook wasn't exactly going to take on Saffron. They may not have been super smart but they weren't totally brainless either. Keep away from Abe, but try to get in on the action that had made him so much money. That's what they figured they'd do. Easy.

Putting girls on the street. How hard was that? Selling speed, smack and dope. A licence to print money and just get someone else to do all the street selling.

The Cross became an out-of-control lawless world that resembled Deadwood in the 1800s, for those who know the television series. An almost lawless miasma of competing interests, all trying to undercut each other, carve their own turf and undermine the territory of others.

As the criminal elements became more scattered, disorganised and unpredictable, craziness ensued on the streets. It made the activities of Saffron and his mates in the 1960s and '70s seem positively civilised. And to an extent they were.

In 1980, Saffron was 60 years old. He still went about his business but was increasingly reclusive. He didn't recognise himself in these new criminal turks and he didn't want to mix with them. He was above that – and this new lot had no respect for what had gone before. In most cases they had no knowledge of it at all and those who did had little respect. They were dumb enough to even think they could take Abe down if he got out of line and flexed his muscles.

Abe didn't care. The criminal times they were a-changin'. It's not that there wasn't a place for Saffron; it was more that he didn't care to be associated with what was coming. He didn't need to be. He was Abe fucking Saffron.

There were other things changing that he did care about, however. Many figures in politics and the police force with whom Saffron had built close and protective relationships in the previous decades, some dating back to the 1940s, were dying, moving on to different positions, retiring or had finally been nailed for pushing the boundaries of legality in their positions.

And there was a new breed of cop who, in many instances, was less keen on bending the rules. There was more investigation and increased checking on licensing. The vice squad upped the ante.

Anyone who was forced to buy $1 plates of slop in late-night rock'n'roll venues knows exactly what I'm talking about. Venues were meant to offer a meal; if they didn't, they were in breach of the *Liquor Act*.

Behind much of this new policing was Sergeant Warren Molloy and a team he assembled to kick things into line in the Cross and surrounding areas. The cops would come into venues and try to get a bourbon and Coke without buying a meal. If that was acceptable, say goodbye to your liquor licence.

A lot of entertainment establishments connected with Saffron were in the cops' sights – the Venus Room (which was then known as the Raft), the Persian Room and Tina's, a restaurant in William Street which did, as Duncan McNab dryly observes, 'all its business across the bar'. Saffron wasn't the specific target, though. The cops were going after everybody.

Abe Saffron continued to attract attention, but nothing really stuck. The whiff of criminality was everywhere in his orbit but he still remained like Teflon when it came to actual charges.

There was carry-on about Saffron allegedly (it was always allegedly) spending time on a regular basis with Deputy Police Commissioner Bill Allen at the latter's playpen in College Street in the city. In parliament, New South Wales Opposition leader John Dowd actually described Saffron as 'a prominent Sydney crime figure'.

Jim Anderson was out there spreading whatever dirt he could on Saffron. This was at a time when there was increased scrutiny on a wide variety of business practices. If something was being investigated usually the name Saffron would appear at some stage. That included tax avoidance schemes and the Nugan Hand Bank inquiry. Everyone sniffed. Everyone assumed Saffron was up to no good. No one could actually pinpoint what no good he was actually up to. Okay, so he had an interest in more than 60 companies. Abe Saffron was simply a businessman with a lot of interests.

Anderson was not going away; this was a man who knew where the bodies were buried. During the inquiry into the disappearance of Juanita Nielsen in which Anderson was a significant (alleged) player, he introduced the notion that Saffron kept two sets of books – one for the taxation department, the other the real story.

Anderson had copies of such books and handed them to Opposition Leader Dowd, who passed them on to the federal police, who couldn't find anything untoward in them. Maybe they were legitimate records of accounts, or perhaps Saffron financially encouraged the people put in charge of the matter to be mathematically challenged.

The accusations seemed dead in the water, or at least those who could have pursued the matter decided that they didn't want to. One thing's for sure: Saffron had a lot more clout in these circles than Anderson did, and a lot more money to buy the aforementioned clout. Plus in the world of criminal activity, it was common knowledge that Anderson and Saffron had had a falling-out.

Confronted with a decision, financially encouraged or not, as to whether to take Anderson's or Saffron's side in this spat, the odds were strong that people would back Saffron Incorporated. His side was much more cashed up and lacked the air of thuggery that Anderson brought with him.

But in mid-1984 the National Crime Authority (NCA) came into being, with Justice Donald Stewart as chair. Established by the government to combat organised crime, its brief was to go after the bigwigs in the Australian criminal network.

There was a long list of individuals who were being looked at – including George Freeman, 'Aussie Bob' Trimbole, Stan 'The Man' Smith, Murray Riley, Arthur Stanley 'Neddy' Smith and Frederick 'Paddles' Anderson – and Abe was on the list too, jockeying for first place

There was also a belief that Saffron was deliberately trying to present an even lower profile than in the past. In his 1986 book *Disorganised Crime*, author Richard Hall suggests that by the early 1980s the federal police were under the impression that George Freeman was taking over from Saffron as the principal figure in the Cross. They suggested that this was actually by agreement with Saffron. At this stage Saffron was in a position to just sit back and let the money keep rolling in; the incentive wasn't there for him to go into bigger ventures. Been there, done that.

George Freeman was also near the top of their target list, but the NCA and the Australian taxation department still had Saffron in their sights, too. They wanted him. They assumed he was involved in bad things and they were intent on finding out what those were.

There was undoubtedly a strong sense of frustration among those in the NCA and tax department whose job it was to try to unravel Saffron's business affairs. There were so many theories, so many connections that didn't add up and so much pointing to Saffron's involvement in all sorts of illegal matters, but they had no evidence to charge him. Not the slightest. And they were looking and looking and relooking. They wanted Saffron badly, but could they nail his business affairs to arrest warrants? No they could not. At least, not yet.

* * *

Nothing stays the same in a city, that's the very nature of urban growth. As the 1970s came to a close anyone expecting to experience the already romanticised Cross of the previous decades was kidding themselves. It was for the most part gone, in keeping with the overall changes in Sydney. There was movement on them there streets. This was my era and while Abe was still a big player around then, I had no idea about it.

Abe and I were both customers of the ANZ bank in the Cross. Maybe we stood in line together waiting for a teller's attention. Who knows. Somehow, though, I think he would have been more of the type who was quickly ushered into the branch manager's office. Saffron may have had more clout than any of the rock stars I was interviewing at the Sebel Townhouse, but unless you moved in his circles he was largely an anonymous figure, and for the most part he continued to fly under the radar. He had money to count, properties to buy, meetings to go to. Another guy going about his business among the denizens of the Cross. It was that type of place.

But in the 1980s there was a new breed of entrepreneur moving into the Cross. They were faster, more aggressive and for the most part not all that bright. They wanted easy money and good times. More disturbingly, they didn't mind how they got it. They were prepared to deal violently with anyone who got in their way – like the razor gangs, but more thuggish, a new breed of criminal coming through expanded the ranks of the vicious. They were bred on bad drugs and violent television shows influencing them on how to behave.

The drugs made them edgier and more unpredictable and there were a lot more guns and other weapons around. The cops were as greedy as ever and increasingly malleable if envelopes containing the right amounts of money came regularly and on time. The golden age of police corruption was blooming.

The drugs changed and heroin ruled. The music changed. The entertainment venues changed. The clientele changed.

Fights on the street and in venues were more common. Kings Cross was edgier than ever – as a music fan you always kept your eyes open and your wits about you as you strolled from one venue to another.

Saffron continued to rule, though, and the cash kept rolling in. His position was clear: Abe was the boss. He didn't mess or mix with the newcomers unless they got in his way. He didn't need to. He was above the riffraff. And if any of them stepped out of line, Abe wasn't going to bruise his knuckles on these little pretenders. He had others who could take care of that stuff and send whatever message was required. For Saffron it was like flicking away insects: don't annoy me … ever.

Such was his increased perception as an almost folk hero – at least to those who weren't on the receiving end of his reminders and hadn't got in his way – that Saffron was even celebrated in a song 'Heartbeat of Sydney' by Edwin Duff, which includes the line 'Abe is the Boss'. Abe would have loved that. Much better than 'Abe is Mr Sin'. Still, there were problems. A few issues including the disappearance of Juanita Nielsen lingered and the smell was bad.

CHAPTER 12

LUNA PARK

Just at the time the spotlight was turned on Saffron, another allegation emerged. Talk in late 1979 and the early 1980s was that Abe Saffron had something to do with a massive tragedy that still looms large in the public consciousness of many in Sydney: a fire that occurred on 9 June 1979 on the Ghost Train ride at Luna Park on Sydney's harbour, resulting in seven deaths. The suggestion was that Saffron was somehow connected via the companies that operated the park.

Rumour-mongering and innuendo went on for years, but it really came to the fore in 1984 due to Martin Sharp's *Luna Images: The Face of Sydney* exhibition at the Ivan Dougherty Gallery.

Sharp was the pre-eminent Australian pop art figure of his time – a local version of Andy Warhol and Roy Lichtenstein if you will. Active in the Cross in the days of the artist hub that was the Yellow House, Sharp had spent significant time in London and had worked on the controversial *OZ* magazine in the 1960s with editors and close friends Richard Neville and Richard Walsh.

Sharp had done album cover art for the legendary English blues rock band Cream and even co-written a couple of their songs, including their best known hit 'Tales of Brave Ulysses' with the band's guitarist Eric Clapton.

Sharp's distinctive paintings and screen-printed poster art were highly sought after and he was considered one of the leading lights in the Sydney bohemian art world with his house Wirian in Bellevue Hill in the wealthy eastern suburbs, a mecca for such types and party central for many visiting international musicians and artists.

Sharp would develop a fanatical interest – we could call it for what it was, an obsession – in American-born singer Tiny Tim and promoted his performances in Australia, released his records and documented his career with a degree of detail that would border on a magnificent mania.

Tiny Tim was an American singer known for his falsetto and encyclopaedic knowledge of popular songs. He had the ability, usually accompanied by ukulele, to recall and perform thousands of songs at whim. He became globally known in 1968 for his version of the song 'Tiptoe Through the Tulips'.

In January 1979 Sharp promoted a performance by Tim at Luna Park, which would claim the world record for the longest non-stop singing marathon, singing for two hours and 17 minutes and performing portions of more than 200 songs.

Sharp was also completely besotted with Luna Park and its history and mythology. In the early 1970s he was involved with the restoration of the place in his capacity as an artist and much later, through the 1980s and '90s, he would be heavily involved in ongoing activity to keep the park and its location out of the hands of developers, many of whom were naturally interested in one of the most desirable locations on Sydney Harbour. Sharp would in fact head the Friends of Luna Park activist group for much of this period.

The fire in the Ghost Train ride at Luna Park killed six children, and one adult: They were Richard Carroll, Jonathan Billings, Seamus Rahilly and Michael Johnson, all friends, all 13 years old; and Craig Godson (4), Damien Godson (6) and their dad, John Godson (29). Jenny Godson stood outside the Ghost Train as the horror unfolded; she waited for her entire family who never made it out. The unimaginable grief Jenny Godson experienced. The grief that affected many lives.

Sharp's antennae were up. He was personally shattered by the tragedy – as were most people – and wondered what had happened and wanted to know why.

According to Lowell Tarling in *Sharp: 1942–1979* and *Sharper: 1980–2013*, his two-part biography of the artist, 'Martin came to believe the fire was the collective negligence of the entire City of Sydney. But the cause, Martin believed, was a deliberate criminal act.' Sharp believed that Abe Saffron had organised a criminal bikie gang to set the fire – to destroy it so developers could move in.

Tarling quotes Sharp in a 1983 interview as saying, 'Juanita Nielsen disappeared from the Carousel Club at the Cross – that was the connecting bond between her and Abe Saffron. (Plus you get the same fairground imagery –

the Carousel, right?) He's also the secret figure behind Luna Park.'

In the book there are accusations that in the early days of Kings Cross, when Sharp and others established the Yellow House, the police tried to shake the occupants down only to find that none of them had any money and it wasn't that kind of establishment.

Sharp also includes the claim that Saffron wanted Gretel Pinniger (Madam Lash) 'rubbed out' but that 'one of her suitors, Lennie McPherson, stepped in and calmed the waters'.

The Tarling book cites a woman who visited Sharp's house in Bellevue Hill and who said that she used to work at Luna Park in the Magic Shop and that, 'Abe got me the job there. He runs it with two Sydney businessmen.'

That was enough for Sharp, who was already obsessive about the fire, Luna Park and Saffron, to put it mildly. According to Tarling, Sharp started to dig deep. He'd gathered newspaper clippings and photographs, plus 'extracts from occult encyclopedias, metaphysical indicators, symbolic evidence and Biblical verification. Examples: (1) the name "God-son", (2) $13 price tags at the Magic Shop, (3) the Pope on a train to Auschwitz for the first time ever, (4) Bob Dylan recording his *Slow Train Coming* album, and (5) Saffron's Jewish connection'.

Sharp's *Luna Images* exhibition featured a number of images with the name 'Saffron' contained in them. 'It's a bit of a complicated exhibition to understand,' Sharp said at the time. 'It takes a lot of hard looking.' Saffron's name 'though small, was peppered throughout. The devil was in the detail.' In Sharp's mind, literally.

Then Sharp came into contact with someone he knew only as 'Mal', who had done time in Long Bay jail. There Mal said he overheard a group of inmates talking, trying to outdo each other with claims of their exploits. Mal overheard one say that they'd 'torched the park for Abe'.

Sharp tried to get media to run stories linking Abe Saffron and the Ghost Train but potential contenders such as *Rolling Stone* magazine and *The National Times* turned him down. It was too volatile a subject, and Saffron too litigious to stir up.

Eventually, in 1985, Sharp found himself with Superintendent Ernie Shepard of the New South Wales Police Internal Security Unit (ISU) in Sydney. In the conversation an individual known as 'Scar' was mentioned who had apparently said he'd 'torched the park for Abe'.

Not long after this, Shepard left that job and Sharp lost his contact in the police department. Soon afterwards, Sharp's associate, photographer John Barker, received a death threat and was told to 'stop going to Martin Sharp's or you'll wind up like your brother'. John's brother Michael Barker – also a photographer – had been working on 21 November 1980 with Friends of Luna Park, an affirmative action group lobbying against developments at Luna Park, when he was killed in a hit-and-run accident. The call to John Barker made it very clear that the death of Michael had been a murder. Who knew about Barker, his brother and Sharp's relationship? Not many people.

The Friends of Luna Park believed that the Ghost Train fire was arson and that the perpetrators had been commissioned by Saffron, who was then in control of

Luna Park through his solicitor David Baffsky and his cousins Harold and Colman Goldstein. Even though they apparently had no previous experience in running fun fairs and parks like Luna Park, they'd won the lease from the New South Wales government.

On 1 June 1985 Sharp stated: 'The fact that John Barker has today been threatened implies that we are indeed on to something with this case.'

At the time Sharp went on to drive around Double Bay for three days before coming up with what he believed was the answer. Sit tight, reader.

Abe Saffron had three cars. Numberplates: ABE-111, ABE-222 and ABE 333.

Add it up and it equals 666. Case closed.

Not surprisingly, even a few of Sharp's friends were beginning to think he was going a little bonkers.

Sharp's fixation endured and he continued to add to his obsessively detailed files on Saffron. Part of the file was a page from the Sydney phonebook with the number of Arcadia Amusements, the company that supplied vending machines to Luna Park, and one that also involved Saffron's son, Alan. That phone number ended in 666 – the number of the Beast.

Sharp's file was entitled 'Criminal Connections: Saffron, The King in Yellow'. According to another Sharp biographer, Joyce Morgan, in her book *Martin Sharp: His Life and Times*, 'it was a reference to the colour of his name, but also an allusion to a theme in a book of supernatural short stories by nineteenth-century American writer Robert W. Chambers. The King in Yellow, referred to throughout the stories, is a fictional play that induces despair or madness in anyone who reads it.'

Sharp made an unfinished film about the Ghost Train fire and singer Tiny Tim – and according to Morgan it contains elements of nightmare. 'Part-documentary, part-visual collage, the film's uniting thread is Tiny Tim's singing marathon at Luna Park, but it is also intertwined with the fire and Martin's response to it. In the film Martin alleges there was a cover-up and that the police had told him this at the time but were powerless to act.'

In the opinion of Sharp and others, 'the Abe Saffron team' had not given up on plans for developing Luna Park. There were plans for floating restaurants, cinemas, cafes, a 200-room hotel, a 1200-space car park and an office block over Coney Island.

Parts of Luna Park were sold at auction in 1981. At this stage a consortium called Harbourside Amusements was close to securing the 30-year lease. Sharp attended the auction, which raised half a million dollars. He spent $9000 buying memorabilia and rides including Coney Island's Turkey Trot, Barrels of Fun and the Joy Wheel.

Much of the park was bulldozed to create space for new rides when it reopened in 1982. The park was closed again in 1988 before reopening in 1995. There had been plans drawn up by a new lessee for an adult entertainment centre with high-rise buildings.

At one stage the Corporate Affairs Commission did its best to unravel the business of Luna Park. It concluded that in the aftermath of the fire, Harbourside Amusements, the consortium who then leased the park and its activities, included two of Saffron's cousins as directors and another relative as company secretary.

What couldn't be established in any way was that Saffron was directly involved, or that he stood to gain from the channelling of funds in his direction. There was simply no evidence. Either Saffron was even smarter than assumed or there simply was nothing going on. And you could bet there were serious attempts to join the dots that could be joined.

A few years went by and Sharp softened his position on Saffron's involvement in the Luna Park fire and his position became that others were definitely involved in the fire, possibly more so than Saffron.

Around this time – either late in 1989 or early in 1990 – Sharp was heading to a lunch date at DBs, a restaurant in Double Bay. As Sharp recalled: 'I noticed this person looking at me, smiling. I turned around to save us a spot and he – Abe Saffron – is sitting right in the middle of this restaurant … I was taken aback. I … shook his hand and said, "Hi, how are you?" It was a strange meeting, quite good-natured in its way. What was I to do? Keep walking? Go somewhere else? It could have been set up of course – couldn't it? Or was it just chance? The thing was – it was as if Saffron was expecting me.'

* * *

Certainly, there was one Saffron connection to Luna Park. When Alan Saffron, who had the amusement machine business Vendomatic, heard that the park's contract for amusement machines was up for renewal, 'we targeted what we knew would be a great deal. There were numerous new pinball machines and video games on the market, and if we secured this contract, it would ensure the continued success of the company.' Soon Vendomatic had more than 100 machines at Luna Park.

At the time the fire occurred, the park was leased to property developer Leon Fink and a partner, Nathan Spatt. They had wanted to purchase the park but reckoned they'd been thwarted by the then Labor government led by Neville Wran.

Everyone had an opinion about who was behind the fire. If asked, most people would answer with a variant of 'Oh, Abe Saffron did it, he's a crook,' or 'Abe Saffron set it up.' That was the prevailing wisdom even though there was not a skerrick of evidence for it. Even the 'criminal' bit was off the mark in those days as Saffron hadn't actually been convicted of anything major. It was another case of Saffron's reputation being smeared by rumours and inferences.

Slowly over the years, the tragedy drifted into distant memory – but not forever. The Luna Park fire still loomed so large in people's imaginations that it was never going to completely go away while the mystery and rumours lingered. For the families of those who lost their loved ones in that fire, the desire for answers and justice was always alive.

In May 2007 the story was back in the headlines when *Sydney Morning Herald* investigative journalist Kate McClymont interviewed Saffron's niece Anne Buckingham. This niece had an axe to grind. She was a little like Donald Trump's nemesis, his niece Mary Trump. There was clearly no love lost in both cases.

Using a strange expression, Buckingham reckoned that Uncle Abe 'liked to collect things' and that one of the things he intended to collect was either Luna Park or the property that it was on.

A further 14 years later the Luna Park genie was unleashed again in a three-part documentary aired on ABCTV. Entitled *Exposed: The Ghost Train Fire* it was as sensationalised as the title suggested. The thrust of the series was simple. It was the old theory: where there's fire there must be Saffron.

Interviewed for the show were people such as James Swanson, a former licensing magistrate, and former senior police officers Steve Bullock and Paul Egge. They made no secret of their belief that Abe ordered the fire and that this activity was covered up by a bunch of corrupt cops and government figures. They didn't name too many specific names beyond the tried-and-tested Robert Askin and Neville Wran. Saffron could not be reached for comment because, well, he was dead and in no position to defend himself.

Mind you, if he were still alive and approached to appear in the series, Saffron would most probably have shrugged his shoulders and said, 'They can say what they want, it's got nothing to do with me.' That was Abe's way. And then he'd sic his lawyers onto them.

The ABC show posited that the whole thing was about control of the land that Luna Park continues to sit on. Was there much evidence presented? Not really. Opinions? Lots of them.

The ABC was widely criticised for airing the program and at the time of writing the Luna Park fire is once again relegated to a part of Sydney's tawdry history and a fascinating unsolved crime.

We await someone getting out a ouija board, contacting Abe in the afterlife and getting his views on the subject. Maybe he's had time to reflect.

An independent review of the ABC documentary concluded that the program provided no substantiated evidence of a corrupt relationship between Neville Wran and Abe Saffron; it was drawing a very long bow to say that Wran was involved in covering up Saffron's alleged involvement in the fire.

Years come and go. Every time the Luna Park fire is mentioned, you can be pretty sure that you'll hear the name Abe Saffron in the same sentence, but the fact is that he has not been and maybe will never be directly connected to it.

* * *

The disappearance of Juanita Nielsen and the Luna Park Ghost Train fire – two terrible events that loom large in the public consciousness and two events that, despite the passing decades, have still not been fully resolved. The name Abe Saffron hovers around both but there is no tangible evidence to connect him with wrongdoing in either matter. Circumstantial, perhaps? Maybe he actually didn't have anything to do with them. If he did, it's further evidence that he was masterful in covering his tracks and keeping at a careful remove from events in which he was involved. The thing I have learned about Abe Saffron, the smoke was dense but the fire was never found.

CHAPTER 13

THE END OF ABE

Let's go back to the years after the Luna Park fire and the inquiries into the other fires – the ones at properties that could be directly connected to Saffron.

By this time, Saffron was not the overt presence around Kings Cross that he once was – and he didn't really want to be. His power was somewhat diminished as a new breed of politician and new judges and magistrates came through the ranks, largely replacing those whom Saffron had traditionally had in his pocket.

The New South Wales Police Force was still a long way from squeaky clean but it wasn't nearly as corrupt as it had been; a lot of the bent and on-the-take cops had been weeded out or had left the force, which also made things tougher for Saffron and his ilk.

But Saffron Incorporated had enjoyed a dream run. At 60 years old, Saffron was a very rich man. Through luck and good management, and by astute under-the-counter and illegal methods, Saffron had kept himself out of the clutches of the law and therefore out of jail.

Did he think that he was immune from prosecution? After all these decades, did he assume that he had everything under control? Or did he expect that the forces of the law would once again descend on him and this time catch him in a net that even Abe Saffron, with all of his contacts, couldn't escape?

Did he ever imagine that it would be his former deputy-turned-nemesis, Jim Anderson, who would bring him down? And that those sets of books and the financial records Anderson had passed on would get a second or third viewing and be found significantly wanting?

Anderson had kept on the case and played a key role in these inquiries into Saffron's financial affairs. Eventually his efforts to bring Saffron down bore fruit. Team Anderson had their win. The books did look to be dodgy. Saffron had been playing free and easy with his accounting and had been not exactly forthcoming about his real income.

Abe had ignored American statesman Benjamin Franklin's wisdom about only two things being inevitable – death and taxes. He'd managed to avoid any legal connection to anything unlawful for decades, and perhaps he thought this would always be the case.

So what got him in the end? Not being exactly straight up in his relationship with the tax department. Or at least that's how the tax department viewed it when they eventually had a forensic look through his books.

In the middle of November 1984, the National Crime Authority again approached Anderson. Saffron was 65 –

retirement age back then. Anderson and other associates and former associates of Saffron's were interviewed at length. No doubt the others provided useful information, but Big Jim was the one really holding the cards.

The NCA also went back to earlier material compiled by Sydney Detective Sergeant George Slade, who had been working for the New South Wales Bureau of Criminal Intelligence. Slade had spent three years investigating Saffron Incorporated after being instructed to do so by his boss, Detective Superintendent Ray 'The Blizzard' Blissett.

Slade reckoned he hadn't found anything incriminating in Saffron's world, but Blissett refused to let it rest, explaining in vague terms that there was pressure being applied from above to come up with something to charge Saffron with.

It wasn't the usual way to conduct an investigation, but Slade approached Saffron about having a meeting, which occurred at the home where Saffron spent time with his mistress Rita Hagenfelds and his daughter, Melissa. It was the home he was at when he wasn't with Doreen. Apparently, Slade showed Saffron all the information he'd collected, which resulted in Abe expressing how impressed he was with the work done and even offering to correct a few mistakes in the files.

At this time, word on the street was that Anderson was making overt moves to have Saffron killed. Outside of Anderson and some other rivals, no one really wanted that. Getting rid of the King of Kings Cross would almost certainly result in a scramble for power and all sorts of things could go wrong. Turf wars were rarely, if ever, sedate affairs. The cops weren't at all keen on a situation where more-brutal and harder-to-manage men like George Freeman, Lennie McPherson and Neddy Smith were driving and controlling organised crime in Sydney. They were bad enough without more power.

Slade stressed to his superiors the importance of ensuring that Saffron wasn't topped by associates of Anderson's, and that Saffron didn't instigate a counter move and have Anderson taken out. The NCA went through Slade's dossier to see if there was anything that had been missed. They issued search warrants on Saffron's home and that of Tosha Maksimovich. They also raided the warehouse space in Surry Hills where Saffron had moved his business when he needed more space than he had at Lodge 44 in Edgecliff.

Saffron may not have been overtly busy but that hadn't stopped his business interests growing. The NCA even set up surveillance across the road from the warehouse. They wanted Saffron badly – but they found nothing of consequence.

Meanwhile, Jim Anderson's hate for his former boss had not cooled. He continued to funnel information to the NCA and eventually they had something they could act on. I can't help but wonder if this information was an exchange for his freedom from prosecution in the Juanita Nielsen disappearance, or any other manner of criminal involvement the police were aware of.

On 5 December 1985 Saffron was arrested. The charges were conspiracy to defraud the Commonwealth between 1969 and 1981 and a further 12 charges of making false declarations to the tax department in the years 1975–81. Saffron was 66 years of age and surely thought he'd beaten them all.

Out on a bail of $250,000, Saffron handed over his passport and reported to police three times a week. His trial was set for October 1987. He was effectively out of action and kept an even lower than usual profile. It was the perfect time for others to step in – which is exactly what they did. In came Louis and Bill Bayeh, who were in the drug business. As Duncan McNab writes: 'At the unlovely Sweethearts café on the Darlinghurst Road strip, the Romanian connections busied themselves in the import and distribution of cocaine. The supposed glamour and hierarchy of the past was just that – a thing of the past. The new business was strictly about money, and any hiccups in the cash flow were dealt with quickly and violently.'

I saw an incidence of this first-hand once, and it terrified me. After an all-night session at the Kings Cross home of a comparatively small-time cocaine dealer I knew, I was hanging around late morning in a jittery state when an incredibly solid, don't-fuck-with-me looking chap burst through the front door and made a beeline for the friendly, mild-mannered dealer, who suddenly looked petrified. The two retired to the bedroom, where thankfully the required money was all present and accounted for. Ten minutes later, Mr Really Scary walked out of the room and straight back out the front door.

These were not people to be messed with. They had a code and way of doing business that you immediately sensed you didn't want to get on the wrong side of. After protracted delays with the Saffron trial, on 5 November 1987 he was informed that he had been found guilty on all tax-related charges levelled at him. Judge Loveday of the New South

Wales District Court sentenced Abe Saffron to three years' hard labour and specified that he had to serve a minimum of two years and three months. Team Saffron immediately launched an appeal and Abe was allowed to remain on bail until the appeal was finalised.

Close to a year later, on 28 October 1988, 69-year-old Saffron lost his appeal, was handcuffed and escorted to a van headed to Long Bay jail in Sydney.

In his book on George Freeman, author Tony Reeves suggests that Saffron's jailing represented the end of an era in Australian criminality: 'The empire, built up over more than three decades, would last a little while yet, but there would have been signs that it was beginning to crumble. Despite their denials … [the old crime bosses] were slowly becoming members of a fading generation as younger crooks took over their traditional territories.'

While in Long Bay, Saffron continued to oversee his business interests via phone and instructions whispered or barked to visitors. Old habits die hard and in June 1989, Saffron convinced prison authorities that a stage show from the Les Girls entourage was just what the inmates needed. As part of her continued defence of Saffron, in her memoir Carlotta states that the Les Girls appearance was not because Saffron had organised it. She doesn't say who invited them but is adamant that it wasn't Saffron, despite what the media claimed. Catering for the performance was not the usual prison fare, but takeaway from a none-too-shabby Chinese restaurant in Kensington. Even in jail Abe Saffron wielded serious clout.

Saffron was moved to the Emu Plains Prison Farm at the end of 1989, but he was returned to Long Bay for the end of his sentence and was released on 11 March 1990. When he walked out of the prison gates, he had served one year and five months. He was prohibited from being a company director until 1995.

The man led a quiet life after being released from prison, working from his inner-city office situated in a Victorian villa in Potts Point, not far from the territory he used to rule. On the wall were two photos: one was of Al Capone and the other, the now infamous photo taken of young Abe at one of his clubs through the raised leg of a dancer.

Alan Saffron writes that his father never lost his taste and desire for younger women. 'In fact, when he was in his seventies it got a little embarrassing when he would gaze intensely and obviously at young waitresses. He was no kindly old grandfather type. Strangely, the young ladies would smile and flirt back. He was charming, with a silent power, even before he threw the black American Express card on the table.'

And if you're wondering, a black American Express card is reserved for the company's wealthiest clients. You can't apply for it. You just get it when you become the sort of person for whom, in theory, money is no object. And American Express doesn't have to worry about your ability to pay your bills.

Author Peter Rees wrote that Abe grew old 'with a wry sense of humour, but any humour disappeared at the mention of Jim Anderson'. In a curious twist, after the first edition of his book about Juanita Nielsen was published, Rees wrote that he received a call from a guy who identified himself only as 'Cliffy'. Cliffy told Rees that he had worked at the ANZ bank in Kings Cross that Saffron visited every Friday to make his deposits and do other banking.

Cliffy apparently had a remarkable memory and said he had been in the back room of the branch on the morning of 4 July 1975 when Abe was there doing his thing. Cliffy says that someone came to the door, looked directly at Abe and said, 'It's done.'

Given the date, Cliffy supposed this was a reference to the disappearance of Juanita Nielsen. No one could back this up, of course. Cliffy went on to suggest that he knew that Nielsen's body was buried at the back of Lodge 44, Saffron Central. Cliffy added that renovations were being done at the property at the time, which had made it easy to bury a body.

Rees naturally wanted to meet Cliffy, but the guy with the good oil on the matter never called back. Rees did take a wander around the property and concludes that it would have been difficult to bury a body there without being seen – and of course if anyone thought this was seriously the final resting place of Nielsen it would still be possible to excavate the site.

As quiet and private as Saffron tried to be, his reputation by this time was loud. So loud indeed that it had seeped into the community consciousness, helped along by more than a decade of media attention and a stint in the can. Cliffy was a typical voice of the popular chorus.

In his dotage Saffron had become an easy and convenient tie into the criminal world and every nefarious mystery rattling around in the Sydney Harbour breeze. And maybe even an opportune distraction, because the times they were a-changing.

* * *

By 2005 Saffron wasn't doing so well. Richard Walsh wrote a piece in which he argued there were two Abe Saffrons: there was Abe One, 'notorious owner of strip joints and other dubious enterprises'; and Abe Two, 'part-time philanthropist' and quiet ladies' man.

In researching this book and digging deep, I have concluded that Saffron's character was intriguing and complex on many levels. The public perception was of a tough, not-to-be-messed-with figure who controlled a vast network of businesses, and he was involved in many things you did not want to know about.

Then there was charity worker Abe, who did lots of good community work, often alongside his wife, Doreen. Saffron was a respected figure at the Benevolent Society and was reportedly a regular contributor when the rabbis required cash for various matters. Moriah College had a science laboratory that was funded by Saffron.

Undoubtedly there are many other examples of his charitable behaviour. In keeping with his low-key approach to his other business activities, Saffron wasn't one to make a big deal about his charitable activities, either. Let's face it, how many of the recipients really wanted it known that significant parts of their funding were courtesy of the King of Kings Cross or the man alleged to be 'Mr Sin'?

As far back as the late 1940s there is evidence of his philanthropy. For instance, he organised a Christmas party for children with disabilities at the Roosevelt. Reportedly it could have been the end of Abe, as the microphone he was using to give a speech short-circuited and slammed 200 volts through him, leaving him lying on the floor unconscious and very blue. Saffron was rushed to hospital where it was discovered that the current that had surged through his body had fractured his spine.

So how did a man who had always been at the centre of things spend his retirement? How did he fill his time? Anyone who thought he'd relax at home with immediate family, particularly Doreen, didn't know Saffron well. His wandering eye and desire for other women had not faded as the years went by. He still loved Doreen, but he didn't by any stretch of the imagination treat her well and with the degree of respect that you would expect. Doreen, on the other hand, always stood by Abe despite the indignities he constantly put her through, including multiple affairs, long and short term, and casual sexual encounters.

Let's not pretend the man was completely removed from what he'd built, though. There was business to attend to. There were still lots of properties and other interests to deal with.

Two significant emotional blows were heading his way. His brother Henry died in February 1999, and then in September that same year, Doreen finally left Abe. On 3 September, aged 77, Doreen died. On her grave was inscribed, 'YOU WERE A LOVING, CARING, LOYAL & WONDERFUL LADY WHO WAS ALWAYS THERE FOR US & WILL REMAIN IN OUR HEARTS FOREVER & EVER. WE MISS YOU SO MUCH.

'ONE LIFE, ONE LOVE'............ABE

Soon after Doreen's death, Saffron travelled to America, hanging with Alan and his family in Santa Monica in Los Angeles. While there, Abe's health took a turn for the worse, resulting in three operations and the insertion of a pacemaker. The American health system being what it is, Saffron's bill was US$4 million. Not that such a bill was really an issue for Abe, of course. As soon as he was well enough to travel he returned to Australia. The spark of Abe's life was flickering.

Six years after his mother's death Alan returned to Australia. His father was dying. I'm not saying the son figured that visibility at this time would increase his financial prospects, but the thought did cross my mind.

Abe Saffron died in St Vincent's Hospital in Sydney on 15 September 2006. He was 86, almost 87. The cause of death was complications from an infected leg. It was a quiet end for a man who had been the catalyst for a wild, eventful ride. His headstone read:

ABRAHAM GILBERT SAFFRON 6.10.1919–15.9.2006

LOVING HUSBAND OF DOREEN, BELOVED FATHER OF ALAN, CHERISHED GRANDFATHER OF DAVID, SAMUEL, ADAM, REBECCA AND DANIEL.

DEVOTED BROTHER OF PHIL (DEC'D), HENRY (DEC'D), BERYL (DEC'D), AND FLORA.

LOVING FATHER TO MELISSA AND ADORED GRANDFATHER OF KOBY, JAI AND SAGE.

ADMIRED AND RESPECTED BY ALL WHO REALLY KNEW HIM.

GREATLY MISSED BY HIS FAMILY AND FRIENDS.

'I DID IT MY WAY.'

CHAPTER 14

ABE'S LEGACY

After Abe Saffron died a whole lot of shit hit the proverbial fan, particularly when it came to his will. There were a fair few players in this caper, all of whom were secretly hoping that the lion's share of what was assumed to be a very big pot was heading in their direction. Alan in particular, despite his tempestuous relationship with his father, was betting on this being his big payday. Only son, and all that stuff. Doreen was gone. It was gonna be his, right?

How much loot were we talking here? Everyone assumed that there were many, many millions involved, but very few people knew for sure so it was a game of estimates. Lots of people had theories but they were all based on guesswork. Was the estate worth $20 million, or $100 million, or more or less? What had Saffron done with his assets that few knew about? It seemed unlikely it was going to be bequeathed to the RSPCA, but stranger things have happened.

Most disappointed – brutally so – when the will was read was in fact Alan, who ended up with $500,000. Not a tiny amount but clearly nowhere near what he was expecting.

Saffron biographer Duncan McNab talked to Abe Saffron not long before he died, and told me that Abe's view was that he'd invested and/or given millions to his son over the course of his life and Alan had managed to screw up pretty much every business venture he turned his hand to, so he wasn't going to get much more to waste away.

Saffron's will gave $1 million each to all eight of his grandkids, five of whom were Alan's kids. So, in effect $5.5 million was coming to his son and direct family. You'd have thought Alan would be pretty happy about this, but no. He was furious, partly no doubt because the will was set up in such a way that he couldn't get his hands on the money going to his children, although he would later make some efforts to get around that.

The big winner in the great will allocation stakes was Teresa Tkaczyk, whose long-term commitment to Saffron as both secretary and mistress resulted in her post-Abe life being taken care of to the tune of $1000 per week for the rest of her life. Nice. Then throw in properties in Surry Hills and Elizabeth Bay in Sydney and another apartment on the Gold Coast, and the payout was very nice.

Also doing well in the divvy-up was Melissa Hagenfelds, Abe's daughter by his former mistress Rita Hagenfelds. Melissa ended up with $1000 per week and took home apartments in the salubrious Sydney suburbs of Elizabeth Bay and Centennial Park.

There was also speculation that various charities received up to $10 million, reinforcing Richard Walsh's theory that there were two Abes, the crook and the philanthropist.

Five years after his death in October 2011, it was revealed that Saffron was the father of another son – a man called Adam Brand (not the singer, another Adam Brand), whose mother was a former Kings Cross stripper. She was 22. The *Sydney Morning Herald* reported that social workers had declared her an unfit mother, taken her 13-month-old son away from her and put him up for adoption. Abe knew about his son and held onto a card sent to him by Adam's mum, Christine, in 1974. The card included a photo of her with baby Adam. After Abe's death, Teresa Tkaczyk handed the card to Adam, who had only recently discovered who his father had been. I wonder if there are any other children out there still to learn that Abe Saffron was their father?

With Abe dead and the threat of defamation suits gone, publishers Allen & Unwin released the first major biography of Saffron, by investigative journalist Tony Reeves, who had also written books on George Freeman and Lennie McPherson. A nice gift set for any aspiring Mr Big.

The next book about Abe was published in July 2008 – *Gentle Satan: Abe Saffron, My Father*, Alan's memoir, who returned to Australia from his base in the US to promote it.

While Alan's book is light on some details, it does provide some interesting insights into his father's character – and his son's attempts to follow in his footsteps. Early on, Alan reveals that the last book his father read was on the life of Virgin Group co-founder Richard Branson. He says that Abe also liked to quote Bill Gates saying that he wasn't going to leave anything to his kids, 'so I should have been aware that my father did not believe in a successor. His successors were godlessness and promiscuity.' Not words that were engraved on Abe's tombstone, but obviously engraved in Alan's heart.

Alan recalled the parade of prominent figures who passed through the family home as he was growing up, giving a taste of Saffron's circle of friends and associates. They included Barry Humphries; Norm Allan, the future Commissioner of Police in New South Wales; Lee Gordon; and Wayne Martin. Alan wrote, 'These were very important occasions for my father as they were when he portrayed his family image to the world – and himself.'

While he might have liked to have been seen as family focused, Abe Saffron was not a family man. It was all about Abe. Abe's family were his business associates and even then there was not the closeness of a real family.

The times he did try to play doting dad were definitely not out of any parenting book I've read. Abe organised for Alan to lose his virginity via a woman from the Venus Room. Immediately after, Alan was confused by why she quickly lost any interest in him. He'd work it out later. Who knows the psychic scars Alan carried but he soon embraced the world of nightclubs and women. Just like dear old Dad.

When he became an adult, Alan's favourite club was John Harrigan's Whisky A Go Go (not to be confused with Brisbane's Whiskey Au Go Go, but more on that later), which he describes as 'the hottest disco in town' at the time and where he would often hang out with his friends. 'The club had numerous scantily clad go-go dancers and they all joined me at the table during their break, where I supplied plenty of champagne for everyone.' He also frequented Sammy Lee's Latin Quarter, the Venus Room and from time to time made visits to his father's strip clubs. Of course he was welcomed everywhere he went and given a special table. Alan probably thought it was all about him back then. But these dancers and people of the night knew exactly who his dad was. Of course they did.

It is not entirely surprising that Alan Saffron developed a predilection for drugs and gambling – and also not surprising that this upset his father, who then allegedly set up for him to be busted and subsequently treated for these supposed addictions via electro-shock therapy.

The most significant revelation in *Gentle Satan* was the claim that Jim Anderson was the main player in the disappearance of Juanita Nielsen. The revelation gives some psychological basis to the war Anderson waged on Saffron. Alan Saffron also said in an interview with the *Sydney Morning Herald* that he'd received death threats over what he might reveal in his book and that he couldn't name everyone and say exactly what he knew as some of the key players were still alive.

He had made specific reference to an at-the-time still-living businessman and a police officer. The *Herald* stated that these figures were named in the manuscript of the book and that Saffron's publishers, Penguin, had that version. According to Alan Saffron, the book would be republished when those figures had died and could be named.

Despite appearing with various covers, there has to date never been a significant re-publication with any added detail, so either one or both of the key figures alluded to are still alive or the publishers don't feel there's enough interest to release a new edition of the book.

Alan did state – and the observations were published a day later in the *Sydney Morning Herald* – that his father was the person who 'controlled the vice trade, including illegal gambling and prostitution in every state and territory except Tasmania and the Northern Territory'. Why Abe Saffron would ignore these two presumably lucrative markets is a little confusing. Alan also stated what was always assumed: that Saffron bribed a lot of politicians and police. This was hardly an earth-shattering revelation or observation. More interesting were the suggestions that Saffron laundered much of his illegal income through loan-sharking and that Kerry Packer was one of many prominent figures who borrowed money from Saffron to cover gambling debts.

I'm not sure I buy this one. One would have thought, quite reasonably, that Packer had the financial resources to cover his own gambling debts.

There are other allegations in *Gentle Satan*, including that Abe Saffron lent money to colourful identities such as Frank Theeman, whose Kings Cross property development Juanita Nielsen was campaigning against. Also on the receiving end of Saffron loans were two people who, once again, it's hard to imagine needing loans from third parties – TNT boss Sir Peter Abeles and property developer Sir Paul Strasser.

Alan Saffron's book also backs up the suggestions that Robert Askin and Norman 'Bill' Allan were on the take in a big way. Alan states that his father paid anywhere between $5000 and $10,000 a week to both men. Even at the low end that's a big whack every year so, if true, one can only speculate about what Saffron was receiving in return to make that investment worthwhile. Both men were known to visit Saffron in his office and Bill Allan made a number of visits to the Saffron home; Saffron reportedly paid for Bill Allan and a female friend to take an all-expenses-paid overseas jaunt.

Some of Alan's claims seem too low level – like that his father was the bagman for the prostitution, illegal liquor and much of the illegal gambling activities in Sydney under the orders of Askin, Bill Allan and others who in turn made sure nothing bad happened to Saffron. All entirely plausible, although it's hard to imagine Saffron doing much of the collecting in person and answering to these men.

The one thing Abe and Alan had in common was that both were always on the lookout for business opportunities. Abe's usually turned a profit; Alan's not so much. For example, in November 2011 it was reported that Alan Saffron had withdrawn $250,000 from a bank account intended for his son Daniel and invested it in a Los Angeles restaurant that ended up on the reality television show *Kitchen Nightmares*. It was another business failure for Alan.

Fourteen years after the death of his father, on 19 April 2020 Alan Saffron died of a heart attack in Houston, Texas. This was during the Covid pandemic that closed the borders of countries and restricted visitors to hospitals. It meant most of his family weren't able to be with him.

Interestingly, the *Daily Telegraph* reported Alan's widow saying his last wish was for her to pass on documents about the Luna Park fire and Juanita Nielsen's death as he wanted closure for the families. Her words were, 'His father was not a good man and he did things he should not have done and I think Alan was at odds with that.'

* * *

It is inevitable that people look for connections when it comes to the family of a larger-than-life man like Abe Saffron. Recently one of his grandchildren has come under the spotlight. At the time of writing, Alan's son David is awaiting trial in the US for what the *Sydney Morning Herald* reported as a '$25 Million Alleged Bitcoin Ponzi Scheme'.

Regardless of what happens to David, it's clear that the Saffron presence in Kings Cross died with Abe Saffron. There are no children or grandchildren looking to follow in their forebear's footsteps and become the King of the Cross.

The Cross is still there, of course, a vastly different place from when Saffron Incorporated ruled. Yet, in many fundamental ways it hasn't changed all that much.

Businesses have come and gone but there's still a plethora of pubs and clubs, drugs are still everywhere and anyone who wants a girl can still pay for some quick entertainment. Factions still vie for control of various business activities and it remains a mixture of glamour (yes, there's still some of that), lights, fast-food joints, neon and underlying tension.

In Kings Cross it's still possible to have a great time or sadly maybe get your head beaten in on a Friday or Saturday night. Depends on how you play your cards and a bit of luck. Just like the old days, if you're in the wrong place at the wrong time, bad things can and quite possibly will happen.

The legacy of Abe Saffron continues to this day. Deals are done, money changes hands for favours, drugs are bought and sold, girls still ply their trade on the Strip, watched carefully by their pimps.

While organised crime dynasties and bit players rise and fall, Kings Cross retains an aura unlike any other Australian inner-city suburb.

Melbourne still has the grimy main drag of Fitzroy Street. Brisbane's Fortitude Valley is still jammed with nightclubs, bars and all manner of food outlets. The same for Adelaide's Hindley Street and other similar precincts around the country. Organised crime continues to flourish close to the surface in all these locales.

Abe Saffron was a trailblazer in this, a man who built an empire with tentacles reaching into countless different areas. He was the leader of the pack in his era. Decades later, his name resonates as one of the most iconic and infamous in Australian history during the past half century.

Questions still remain about what Abe Saffron did, what he knew, and what he made happen, but the truth is – you don't get a moniker like Mr Sin without making deals with the devil.

PART TWO

MUSIC'S UNDERBELLY

CHAPTER 15

KINGS CROSS VIBES

During the Abe Saffron era, Kings Cross was the epicentre of entertainment, glitz, glamour and seediness, but it wasn't the only game in town. There were a lot of other powerful and successful operators all over Sydney – and, like Abe, the majority were not exactly squeaky clean. Abe dominated the Cross, but there were venues and people beyond him where musicians, entertainers and less salubrious figures often mixed.

One of the longest running, best known and most successful was Chequers, situated in downtown Sydney. Like Saffron's Roosevelt club, Chequers epitomised class and glamour. Its entertainment was first-class and its clientele were treated to a memorable night out they would remember for the rest of their lives. And like the Roosevelt it was also a hub, a meeting place for people with connections – powerful men with connections they didn't want everyone knowing about. For a long time in the world of Sydney nightlife, Chequers was *the* place, the epicentre of style, entertainment – and organised crime.

Brothers Denis and Keith Wong founded the business in 1959 on Pitt Street and then moved to Goulburn Street where they developed it into one of Australia's premier cabaret venues, one that had a reputation that travelled around the world. It was the sort of joint where people travelling to Australia would be told 'make totally sure you go to Chequers whilst you're in Sydney – we had THE best night there last year.' American publication *Variety* awarded Chequers a gong for being one of the Top 10 nightclubs in the world. If money and influence had anything to do with that award we'll never know – but it was an accolade that no other Australian nightclub could claim.

The club attracted the likes of Sammy Davis Jnr., Dionne Warwick, Peter Allen, Liza Minelli, Matt Monro, Shirley Bassey, Ginger Rogers, Nelson Eddy and many, many others. It was that kind of place. It was classy and sophisticated – both in terms of the entertainment it provided and the types of customers who were drawn to its door. You felt urbane and transported from the everyday mundanity of existence just by walking down the stairs and being shown to your table. 'Would sir and madam like to start the night with a little glass of bubbly – or should I bring a bottle?'

There are claims that Chequers was one of the first restaurants in Australia to offer yum cha and Denis Wong made a big deal, as did patrons about his bombe alaska desert.

Over the years, as the interest in cabaret and crooners waned, Chequers moved with the times and embraced the new-fangled world of rock'n'roll. AC/DC played the club in their early days and Cold Chisel played there long before anyone bar a few hardcore fans really cared who Cold Chisel were.

I first started going to see gigs at Chequers in the late 1970s. I remember it as being downstairs and a little claustrophobic with no windows and it was an essential part of the inner-city circuit for bands and fans. I spent many nights there. The Ramones played there and I was in the audience one night for visiting English post-punk band Magazine.

The Wongs didn't just focus on the one place. They also established the Mandarin Club in the CBD. It was open very late – most probably flaunting any and all licensing laws – and it became a mecca for 'colourful' characters to drink, gossip and discuss affairs of the world. It opened and closed a few times over the years and moved from the corner of Pitt and Goulburn streets to Dixon Street in Chinatown before it closed for good in 2009, the year Denis Wong died, aged 80.

Over the years there have been many terrific yarns around the traps about Denis Wong and Chequers. Tommy Spencer, who played drums in the Chequers house band, told Michael Gormley from the *City Hub* newspaper that Wong was once offered the Beatles for a run of shows for $4000 per week. The story goes that Wong asked how many musicians were in the Beatles and when told four he offered to hire two of them. Apocryphal as it may be, it's a funny story.

There's also the gossip around the night then Prime Minister John Gorton disappeared backstage with Liza Minelli. They were gone for a while and tongues started wagging.

Chequers was also the location for a legendary gathering put on to welcome Chicago organised crime figure Joseph Dan Testa back to the Emerald City in 1969, four years after he first stepped foot on Australian soil. Attending that bash were Lennie McPherson, George Freeman and Milan 'Iron Bar Miller' Petricevic. I don't think Abe was there, nor do I know if he was invited.

Chequers and the Mandarin Club were locations where these sorts of individuals clearly felt comfortable and able to go about their business without being threatened, photographed – or shot at. But it wasn't the only place were dodgy people mixed with regular folk.

* * *

The now iconic and much mythologised Manzil Room in the Cross was a shadowy, shady, often edgy place that really didn't get going till midnight. It was where lots of well-known music industry people, hangers-on and figures who, well, you knew better than to ask who they were and what exactly they were doing there. Best just keep your distance.

Who owned the Manzil Room? Did Abe Saffron have an interest in this most rock'n'roll of Sydney and Kings Cross nightspots? As someone who spent more nights and early mornings inside this institution, I never really gave much thought to who was financially involved. Even if he did have a stake or ownership in the club, it's unlikely that he'd be wandering around the musicians, roadies, dealers, hangers-on and party hounds that made up the late-night clientele of the place.

When I started researching this book, I asked online if anyone had a copy of David Hickie's legendary *The Prince and the Premier* book, because my original copy had gone walkabout.

Someone – let's call him Arthur – contacted me and offered to not only give me his copy but also home deliver it. When Arthur arrived, I sensed immediately by his manner that he'd been around. We got talking about various eras in Sydney nightlife and when I mentioned a particular decade he said he wasn't around at that time. I asked where he'd been and he said, 'I had to leave the country – go overseas – make myself invisible …. if you know what I mean.' I didn't, but I could guess. He seemed like he knew people. He dressed well. Had an air of confidence. It was the middle of the day. He didn't look like the sort of person who was taking a lunch break.

In fact, he came across as the sort of person who was doing okay just by knowing people. In case I wasn't getting the message, he told me that after leaving my place he was heading to Marrickville to have coffee with – let's say it was an identity whose name was connected with the Sydney underworld that even I recognised.

We moved on to discussing the 1980s and the heyday of the Manzil Room. Arthur had worked there in the very early part of the decade, tending the bar and doing other bits and pieces. He'd risen to the point where he was trusted to take the night's takings across the road to the ANZ bank on Macleay Street in the early hours of the morning and deposit them in the night safe.

One night he had his eye on a woman who was at the Manzil Room and at 4 am he wasn't all that keen to leave the club in case she left, or someone else caught her attention.

There was a comparatively new guy working at the club, but Arthur liked him and figured he was okay. He trusted him enough to give him roughly $13,000 in cash and tell him to deposit it on his way home from his shift.

In the early hours of the morning Arthur went home. I forgot to ask if he went alone or with company. He went to sleep before the next night's shift, then mid-afternoon his phone rang. It was Joe Gersh, the manager of the Manzil Room. He was inquiring why no money had been deposited the night before.

Arthur went cold. His stomach started churning. The manager said he had better come to the Manzil right now. Not later. NOW. Thirteen grand was a lot of money.

On the way, Arthur stopped by the backpacker accommodation, where he knew the guy he'd entrusted with the cash had been staying. He was told that his mate had left, moved on, no forwarding address, no idea where he'd gone. The only thing for pretty much certain was that wherever he'd gone he had $13,000 of Manzil Room money with him. Money Arthur was entrusted to put in a safe.

When Arthur arrived at the Manzil Room he was told to go into the manager's office, and from there he claims he was taken to an office behind the office, where sitting at a table was a figure he recognised all too well. The King of the Cross, Abe Saffron.

'Hello Mr Saffron,' Arthur stuttered.

'Don't call me Mr fucking Saffron,' the man who was Abe Saffron said. Arthur had no idea how to address this clearly unhappy individual, so he said nothing more. Saffron explained that this was his venue, he owned it and that the missing money was in fact his.

'What the fuck happened to my money?' Saffron demanded.

Arthur bumbled his way through his explanation of why it was not him but another employee who had taken the money out of the club to the bank.

There was an uneasy silence before Saffron said, 'I believe you – and you can thank Christ I do as otherwise this meeting would have had a very different ending. Now, come back tonight, do your job and if that involves you taking the money to the deposit box then fucking do it, and don't think about getting anyone else to do it. Now get out.'

Arthur insists this was a true recollection of what happened, and that Saffron was the owner of the Manzil Room premises and more. Over the two years I've worked on this book no one has come forward to contradict him, and the key players from that era are either dead or not talking.

The Manzil Room operated at 15 Springwood Avenue in Kings Cross until 1990 when it changed its name to Springfields. Its heyday was definitely the late 1970s and early 1980s; as by the mid-'80s much of the action had moved down the road to Challis Avenue in Kings Cross and a new club named Benny's.

Unlike the Manzil Room, where music was an institution and the majority of bands played three sets a night, Benny's didn't feature live music. To give an indication of the hours that the Manzil operated, a band's first set would start about 11.30 pm, the next at 1.30 am and the last around 3 am.

The action didn't really kick off atmosphere-wise until at least midnight, because the Manzil Room was where you went after you'd been somewhere else. It was never your first port of call.

And while it's fair to say that 90 per cent of the clientele of the Manzil Room on any given night had consumed something other than booze, the drug use there was not nearly as brazen as it would be at Benny's, and the clientele not nearly as flashy. The Manzil Room exuded a grungy, sweaty rock'n'roll vibe and if there was a drug of choice it was amphetamines, whereas Benny's took care of the cocaine crowd.

No doubt wandering around the Manzil Room or sitting in corners playing backgammon until dawn were some shady and colourful Sydney identities, but they were well behaved and discreet. I never saw any hint of violence at the Manzil and I never saw drug deals going down. I certainly took drugs there – everyone did – but I did them carefully and quietly in one of the bathrooms.

There was an air of good times but also the feeling that trouble wasn't far away if you stepped out of line. The bouncers on the front door acted friendly and you knew things would stay that way as long as you behaved.

No one I knew ever expressed any knowledge that we were in one of the houses of Abe. We never even thought about it.

* * *

Everyone in the entertainment caper went to Benny's. It was just what you did – if you could get in. It was a warm, comfortable club where the movers and shakers felt at ease hanging out and talking shite all night. First you had to get past the door person, who had the ultimate decision about whether you had the Benny's vibe – or not.

Deals were done, celebrations held, confidences shared – and a lot of drugs, usually of the white powdered variety, were consumed in the bathrooms and, as the night moved on, openly on tables. Benny's was a clubhouse for the fast-moving figures in the industry.

Pretty much every visiting international artist found their way there. It was, after all, only a hop and two skips from the Sebel Townhouse, so easy to get to and within staggering distance of home base. Australian music industry figures such as Richard Clapton, Michael Hutchence, promoter Michael Chugg and many others seemed to spend more time at Benny's than any other location during its golden era. I wouldn't have been surprised if some figures used it as their mailing address.

Like so many of my music industry cohort, I spent far too many nights at Benny's after the Manzil Room. Arriving late, you'd approach the door where there was a small peephole. You knew you were being checked out. If you passed inspection, the door opened and in you went. No cover charge, just straight to the bar or the bathroom depending on whether your priority was a drink or a line of coke.

As the night wore on it wasn't even necessary to retire to the bathrooms to consume your drugs – and really, it was just cocaine, cocaine and more cocaine. By 2 or 3 am people were just chopping out lines at the table. It was no big deal. Everyone was doing it.

Once I threw a party there and have a vague memory of a doorman driving my partner and me back to our Bondi home at about 5 am. He was driving a white Mercedes. I knew what state I was in, but I didn't stop to think about his condition at that time where night meets new morning.

I remember INXS coming in one night in 1987 after they'd finished recording an album. They were standing on tables, grabbing the ceiling fan blades and spinning around the room. There was behaviour that occurred in that club that would not be tolerated in this day and age.

But Benny's was the centre of much more than random drug-taking, drinking and good times. While the bulk of the crowd at Benny's was fast, flashy and out for fun, there were always other figures around who didn't look like they exactly fitted into that world. And they didn't. Sitting in booths at the club from time to time were people like Ronald Jeffrey Montgomery, who lived in Peru and spent time in a Bolivian jail for cocaine trafficking. An American citizen, Montgomery used false passports and identification to enter Australia, having previously been declared by the Department of Immigration a 'prohibited non-citizen' – that is, someone with no legal right to enter Australia. There were other criminals and drug deals that were instigated inside that club and Ian Saxon, whom I talk more about later, was surely an acquaintance of Montgomery's. I could list more names but I don't want to risk lawsuits!

Needless to say, when one nightclub door closes in the Cross, another one opens to carry on the traditions. When the Manzil Room closed it became Springfields, a new Kings Cross nightspot.

Here, the spirit of Kings Cross nightlife and its intricate links to rock'n'roll lived on.

* * *

Speaking of Kings Cross locations where showbiz and dodgy types mingled, it would be remiss of me not to mention the Bayswater Brasserie in Bayswater Road, which in the 1980s was the place to hang if it was daylight hours.

This was *the* lunch spot for pretty much everyone in the music, television and media worlds, and for many well-heeled characters who would appear to have business interests that meant they didn't really do much beyond have lunch at the brasserie in Bayswater Road.

It was a hang for dodgy cops, too. Certainly, Roger Rogerson was a regular there in the mid-1980s and frequently dined there with the likes of underworld doctor Nicholas Paltos, solicitor Ross Karp and a prominent Sydney businessman – all of whom were to be of assistance to Roger in his activities as a police detective.

Rogerson was well known for his association with organised crime figures, and overall criminal behaviour while still in the employ of the New South Wales Police Force. If there was something dodgy that Rogerson could be involved with – drug dealing, extortion, murder – he was there.

Lunch, I should point out, would start around 12.30 pm on any given day and if you finished before 4 pm, it wasn't really a Brasserie lunch. The afternoon would usually be punctuated by a few quick dashes up the staircase to the bathrooms for a couple of quick lines of whatever pharmaceutical – usually cocaine – was your pleasure.

Often lunch would just move to the cocktail bar at the restaurant or a different location around the Cross, followed by seeing a band and then going to the Manzil Room or Benny's, and before you could say, 'Chop me another one, my friend', it would be daybreak and fuck me, how did that happen – fancy lunch?

Many deals were consummated at the Bayswater Brasserie, which as Louis Nowra points out in his engaging *Kings Cross: A Biography*, was really the only restaurant of significance in the area at the time. Designed to look like a Parisian brasserie, it opened in 1982.

The restaurant was just around the corner from the Hotel Mansion and a few doors down the road from the old offices of Simpsons Solicitors, then and now Sydney's leading law firm dealing with the arts and intellectual copyright. Principal Shane Simpson wrote a book on the music industry and the law and looked after the legal affairs for artists I was involved with, predominantly Paul Kelly.

So it was simple really – schedule a 10.30 or 11 am meeting, then head to lunch at the Bayswater. Dragon singer Marc Hunter had his office nearby on the second floor of a dilapidated warehouse space, which also housed his wife Wendy Heather's fashion business.

And of course the Brasserie was nestled right next to a very significant Kings Cross landmark – a large terrace house which operated as a brothel called the Nevada, which had a huge sign out the front attached to the first-floor balcony boasting that it contained Australia's largest bed.

How big Australia's largest bed was, I have no idea and no one emerged over the years to dispute the claim – therefore it was Australia's largest bed.

It was that sort of area. It's not impossible that Australia's largest bed was housed in a premises owned or controlled by Saffron. Did Saffron dine at the Brasserie? It would seem a bit ostentatious and public for someone like him. Not his kind of place. Leave that venue to the new generation of showbiz crooks who paraded their bling, flash cars'n'clothes and gals. Abe was a businessman, not a show pony.

CHAPTER 16

ORGANISED CRIME AND THE MUSIC INDUSTRY

There are a number of reasons why Abe Saffron found the entertainment industry irresistible. Traditionally until a few decades ago, all business was conducted in cash: jukeboxes (a big deal financially in days gone by), venue and club admission charges, drinks and food at nightclubs and other venues, merchandise, vinyl at record shops, and payments to artists for live performances were almost always cash transactions.

The master recordings and publishing copyright of hit songs were a source of continual cash flow (although in this case rarely in actual cash), more so in the early days of the music industry. They have been compared to the use of rental properties and annuities, except in the music business there was a much more dramatic volatility.

You wanna park cash somewhere? This is what to do. Certainly as Saffron and others learned very quickly, if you're going to move money around – cash money – the entertainment business isn't the worst avenue you could come up with.

Gone to a large extent are the good old days of all transactions being done in cash, but I have vivid memories of a 1980s show on a major league tour of a band I was associated with. The promoter told me I should come and see him after the show. He was quite upfront in stating that the 6000-capacity venue was going to be massively oversold that night and there'd be 'something' in it for me. I didn't realise how much that something was until he took me into a side room backstage after the show and handed me $18,000 in cash. That was my share.

After I recovered from the shock – I was pretty new to the business then – I got to thinking that if he was volunteering this much to me then how much was he pocketing. A lot more than $18,000 was my reasonably educated guess.

There's another story that involves the tax department going through the financial records of an extremely high profile Australian artist. They queried the tiny amount of money the artist claimed he'd earned from a gig in northern Queensland. They'd gone to the hotel and subpoenaed their bar records for the night.

The story goes that the tax department investigator quipped, 'Thirsty crowd then – if there were only 120 people at the show they drank a lot – an average of $465 worth of booze each. Can you explain that?'

Yes, cash was everywhere in those days. Not so much these days as banking and payments have gone online and everything has changed significantly, but the ever-adapting entertainment industry continues to find ways around it –

from selling what are claimed to be industry tickets through to under-declaring the number of tickets sold. As the saying goes, where there's a will there's a way.

And as we've discovered, where there's cash there're criminal figures and bent cops. They can smell a cash business that maybe needs protection, or a blind eye turned to some of their activities happening further afield and yes, they did come a-knocking – on a very regular basis.

There were very few pubs and clubs operating in Australia that weren't paying one or more people to stay in business, especially in the golden era of Australian pub rock'n'roll in the late 1970s and '80s. Many of these venues were notorious for flouting licensing laws in all manner of ways. They swung pretty free and easy with the age of their patronage and it would be easier to list the ones who did pay attention to the number of patrons they were legally allowed inside than the ones who didn't. Venues licensed for 500 patrons would consistently allow 700, 800 or 900 people inside. Many – sadly – also played free and easy with fire restrictions.

I spent many nights in an inner-city Sydney venue that was constantly packed to the rafters and had an entrance through a narrow corridor – and if there was a back exit in case of an emergency, I never saw it. As many of us commented frequently, it was a fire trap waiting to happen as we pondered how close to the door to stand, or whether to venture into the sardine-like mass of humanity who would have been in deep doo-doo in case of a fire.

How did these venues continue to operate? Paying the cops is how, or paying people who would slip that little something extra to the cops.

One music industry figure recalled to me an all-too-familiar scenario when one night he was in the backstage room doubling as an office for the person who ran one particular Sydney city venue. The dishevelled room reeked of pot smoke and other paraphernalia that passed for a good time in Sydney in the 1980s. There was a knock on the door and when it was opened there were two uniformed police officers outside. A bust? Who are you kidding. They were there to collect an envelope waiting for their superior. The guy running the venue reached into a desk drawer, pulled out the envelope and handed it to the cops. No comment on the pot smoke or anything else.

'I sling the cops $250 to open on a Sunday night – which I'm not meant to do of course, but it works out well – after paying the bands I'll usually make a couple of grand from the bar and the door charge,' said the venue owner.

Another music industry figure recalls seeing what were clearly plain-clothes cops visiting another high-profile and successful Sydney venue a few days before Christmas, and watching the venue owner and one of his staff load boxes of spirits, beer and wine into the boot of an unmarked car.

'There was so much weight in the car that the chassis bottomed out on the way out of the loading dock and they had to partially unload to get it into the street, then re-load it. I asked the owner if the cops had paid for it and he looked at me like I was crazy. "You're kiddin', right?" This venue had a 10 pm closing licence but stayed open till midnight every night.'

Later the venue applied for and received a midnight licence – but no doubt the cops found another reason to continue being looked after.

A number of sources have told me that in his police days the infamous Roger Rogerson would regularly drop in for a visit to at least one extremely popular Sydney venue that didn't close on weekends until at least 5 am.

Maybe Rogerson just liked to have a friendly catch-up with the person who ran the venue. Maybe he was suggesting a few bands he'd heard were pretty good that might like a gig. Or maybe he was collecting a big envelope.

This may well explain suggestions that Saffron was none too happy about this popular venue, as he had a significant financial stake in another pub just up the road – one that was floundering at the time because of the nearby competitor.

The story goes that he sent some people down to cause a little trouble, intimidate staff and patrons, and generally create a sense that this was not a safe and friendly place to hang out, in the hope that a significant portion of the customers would migrate up the hill to his pub.

This didn't get very far as the popular venue already had an understanding with members of the New South Wales Police Force and Team Saffron were quickly sent packing.

In Sydney in this era there was still the air of the unregulated wild west about the venues and rock'n'roll scene. From the outside everything seemed legitimate and above board, but beneath the surface things were quite different. People behind the scenes have endless stories – some of them no doubt embellished with the passing of time or completely apocryphal, but many are no doubt based on some form of reality.

'Mate, I remember the night when – and I heard this from one of the people in the room – look, he managed a really big Sydney band, and he went to get his money at the end of the night. He knew that was going to be problematic, so he took a .45 in his pocket. The venue guy had the money there – or some of it – he said he was docking the band a coupla grand for being late and not playing for as long as the contract specified. Apparently, they were ten minutes under. Now, the manager of the band reached for his gun – just to explain that he wanted the full amount – but before he could the venue guy pointed a sawn-off shotgun at him. Game over.'

That was the sometimes brutal and unsophisticated side of the entertainment industry but there were more elaborate scams afoot. There was the much-used cross-selling of business activities. In the US it was pretty easy for places like nightclubs and record shops to be turned into vendors for other businesses controlled by the Mafia. Pick an aspect of the entertainment business – venue construction workers, food and drink supplies, tablecloths, garbage collection – and the requirements could be satisfied by Mafia-controlled businesses.

Before the domination of streaming services and the move to digital music, counterfeiting was a big business that was highly attractive to the organised crime world. Analog music in the form of vinyl records, cassettes and CDs was very easy and cheap to duplicate. Bootleggers could and did press counterfeit records and then sell them at or below retail price. And if a retailer wanted to get their hands on these items, it was always a cash transaction. For the Mafia, it wasn't really duplicating copyrighted music – it was printing money.

These figures knew where the money trail led and that involved working in and around the area where the cash was – as managers, financial brokers or financing artistic ventures for a large percentage in return.

Steve Marriott toured Australia a number of times both with his band Small Faces and later under his own name, but when he visited in the 1980s his Australian promoter Peter Noble recalls that the singer and guitarist had a constant companion: an associate to whom he was instructed to pay money from gigs. Noble was also told in no uncertain terms that no money was to be paid to Marriott. Marriott was by this stage 'owned' by organised crime figures. Senior and less senior English crime figures and high-ranking members of the American Mafia were ever-present in his life.

Marriott's close links to organised crime bosses the Krays stretched back to the 1960s, and from the mid-'70s until his death he was informally managed by Laurie O'Leary, Ronnie Kray's best pal and a senior Kray business associate. The Krays – identical twin brothers – were feared and fearsome gangsters who dominated the world of organised crime in London, particularly during the 1950s and '60s. Like Jim Anderson and Neddy Smith, Ronnie and Reggie Kray were not people you messed with.

Another prime example of how the Mafia infiltrated the music industry is Frank Sinatra. The mob loved Sinatra and while Sinatra never once confirmed – or denied – his connections to organised crime figures, it is certainly well documented that he was very friendly with the likes of Joe Colombo, Carlos Marcello and John Franzese. It has also been strongly rumoured that Sinatra was the liaison between Joe and John Kennedy and the Mafia.

It is not only America where organised crime's association with music is rife, but also in the entertainment scene globally. The yakuza in Japan have run that country's entertainment industry since the end of World War II.

As described in variety.com, 'The Japanese entertainment industry has its roots in a vast night world of clubs, cabarets and bars, which have connections with the yakuza that go back centuries and are still pervasive, despite efforts by the police (who call the thugs *boryokudan*, meaning violence groups) and the biz to sever them. The gangsters provide "security" for these venues, a protection business that keeps other gangs away, but requires a payoff.'

The recent changes in the global music industry in general have affected how organised crime operates within it. Starting about 15 years ago, illegal music downloading and file sharing created serious interference to anyone wishing to make a profit from recorded music, and the tech giants like Apple, Amazon, Spotify and ByteDance have assimilated the lion's share of the money in the music industry.

Even though cashing in on the music business by legal or illegal means is more complex than the good ol' days when cash dominated the scene, there are still many opportunities for financial gain. There haven't been any recent reports about the mob's involvement in the new technologies, but it's a safe bet that they still have a seat at the table and their hands in the till.

Although the mob had a lot of influence in the US, things were different in Australia. The main reason for this is that there was less money floating around from which people wanted a cut of the action. Australia, being a comparatively small country, has most of its entertainment consolidated around the three largest eastern state cities. There simply haven't been the opportunities for the mob, and nowhere near the potential earnings – or skimmings. But there was enough.

In his memoir, *Hey, You in the Black T-Shirt*, promoter Michael Chugg expresses surprise that an industry in this country that had so much cash flowing everywhere didn't attract the attention of global organised crime and gangster figures to the extent that it did overseas.

Chugg observes that in the 1950s and '60s there was a little overlap in that some of the clubs where bands played were owned by what he describes as 'colourful racing identities', but in his opinion none of them 'wanted a bar of the live music business'. Chugg is referring here to the smaller club and pub venues that featured predominantly Australian artists on the touring circuit. The big money was and still is in international concert promotion, which is exactly what lured Abe Saffron and Lee Gordon into the business in the 1950s. But neither of them had any interest in promoting Australian bands in pubs and clubs, as it was small pickings.

In Chugg's opinion that situation hasn't changed much. As he argues, 'Why gamble on a business where you can drop half a million dollars in minutes when you have a steady income from clubs, drugs and hookers. Nowadays, since GST was introduced in 2000 and with electronic ticketing the norm, there isn't nearly as much cash around, which makes it even harder to rort the system.'

Chugg agrees that in this world 'crooks are around the fringes – and I've met plenty of them'. In fact, he considers there are some noticeable similarities between crooks and musicians. Hanging out in a sphere where he's familiar with both reveals that often the crooks are 'weird but they can also be funny and nice people; it's just that their business is being criminal. None of them has ever tried to infiltrate the business. All that *Underbelly* stuff, there's no real music involvement in any of that.'

Chugg is an experienced street-level campaigner and a smart and tough operator. On one level he's right – the direct influence and involvement of organised criminal figures is minimal, but they are also everywhere on the fringes and, often more importantly, using the infrastructure of the music and entertainment worlds for their own advantage.

Chugg did have a couple of memorable underworld encounters. One put him right in the sights of a major Australian organised crime figure: in 1970 Stan 'The Man' Smith pulled a gun on him. Smith was a well-known and feared racketeer and standover man in the 1960s and '70s. Chugg describes how in 1970, Smith bucked the trend of organised crime figures not risking their money and decided to get into rock'n'roll concert promoting, bringing a few overseas artists to Australia. One was a bikie blues band from Canada called McKenna Mendelson Mainline.

During the course of the tour a couple of band members were busted for possession of drugs. According to Chugg, the word was sent to Smith that it was Chugg who'd dobbed them in. Chugg insists he had nothing to do with it and was not even in the country at the time.

That wasn't the way Smith chose to see it. A few months later Chugg was at a gig at the Bondi Lifesaver in Bondi Junction and his buddy Lee Dillow introduced him to Smith. Chugg recalls, 'Smith was almost frothing at the mouth and started laying into me for ruining his tour. We were sitting at a table and he pulled out a gun and held it under the table pointing at me. He was flying, completely off his face, which made it even scarier. I was stoned, so I got increasingly paranoid with every passing second. *Tripping standover man slays stoned, innocent rock promoter.* It wasn't looking good. I just kept talking to him and eventually managed to calm him down … I did what I do best and talked my way out of it. He could see I was telling the truth. That's the only time I've ever had anything like that happen to me.'

Chugg's other organised crime interaction came many years later, when 'Mr Sin' came a-calling. He wanted a meeting with Chugg who, not being a fool, decided to attend. Saffron asked if Chugg was interested in putting together a package tour of American artists Saffron wanted to bring to Australia. Among the artists mooted were Chicago and the Beach Boys. Saffron stumped up the money for Chugg to fly to America and have meetings with the relevant agents and managers, but nothing ever came of it.

Chugg believes that Saffron did financially back a few international tours 'but I think he, like other high-end crims, realised that you can lose money too easily'.

* * *

Chugg wasn't the only one to have an encounter with an organised crime figure at the end of their gun. In fact, confronting and often gun-related violence involving organised crime figures was somewhat commonplace in Sydney, particularly during the 1960s and '70s.

Abe Saffron's man Wayne Martin from the Pink Pussycat was at the right – or wrong – place a number of times. One such time was in May 1967 when he was at the Latin Quarter Club. While there, gun-for-hire Raymond O'Connor was shot in the head in what was at the time an ongoing war between the Sydney and Melbourne underworlds.

As reported in the *Sydney Morning Herald*, a friend said: 'Wayne was at the club when the shooting happened, and the bloke fell into Wayne. Wayne saw blood and thought he had been shot but then a detective who was there told Wayne to "get out of here before things blow up", so he knew he wasn't the one who had been shot and took off.'

That's a cute story, but you have to imagine that Sir Wayne would have known if he'd been shot or not.

One of the legendary crew members I interviewed for my 2018 book, *Roadies*, was Mick Cox. He recalled an incident at a venue in the centre of Sydney in the early 1970s. 'It was a basement place. They had a bouncer up on street level and a ticket office down the stairs. I'm down there, and the next thing I see is the bouncer from up the top flying down the stairs backwards. He's been knocked out.

'It was Neddy Smith and his guys, who were running a protection racket on the clubs. They knocked the chick in the ticket booth out and then came into the club and started bashing patrons. They're throwing tables and chairs around and making a real mess.

'There's a full-on riot, so I tell the band to hide in the kitchen and that's what we do. Then I hear a yell that they're taking the band's gear, so I run out. I grab the first thing I see, which is one of those long steel things you sharpen knives on. What the fuck was I thinking? I also managed to throw a bottle in their direction and yelled, "Leave that fucking guitar there!" And the next thing I hear are the words, "Shoot the cunt", and then I see the guns come out and I run to the kitchen and hide in the cool room until they've gone.

'We knew a couple of figures in the underworld ourselves in those days, so the guitars were returned a few days later … but the amps and speaker boxes were ruined as they'd just thrown them into the crowd and smashed them up.'

* * *

Rock'n'roll, guns and money. That's a fine combination and in 2016 the three coincided spectacularly when Paul DeMarco, who did and currently still plays drums with Rose Tattoo, admitted to his role in a gun-selling racket which also involved ex-bikie boss Hassan 'Sam' Ibrahim. This was a doozy of a story.

The other key players were Sam Ibrahim's sister Jazz Dior and her partner, Elvis Mileski.

DeMarco, who was 58 at the time, pleaded guilty to conspiring to supply firearms. He admitted to selling 13 guns to an undercover police officer between 29 November 2013 and 25 March 2014.

Included in the firepower offered were some heavy-duty items – not just garden-variety pistols. There were two Uzi-style machine pistols and ammunition. Asking price $60,000. Also up for grabs were two .30-calibre revolvers for $24,000 and a Magnum revolver which was a snap at $14,500.

It was clear that DeMarco was at the lower end of the organisational chain. He was the guy taking the risks on the street, not Sam Ibrahim, Mileski and Dior, who it was alleged had planned and conducted negotiations for DeMarco to sell to the buyer – who as it turned out was that undercover cop.

According to court documents reported in the *Sydney Morning Herald*, Sam Ibrahim and Dior were recorded on 14 January of that year discussing what had gone down.

'It lit up like a Christmas tree … as soon as he put his foot inside,' Dior told Sam Ibrahim.

DeMarco would later tell the undercover (and arresting) officer that he had been waiting for a box of brand-new Glocks but that this had turned bad when his gun supplier had been spooked by a laser-beam alarm system when he went to collect the guns. Note to self. Beware of laser beams when collecting gun shipments. The two do not mix.

Apparently, a cat was put inside the location to suggest it was a false alarm activation. Further note. Do not involve cats with laser beams and gun shipments.

A recorded phone call on the night of 12 February 2014 has Mileski telling Dior to in turn tell 'Sam' that he needed another $23,000 for six 'brand new things in the boxes'.

This is taken to mean more guns. The Glocks. This was on top of the $10,000 that had already been paid.

More calls were recorded and provide ample evidence that Sam Ibrahim was getting more than just a little agitated at the ongoing delays in receiving the guns. A number of times he said he would 'cave his head in' in reference to DeMarco. Later, Sam Ibrahim told DeMarco he had an injured hand because he had 'slapped' the person they were waiting for. This does suggest that the slap was a fairly decent one aimed at being a not-so-gentle reminder to get this situation sorted.

But Sam Ibrahim clearly knew that slapping wasn't going to sort the problem. 'You can't fix stupidity,' he said.

Dior and Mileski pleaded guilty to conspiring with each other to supply firearms. Their sentence of 18 months' jail was to be served in the community under an intensive correction order.

DeMarco, who had already spent two years on remand, was sentenced to six years in jail. In February 2018 Sam Ibrahim was sentenced to nine years in jail.

Just another example that most of the time entertainment and rock'n'roll don't mix well with criminals – no one ever wins.

CHAPTER 17

BEYOND SYDNEY

Sydney and the Cross were not the only places in Australia where the worlds of entertainment and crime intersected. Melbourne has more than its fair share of connections between organised crime and the entertainment business.

In 2018 the family of John Wren announced that they would sell the Melbourne site where Festival Hall was located. John Wren made his loot through his involvement with illegal gambling operations in Melbourne. He died in 1953 and was the thinly disguised subject of Frank Hardy's 1950 novel *Power Without Glory*. Like Saffron, he was a seemingly unemotional figure when it came to business and assets.

In fact Wren and Saffron seemed to be similar figures, albeit separated by half a century. Born in 1871, Wren left school at 12 when he joined the workforce but supplemented his meagre income by circulating betting cards and bookmaking. He became extremely successful at the latter and was, in the 1890s, allegedly earning over £20,000 a year – a massive amount of money in those days.

Like Abe Saffron, he could be generous to those in need. He also employed former criminals to do the work of collecting debts and keeping people in line. Anyone who crossed him was sorted out quickly, often with the use of brute force from others. He had the power to have potential legal matters 'sorted' before they went to court and like Saffron was strongly rumoured to have significant politicians and judges in his pocket.

Again, like Saffron, rumours constantly circulate around Wren. It was speculated that he had something to do with the bombing of Sergeant First Class David O'Donnell's home. O'Donnell was extremely active in a crusade against illegal gambling, particularly the operations of Wren, and his relentless, incorruptible efforts to close the Collingwood totalisator and other gambling houses made him almost legendary in Melbourne.

Wren became involved in boxing promotions in 1904 acquiring the Festival Hall venue initially for boxing matches.

The venue was rebuilt for boxing after the original structure was destroyed by fire in 1955. Since then it had become one of the most iconic venues in the city. Among other things it was the venue where the Beatles performed in 1964. In Sydney they performed at the Sydney Stadium in Rushcutters Bay, another venue better known for hosting boxing bouts and as such a mecca for prominent businessmen many of whom were not prepared to explain what prominent businesses they were involved in.

Though there were clear parallels between Wren and Saffron – there were also significant differences, not just because of the eras they existed in.

Melbourne has always had and continues to have a very significant world of organised crime operating in its midst – you only have to look at the dozens and dozens of gangland shootings over the past decades.

Powerful figures rose, and were shot down. No one like Saffron appeared in the golden era of criminality – there was no single figure who dominated the Melbourne landscape. Unlike Sydney, Melbourne had networks of often family-orientated criminal factions such as the Carlton Crew, in particular, along with their rivals in the Honoured Society and the Calabrese family. And every major city had its outlaw motorcycle gangs with their myriad criminal tentacles.

No one has dominated any other city the way Abe Saffron controlled Sydney for such an extended period of time. And, if Alan Saffron is to be believed, his father also had more than just a passing interest in other capital cities, too.

* * *

In Brisbane, the 1973 fire at the Whiskey Au Go Go nightclub in the entertainment-orientated suburb of Fortitude Valley was the largest modern-day mass murder Australia had experienced up until that time. It was horrific. Fifteen people died.

This wasn't just the bad guys killing each other, this was collateral damage on an unimaginable scale. Still largely unsolved, it is an event that continues to spotlight the complex intricacies and the multi-layered interactions that come together in the criminal underworld and the world of entertainment. The cops and the robbers, the bosses and their muscle. The turf wars and the crews for hire.

Fortitude Valley became a place where entertainment and crime met, coalesced and thrived. It was and, continues to be, very much the Brisbane equivalent of Kings Cross but with less overt emphasis on strip clubs, illegal gambling and prostitution. But there were still lots of all these things – something which came to light in the Fitzgerald Inquiry in the late 1980s.

The area is bright, garish and loaded with pubs, clubs and restaurants. It's the sort of area Saffron would have relished an involvement in, but how could he have managed that? Why would he? The Queensland Police Force were a law unto themselves and a succession of conservative governments exhibited more than just a bit of corruption. So many palms to grease. So many envelopes to hand out.

There was also another ensemble of shady businessmen, tricksters, would-be competitors and thugs. Tough guys, hard men and some monsters – a microcosm of complex relationships that seemed to be part of the bedrock of the entertainment world. Better to stick to the turf he knew and ruled unless you have a network of trusted allies or lackeys on the ground. Saffron's involvement in these interstate networks has never been fully explored.

But of course, if anything bad happened, like the fire at the Whiskey Au Go Go, eventually people would start to speculate and wonder if Abe Saffron had anything to do with it. That was just the way people had grown to think. Trouble in a nightclub plus criminal involvement – well, Abe must have his finger in it. Was there a Sydney connection?

Yes there was – but not necessarily a Saffron one. But who really knows for sure?

The Whiskey Au Go Go was situated on the first floor of a building on the corner of Amelia Street and St Paul's Terrace in Fortitude Valley. It looked like a typical commercial building on the outside and it still does. There were many windows that would have let in gallons of sunlight in 1972 if they weren't covered with thick, dark curtains essential for that sensual aesthetic nightclub feel. An atmosphere of mystery, a covertness common to all night-time dens that could trick guests into forgetting that in fact they were in a pretty ordinary building near downtown Brisbane. The space had previously been home to another venture called Celebrity Cabaret, which was forced to close when things became financially difficult for the owners.

From the get-go, the financial health of the Whiskey Au Go Go was dubious. This fact was revealed at the inquest many decades later.

With an eye out for opportunity and suitable premises available, former band manager and booker John Hannay talked two associates into renting the premises and opening a new nightclub in the busy precinct. The two associates would also open Chequers nightclub on Elizabeth Street. And Hannay would start up his own restaurant bar on Brunswick Street called Alice's.

The Whiskey Au Go Go opened its doors for business in March 1972. John Hannay ran the club and kept the books. So far, so good. Another club. Another merry-go-round. Business looked to be good. But the relationship between the two associates and Hannay fell apart. On their account Hannay had his hand in the till. Hannay was fired.

So where does Sydney come in? First up, enter John Andrew Stuart, one of those figures known as a career criminal. They don't know how to do anything else or just can't see any other way. And they aren't very good at what they do, or they just don't have the friends and the smarts to stop them spending more time in prison than out. Stuart was violent when needed. Erratic. Loud.

Released from a New South Wales jail in July 1972, where he'd been housed for the 1966 attempted murder of another criminal – a bloke called Robert Steele – Stuart headed back to home base in Brisbane and started mouthing off about Sydney-based crime figures who thought there was easy money to be made by shaking down clubs in Brisbane. Who was he referring to? Was it just big talk? Was this evidence of the tentacles of Saffron Incorporated moving across another border? Or some other entities sniffing a lucrative opportunity? Were they already there? Author Matthew Condon says that Paddles Anderson and Lennie McPherson had definitely been north for a visit just prior to the fire and had met with the two associates. Then after the fire, Roger Rogerson was dispatched from Sydney with such urgency he arrived at the site before the bodies had been removed.

For some reason Stuart mentioned this to journalist Brian Bolton and Detective Basil Hicks. Maybe he was trying to earn some brownie points by tipping them off, or just simply big noting himself about knowing people who knew people who did stuff. Perhaps Stuart did know things, though. Towards the end of 1972 he told Bolton specifically that first an empty nightclub would be firebombed, and that this would be followed by an attack on the Whiskey Au Go Go – but that this bombing would happen when the joint was packed with customers. Apparently, Bolton wrote about these alleged threats and told the Queensland police commissioner and police minister.

Erratic and foolish, Stuart simultaneously tried to tell the police and media, warn the two associates and threatened them himself. He also tried to stand over Hannay. He was all over the place, and clearly annoying both the crims and the cops. Then things began to get horribly real and more troublesome for Stuart, when the Torino's Nightclub on Ann Street, a short walk from the Whiskey Au Go Go, was destroyed after an arson attack on 25 February 1973. Given what Stuart had told the journalist and the police, if a few warning lights hadn't turned on, they should at least have started to flicker.

This wasn't the first fire. A few weeks earlier, Alice's Café in Brunswick Street owned by John Hannay, now the former manager of the Whiskey Au Go Go, was set alight. Conveniently all the bookkeeping records for the Whiskey Au Go Go were destroyed in the blaze. Books that may have revealed what the two associates had suspected, that Hannay had siphoned a lot of money from the club, were now a pile of ash.

And then there was another. At precisely 2.08 am on 8 March 1973, all hell broke loose at the Whiskey Au Go Go. A fire started when two drums of petrol containing four and five gallons (15 and 19 litres) of fluid were ignited in the foyer of the building. Clearly they were placed there deliberately. The burning petrol did what burning petrol does and sent carbon monoxide slowly and insidiously up to the main room of the venue on the first floor.

Have you ever entered a nightclub or a venue like I often did, looked around and thought to yourself, 'I hope there's not a fire in here – getting out is not going to be easy'? Such was the case with the Whiskey, where the only alternative way out was the rear stairs which – as with most venues – the owners probably never expected to need to use in an emergency. Lighting was poor and rubbish was everywhere, including a crate of empty bottles waiting to be carried down for rubbish collection.

At the time the fire started there were around 50 patrons, some bar staff and entertainers in the upstairs area. Chaos broke out. Some people hurled themselves from broken windows, dropped to an awning and fell almost five metres to the ground. Others got out through windows that they smashed in the men's and women's bathrooms. The dark drapes hid the windows at the front of the building that might have been lifesaving.

According to reports, those in the club had further difficulties leaving the building. Aside from the panic and confusion, there was a large quantity of grease covering their escape path – then add in a 1.8-metre fence that was blocking the side alley. The odds were stacked against everyone trying to get out.

In the aftermath of the fire, the bush telegraph of rumours had it as definite fact that whoever had been responsible for the fire had added the grease deliberately, but that was proved to be incorrect. The reality was that the staff at the club stored their used oil containers outside near the wall where the escape route was. As you'd imagine in the mayhem brought on by everyone trying to escape, those containers were knocked over and the grease quickly spread all over the floors and stairs. The venue had no fire exit plan or procedure. It was deadly chaos.

The end result of this, intended or not, was that 15 people died, all from carbon monoxide poisoning. By the time the firefighters, police and ambulances arrived with sirens screaming, all were dead.

Two of those who died were in the six-piece band Trinity, who were the support band that night for the Delltones; the remaining casualties were three Whiskey staff members and ten patrons.

Not surprisingly, it took only a short time before the Queensland government offered a $50,000 reward for anyone who came forward with information to resolve the tragedy. And who did they consider the prime suspect? John Stuart, of course – as he'd been the person who'd told them what was going to happen. Yet they'd done nothing to act on his information. He had also threatened Hannay, his two associates and others.

The police investigation would at various times look at some of Brisbane's most prominent criminals, gangsters, bosses and violent offenders, but they had their sights set on Stuart. He proved to be an easy catch. Bringing in Stuart and his alleged accomplice, James Richard Finch, not only took the heat off the police, but it also took the spotlight off the other criminal forces currently at play in the Valley and in general.

It was strongly inferred that there was political and police corruption – the suggestion being that a group of officers were using fire to help some club owners cash in on the insurance, and taking a cut of course. A close investigation into the fire might have exposed those things earlier. And a lot worse. The community needed to be appeased, and quickly.

Stuart had an alibi for where he was on the night but the cops were out for him. They trumped up supposed evidence that he'd threatened someone with a knife and arrested him. They also nabbed Finch at a shopping centre in the suburb of Jindalee. Why him? Well, back in 1966 Finch had been jailed for 14 years after being convicted on two matters – malicious wounding with a firearm and being in possession of an unlicensed gun.

The allegations at that time were that Finch had fired his gun twice during a scuffle at a petrol station in Sydney's Oxford Street, Paddington. Two men had been injured. How does this link up with a fire seven years later? Stay with me.

After the fracas, Finch had given his gun to Stuart. That's the connection right there. The two had known each other for many years and at Finch's trial the police had claimed that not only was Finch 'an active young criminal' but was also an 'associate of the most violent criminals in Sydney'.

Finch was out and about after serving seven and a half years in jail. But it was drawing a fairly long bow to connect them with the first Brisbane fires. Mind you, Stuart had told everyone who cared to listen what was going to happen.

In a move that will surprise no one, both Finch and Stuart were adamant that they were innocent. Charged with arson and 15 counts of murder, Stuart was volatile and aggressive as he was transported to his court appearance and required six detectives to keep him under control. Finch was a comparatively easy case and only one detective was required to get him to sit quietly.

Finch told everyone who'd listen that the police had presented him with a confession document and had beaten him until he signed it. In his book *Dodger*, Duncan McNab says that Roger Rogerson and his Sydney colleague Noel Morey were present during Finch's police interview with four Queensland detectives. Getting an airtight record of interview, a verbal, was a Rogerson special. Any talk about Sydney heavies dissolved from the narrative, with mention of Stuart coming back from Sydney and starting his own standover chapter in Brisbane being his own idea.

The argument from the prosecution was that Stuart had dragged Finch into this activity. After being released from jail Finch had returned to his home country of England, not returning to Australia until 12 days before the first bombing at the behest of Stuart.

It was claimed that Finch had confessed to police and told them all about Stuart's involvement. The claim was that Finch had set the fire and that Stuart was the one who was involved in putting everyone off the scent with the suggestion that those bad criminals from the City of Sin, aka Sydney, were behind all this and it was all about extorting payments from Brisbane venue owners.

Stuart and Finch were clearly loose cannons. People do strange things in custody to avoid their time in court. For his party trick, Stuart swallowed metal and was hospitalised, as a result missing most of his trial. While in custody, he underwent five operations to remove objects not normally found in a human stomach.

Finch upped the ante and amputated one of his fingers during the trial.

The antics didn't help. Both men were convicted of the murder of one of the patrons, Jennifer Denise Davie, on 23 October 1973. In the minds of the jury, the Whiskey Au Go Go fire was deliberately lit – but they sided with the viewpoint that it was in fact part of a terror campaign aimed at venue owners with the intention of extorting money from these owners under promise that their venue would not suffer a similar fate.

Both men were sentenced to life in prison and were sent to Brisbane's Boggo Road Gaol, where they maintained their innocence and embarked on whatever legal means were open to them to get released. Both also exhibited extreme and unpredictable behaviour, which included Stuart sewing his lips together with paperclips. This incident happened during a warders' strike when the police took over the running of the jail.

Stuart's logic was simple – he could not be compelled to answer anything if his lips were stitched together. Finch was verbally abusive and in one outburst poured toilet waste over warders. Never a winning move.

Appeals went on and on, particularly by Finch, but they increasingly fell on deaf ears.

John Stuart died on 2 January 1979, found in his cell after a six-day hunger strike. The paperwork stated acute heart infection as the cause. There were claims he was murdered, but that's not unusual when a violent criminal dies in custody. Swallowing metal on a regular basis combined with an unpredictable and fragile mental state wouldn't have helped prolong the man's life.

According to some reports, police considered Stuart 'Australia's most violent criminal'. In my opinion, there's a fair bit of competition for that mantle.

Two years later, after a decade and a half inside, James Finch was released. Part of the deal was that he be deported back to England.

But it wasn't over. In October 1988 Finch confessed to starting the fire at the Whiskey Au Go Go. What was in it for him? And why now? Is it relevant that Finch had a long connection with Neddy Smith, from his time at the Gosford Farm Home for Boys to the jail time they both spent at Grafton and Long Bay? Did Neddy Smith's connection with Rogerson have something to do with it? Was he paid off to take the rap … again? In an interview videotaped by *The Sun* newspaper, he claimed that he'd tipped the two drums of petrol into the doorway of the club prior to the firebombing. Obviously not exactly cognisant of the concept of contradictory evidence while saying he did it, he also hadn't given up on the claims that he was forced to sign his confession. Added to this, he repeated that a policeman who was named in the original inquiry had actually ordered the bombing. That's a significant accusation and one with absolutely no evidence to back it up.

Finch later withdrew his confession. At the time, he was interviewed by Jana Wendt on *A Current Affair* and it became obvious that he was unaware of the implications of being found guilty of only one murder. There were another 14 with which he could be charged and which may result in him being extradited back to Australia. At this point Finch had an attack of the vagues. Having been made aware that he could be extradited to face further charges, he decided he didn't want to come back to Australia for multiple murder trials.

There's a disturbing side note to this story. In 2017, a certain Vincent O'Dempsey and his accomplice Garry Dubois were charged and convicted of the manslaughter of a woman, Barbara McCulkin, and the rape and murder of her two daughters, Vicki, aged 13, and 11-year-old Leanne in 1974.

On 2 June 2017, following the conviction and sentencing of O'Dempsey and Dubois for the McCulkin murders, the Queensland Attorney-General announced the re-opening of the coronial inquest into the Whiskey Au Go Go fire.

How are the two cases connected? The story is that there was allegedly evidence that McCulkin had been killed as she might have been able to implicate O'Dempsey and Dubois in the Whiskey Au Go Go firebombing. It was claimed that McCulkin's husband, Billy, was a prominent gangster and was part of the crew that did the Whiskey Au Go Go job, together with O'Dempsey. Billy's violent marriage to Barbara was over, and that meant she was a loose cannon who was required to be 'shut up'.

One allegation was that the firebombing of Torino's nightclub was in fact an insurance scam that was organised by Dubois, and ordered by O'Dempsey, and that the Whiskey was a separate job involving O'Dempsey, McCulkin and two others.

In the opinion of Justice Peter Applegarth, 'It was clear Barbara McCulkin knew enough about each of the pair's roles in the nightclub bombing at the time for them to want to silence her.'

O'Dempsey refused to answer questions or cooperate in any way at the inquest. A long list of individuals appeared – even Roger Rogerson, who couldn't remember on whose orders he was dispatched to Queensland.

One witness to the fire was a woman by the name of Katherine Potter, who had been outside the Whiskey when everything went down. She stated that she looked over at the entrance to the venue and reportedly saw a black vehicle pull up, and three men get out. Two of them retrieved drums of fuel.

Potter told the inquest that she had reported what she had observed to police the next day, and that around a week later she was visited by police officers at her home, who asked her to rectify her statement regarding how many men she had seen. They wanted her to have seen just two men. When she refused to change her statement, they accused her of lying.

It's not unreasonable to believe, as many do, that the responsibility for the Whiskey Au Go Go firebombing goes much deeper than Stuart and Finch, two seasoned criminals in Brisbane who honed their skills after some time cavorting with the who's who of the Sydney underworld. Or the other despicable consorts McCulkin, O'Dempsey and Dubois who more than likely did the job. But who was behind it? The Whiskey Au Go Go and Chequers clubs were already in liquidation by the time of the fire, so if it was some type of standover or extortion, did those standing over know of the financial unfitness? Was that somehow relevant or not? Did insurance play any part? It is reasonable to say that corrupt police had a lot to do with obfuscating the situation and that more prominent and powerful criminal figures were involved. Roger Rogerson's race to attend the scene and be at the initial interviews of Stuart and Finch may suggest he was there to protect Sydney figures involved.

In a 2025 postscript involving fires, organised crime and Brisbane venues – but this could happen in any city where nefarious activities are being engaged in – sometimes you can be innocently going about your business in the entertainment industry and get caught up in criminal activity.

On Boxing Day 2024, Brisbane venue Tomcat was on the unwelcome receiving end of a firebombing of a convenience store in Fortitude Valley, which police believe was connected to the illicit tobacco trade in Queensland, illicit tobacco being the modern-day equivalent of the sly grog trade.

The venue, located above the targeted convenience store, sustained a significant amount of smoke and water damage in the explosion, resulting in the venue's closure for four months and obviously a huge loss of income for the owners and artists booked to appear there.

Clearly the outcome could have been much more severe. But it illustrates that the use of fire is a common method of dealing with competition or solving a criminal's problem.

CHAPTER 18

WHEELING AND DEALING

Back in the 1970s and '80s, and even to this day, if an organised crime syndicate wanted to move large quantities of illicit substances – marijuana, speed, cocaine, meth – around the country and give themselves a pretty good chance of not being detected, they could do a lot of much sillier things than connect with a rock'n'roll band. They could even just approach their road crew members, involve them in the transportation of the cargo and reward them handsomely for their efforts to transport it around the country. This is still the case now, but it was particularly common in the 1970s.

Bands crisscrossed the country constantly in the golden era of Australian pub rock'n'roll, the bigger bands carrying their gear and sound equipment in usually at least one and often many large trucks.

In the era of big international tours, it wasn't uncommon for the biggest artists to have up to 50 large semi-trailers travelling between cities. That's a lot of vehicles and a massive amount of equipment – but even one truck carting the gear for a band has a lot of space and equipment in which to conceal large amounts of things that were not part of the band's inventory.

Say Quantity X needed to get from Brisbane to Melbourne. Stick it inside a couple of large speaker containers, plant them midway through the truck and off you went. Delivery in under 24 hours at the rate Australian road crews drove and worked.

Chances of the truck being stopped? Possible, if the driver was speeding. Chances of the cops saying, 'Empty the truck and let's see what you have in there'? Fairly slim. And they'd have to have a damn good reason to detain a band's crew for a day or two to go through a truck full of speakers and other gear while a manager is in their ear about the loss of income if the equipment didn't arrive on time. It was much safer than trying to transport contraband by air, putting it in the boot of a car, or travelling with it on a train. There was little chance of detection unless there was a tip-off, in which case everyone involved was screwed.

It would be comparatively easy to engage in this sort of activity without other road crew members or the bands they worked for having any idea what was going on.

All sorts of things found their way into the back of bands' equipment trucks as they traversed the highways of Australia. I know from experience. When I was offered the job writing for *RAM* magazine in August 1978, I needed my worldly possessions moved from Adelaide.

RAM's editor Anthony O'Grady made a call to the management of the Angels, who were playing in Adelaide at the time. The next day their road crew came to my home, collected a large array of boxes and bags belonging to me, put them in the back with the band's PA and equipment, and began the trip to Sydney – via Melbourne and a number of other stops for gigs.

There was nothing illegal in my possessions, but what if there was? No one checked. There were no sniffer dogs. Nothing.

During the extended interviews for my 2018 *Roadies* book, I heard many stories of road crews 'liberating' Space Invaders and cigarette machines from venues as they loaded equipment out at the end of the night when there was little security around. It was simple for them to unplug these machines, cover them with a cloth and load them undetected into the back of a truck, drive away and later forcibly open them up and take the cash and bounty from inside before rolling them down a hill to rot away.

Over the years I observed all manner of things being casually loaded into the back of trucks carrying band equipment – sometimes extra-big garbage bags that contained green plants with a very distinct smell.

Many road crews in the 1960s, '70s and '80s carried firearms in the backs of their trucks. They were used sometimes for killing-boredom activities like shooting at road signs, but also often to protect themselves from violent assaults as they were leaving venues, particularly in regional towns and cities where the local lads, seven schooners to the wind, considered them fair game.

* * *

You hear different stories about why some people end up in the criminal world. Whether they were just passing through, or permanent fixtures like Abe and his associates.

It can be a weakness for sex or gambling, greed, family ties, pathological viciousness, a need for financial security, or just plain old stupidity.

There are, however, stories about the coincidental criminal. Those who find themselves at a place and at a time faced with a temptation, and maybe a revelation. Sometimes pawns and sometimes maestros, showing entrepreneurial genius ahead of the pack. Recognising an opportunity and going for it. Like when you start hanging around your favourite rock band and you realise that a big percentage of their time is spent driving up and down the coast and from state to state playing shows – and you need to move certain things as discreetly as possible between cities on a regular basis.

At least two individuals in my orbit in the 1980s who worked as tour managers were well known as prominent cocaine and speed dealers. It's not hard to imagine how they transported their wares around the country, when only an idiot would pack them in a suitcase or briefcase and attempt to take them on a plane.

This was the era of long-haul drives by road crews and trucks loaded with sound systems, amplifiers, band gear – and anything else that would fit.

'Hey Billy – throw this in the truck will you, I'll see you in Sydney.'

With the benefit of history and hindsight, the revelation that there could be a connection between a touring band and transporting goods, that is illegal goods, around the country seems obvious. But with the whirl of the rock'n'roll revolution and all the bells and whistles, strobes lights and fog machines, what seems obvious today was really an epiphany for a few movers and shakers close enough to the action to recognise the enormous potential. It was hiding in plain sight, with the band and most of their crew none the wiser. But eventually the secret gets out. People get loose and sloppy.

One example is the gossip and headlines around a bloke called Greg Ollard. Like so many others who were mesmerised by the charismatic lead singer Marc Hunter, Greg was a Dragon fan. Dragon had a string of extremely successful pop/rock songs such as 'April Sun in Cuba', 'Are You Old Enough' and 'Still in Love with You', and by the late '70s they were a significant live drawcard and touring internationally.

It turned out that Greg Ollard was a mate of Dragon's New Zealand manager, Graeme Nesbitt. Ollard had worked for EMI records in New Zealand and the intersection of music and crime again shows its head. Nesbitt had told Ollard that he could crash with the band on a temporary basis while Ollard set himself up in Sydney.

Ollard had done a bit of buying and selling of dope back in Wellington and was already well connected with a man called Terry Clark, a particularly ruthless and nasty piece of work who would go on to head the Mr Asia drug syndicate, an organisation whose main activity was importing heroin into New Zealand, Australia and the United Kingdom

Clark was the second most prominent figure in the organisation, but he became head of the syndicate after he ordered the murder of Marty Johnstone, known as Mr Asia, in 1979.

Ollard had met Clark when both were in Wi Tako Prison (now Rimutaka Prison) north of Wellington. When released, Clark kept a low profile but was active in the distribution of drugs in New Zealand and relied on people like Greg Ollard to do the collecting from wholesalers and importers on his behalf. Their biggest line of work was in Thai sticks (dried cannabis wound around a stick), which were a big deal in New Zealand at the time and preferred over LSD and heroin, both of which were around.

According to reports, Greg Ollard was a likeable chap who wasn't short of a dollar, which makes you wonder why he needed to stay in share accommodation with a bunch of poor musicians, who were at this stage existing on a very hand-to-mouth, day-to-day basis in Sydney.

There's the 'aha!' moment. It seems highly likely that Ollard was deliberately targeting the band to give him access to a transportation channel as the band toured around the country. The band didn't need to know a thing. It was the vehicles that were of interest to him.

When Ollard lobbed into town the members of Dragon had no idea that Ollard was a lieutenant in a drug ring or that this ring would play a significant role in the sea of heroin that began to flood into Sydney, particularly around the Kings Cross area. And they didn't know that heroin would hit them so hard.

When Ollard moved away from Dragon Central to his own place, a small flat in Kings Cross, he frequently threw parties where, among other things, there was free tequila and heroin. You only offer free heroin at a party if you have a LOT of heroin around you. And of course he invited the band to these shindigs. Sadly, this was the beginning of a flirtation with heroin for Marc Hunter and Neil Storey and ultimately a full-blown addiction for Paul Hewson.

Because Ollard had access to significant quantities of cash, much more than the still-struggling members of Dragon, he would frequently pay for the essentials – food, drinks and petrol. 'I've got $400,000 in cash now,' he once remarked to a friend in Palm Beach. 'And when I've got a million I'm going to quit.'

In a not-uncommon experience with rock'n'roll bands, Dragon hadn't been in Sydney long before their equipment was stolen. Coming to the potential rescue was Ollard, who offered to reach into his pocket to pay for new equipment. Perhaps sensing that Ollard was trouble, or worried about where the money was coming from and what the long-term implications might be, Todd Hunter, Mr Sensible, preferred to do a hire-purchase agreement with Farrell Music. He convinced his bandmates that this was the way to go.

Greg Ollard was, to put it mildly, an interesting character who constantly seemed to be around bad things. And did bad things. One story went that Ollard mouthed off about killing a woman and dumping her body in Sydney Harbour. Sure, this could have been bravado and bragging, trying to show he was a tough guy to a couple of people in the front bar of the pub after a few too many, but there could also have been some substance to his claims. When a woman's body was recovered from Sydney Harbour in January 1976, the bravado seemed more driven by fact. The body was identified as Maria Hisshion, a fashion designer from Melbourne who was suspected of being a drug courier. The brag might have been sickeningly true. Was this the woman Ollard claimed to have killed? The allegations reached New South Wales Police but the word was that there wasn't enough to go on to investigate the matter further.

Meanwhile, things were looking up for Dragon and a change of management would put a spotlight on Greg Ollard. He'd made the classic mistake of an associate who thinks that they're actually part of a band, whereas they, in fact, work for the band. The new manager wasn't having a bar of that. He made it very clear that Ollard's relationship with Dragon was officially over. No sixth member. No financier. No nothing.

In September 1976, Dragon released 'This Time' (complete with a video filmed in and around Kings Cross), which propelled them several steps up the rock'n'roll ladder. It had only been out for a fortnight when 22-year-old Neil Storey, the Dragon drummer, was found dead from a heroin overdose. The band survived that shocking tragedy but Ollard pretty much disappeared from the band's orbit after that. He wasn't wanted.

Greg Ollard disappeared from everyone's orbit in November 1977. Evidently, he had started to distance himself from his Mr Asia syndicate boss and he told people he wanted to cash in his interests in the syndicate, a settlement worth several millions of dollars. This clearly didn't go down well. There were also whispers that Ollard was under police surveillance, which was mentioned later in the 1983 Royal Commission of Inquiry into Drug Trafficking report.

Ollard knew where the bodies were buried and the risk of him turning on the syndicate to name names and methods of operation was real. But there was also the risk he'd go direct to the clientele and cut out the middlemen. Either reason was enough for Clark to decide to kill him.

A meeting was arranged between Ollard and several Mr Asia figures in a Melbourne hotel-motel. After that meeting, Ollard and his de facto wife, Julie Theilman, were never seen again.

What happened to them? For five years no one knew for sure, but no one believed they'd headed off for a quiet retirement in a remote area of another country. Police believed they were both executed by Clark. Ollard's remains were found in the Ku-ring-gai National Park on 16 August 1982; the skeletal remains of Julie Theilman had been found three days earlier in the Blue Mountains.

So, don't blame the band or the hard-working road crew. More often than not they were oblivious to what was going on. All that was required was one vulnerable individual who would happily accept a wad of cash in exchange for placing a few extra items – carefully disguised – in the back of the truck.

* * *

I remember seeing Ian Saxon in full flight one night in 1989 at a Greek restaurant on Bondi Road, a few blocks back from the iconic beach. Saxon was tour manager for the Gipsy Kings then, who were touring for Michael Gudinski and Michael Chugg's Frontier Touring Company. It was the end of a successful tour – the Gipsy Kings were a big deal at the time – and Frontier were shouting dinner.

I was a Bondi resident at the time so it was an easy wander to this casual dinner for the band, the promoters and a few supportive media types. I ended up sitting next to Saxon, who seemed an outgoing, gregarious, funny, engaging guy. Few who knew him had even the remotest idea that there was another side to him. I certainly had no clue that I was dining beside a serious drug dealer. At no point did he even so much as hint that he was holding drugs that I might enjoy – and in those days I enjoyed a variety of illicit substances.

Saxon worked the room with a big smiley demeanour that stuck with me. Nice guy, I thought. Typical tour manager. On top of everything, attending to every request and demand from the artist and the promoters with a 'No problem – is that the worst you can throw at me?' attitude.

Not long after the dinner, Frontier Touring Company hit the headlines for reasons they'd have preferred not to. It all came through their association with Saxon, who was arrested on several heavy-duty drug-related charges – more than being busted with a couple of joints and a few grams of coke while driving home through the eastern suburbs of Sydney.

As would be revealed, Saxon had a long association with and was a significant player in the organised crime world in Australia. When arrested early in 1990 after investigations by the National Crime Authority, Saxon and several associates were charged with the importation of 10 tonnes of cannabis with an estimated value of $77 million.

The search warrant executed on Saxon's apartment in Darlinghurst resulted in the seizure of two kilograms of resin, and $192,000 in cash. A subsequent raid on a garage rented by his brother Lloyd turned up $7.5 million in cash. And this was just some of it. A subsequent order was made against Ian Saxon demanding he pay the Australian government $78 million in laundered profits after only $11.25 million had been recovered.

Saxon and co. had been at it for a long time, in fact some figures suggest that for two decades the network that included Saxon had been serious marijuana importers, bringing shipments into not only Australia but also the United States, the United Kingdom and Canada.

The fact Saxon had ended up around part of the international music touring world wasn't all that surprising. Born in 1943 in Auckland, New Zealand, he grew up around music, his father being a talented pianist. Saxon had learned saxophone and guitar before becoming known as the 'singing compere' and working the cabaret circuit in his home city, while supplementing his income by dealing pot.

Saxon moved to Sydney in the mid-1960s and continued to learn about the world of performing and promoting. John Harrigan, a prominent figure in the music industry at the time, put Saxon on the road with two bands he managed – Ray Brown & The Whispers; and Billy Thorpe & The Aztecs. It was during this period that he encountered a brash and ambitious 18-year-old Michael Chugg who promoted these bands at dances in Tasmania. Along with this, Saxon worked in the Latin Quarter nightclub in Pitt Street in the Sydney CBD.

During this period Saxon found himself onstage with some of the biggest names in Australian showbusiness and also mixed with many of Sydney's most notorious figures in the crime and entertainment business, Abe Saffron being more than likely one of the people he rubbed shoulders with. And who knows how much or little Saffron inspired him.

He moved around a bit. After a stint back in New Zealand where he formed Ian Saxon & the Sound, the singer and comparatively small-time drug dealer then toured with his band, whose line up at one time included star in the making Colleen Hewett. Among the tours they did was one with Johnny O'Keefe.

Their work included a residency at the Chevron Hotel in Kings Cross but after releasing two singles in 1970 they disbanded. Saxon found himself work as part of the 11-piece band SCRA (Southern Contemporary Rock Ensemble). Music alone was never going to cut it for Saxon, however.

By the mid-1970s Saxon had moved on again and relocated to California, working on the fringes of the music business and buying and selling drugs. His first significant brush with the law was when he was arrested and later convicted in 1976 of possessing around an ounce of concentrated cannabis. Not the hugest of amounts but he was fined $500 and put on probation for three years.

As documented by Clive Small and Tom Gilling in their 2017 book *The Dark Side*, Saxon spent 1978 travelling to Europe and Pakistan where he encountered a number of Australian drug traffickers, including one figure known only as 'Mr Andrews', a court-ordered pseudonym. He also met a number of other figures who knew a lot more about the drug trade than he did – but he learned quickly.

While based in the US, Saxon flexed his drug-trafficking muscles with a number of cocaine shipments to Australia, which he did with his friend and smuggling partner, Gary Morton. The two men were arrested in Tahiti in 1980 and convicted of importing cocaine and some other items that they hadn't declared.

Saxon was jailed for four years for the attempted cocaine importation, a deal whereby he'd bought the drugs in California and if successfully landed and sold in Australia would have netted him roughly five times his initial investment. There wasn't a lot of cocaine in Australia at the time, it wasn't easy to procure, and the price was high. On the 'Oops, I forgot to declare it' charge, Saxon earned a fine of around $800,000 or two years in jail.

'The Frontier Touring Company had taken off,' he told New Zealand journalist John Dix in 2016. 'I knew Chuggy from Tasmania and I met Michael Gudinski during SCRA. They give me the smaller acts to tour manage, those foisted on Frontier by agents. I think Suzanne Vega was my first tour. Same thing with Jimmy Buffett. Gudinski didn't want to know but Buffett had the same management as the Eagles and Fleetwood Mac. I also did Herbie Hancock, solo: just me, Herbie and his production manager. Herbie shared the same manager as Fine Young Cannibals who Gudinski had his eyes on.'

Saxon also toured with John Mellencamp (aka John Cougar/Johnny Cougar), Billy Joel, Bon Jovi, Iggy Pop and Poison. Despite not being a permanent staff member or partner in the company, he was clearly more than just a casual, occasional tour manager. He was really likeable and good at his job.

Michael Chugg says in his book, *Hey, You in the Black T-shirt*, that Saxon's title was 'Musicians' Liaison'. Chugg noted that the Kiwi always seemed to have a lot of money around him, and owned property in Sydney and a boat named *Rolling Thunder*. He also says that he and his associates had an inkling about what Saxon was involved with but absolutely no idea of the scale of his operations.

Early in 1989, before the Gipsy Kings tour, it became obvious that not only was Saxon very good at his job but he also had the supreme trust of the Frontier partners, as he scored the gig as tour manager for probably the most prestigious tour the company had ever done – Frank Sinatra, Liza Minnelli and Sammy Davis Jr. Another link to Abe – cranky Frankie.

Behind the scenes, though, Saxon was involved with some powerful figures in the drug trade. Seriously powerful. But we'll get to that soon.

In 2000 I talked to Chugg for my book *The Promoters*, a good ten years after the Saxon drama had gone down, and it clearly still rankled him. 'That was fucked,' was Michael Chugg's quick response to the mention of Saxon and the way the company's reputation had been significantly tarnished by their involvement with him as a tour manager. It hadn't been good for the touring company. Not one bit. And just to be clear, I'm not in any way saying that Chugg and Frontier were at any time aware of or involved in any illegal activity.

Chugg considered Saxon to be one of their best tour managers, with real empathy for dealing with artists, their management structure and technical crews. He could do more than book hotel rooms and flights, in other words.

Things finally came unstuck for Ian Saxon when he was employed to tour manage the American singer-songwriter Tracy Chapman. She was coming to Australia for the first time in 1990 on the back of the huge success of her debut self-titled album and its lead single, 'Fast Car', one of *the* records of the late 1980s.

It was the night of Saxon's birthday and Chugg and a bunch of his cohorts had organised a celebration at Sabatini's restaurant in the Sydney suburb of Surry Hills. At 8 pm there was no sign of Saxon. An hour later he still wasn't there. Same at 10 pm and then 11. Chugg and the other diners had by then assumed Saxon wasn't going to show. This was of course in the days before mobile phones and text messages.

At midnight, with the celebrations for the non-appearing tour manager in full flight, there was a call from an associate telling Chugg that Saxon had been arrested. By this stage of the night Chugg was 'a bit wasted' but decided, along with the other dinner guests, to head straight down to the police station where the birthday boy was being held. He walked in and saw Tracy Chapman itineraries all over the desks, along with a large amount of American currency and a briefcase.

Chugg confronted the police officer who appeared to be in charge. 'I said to the copper that I wanted everything there,' Chugg said. 'It was mine and I had a tour starting the next day.'

The police officer looked over his glasses and stared at Chugg for a few moments before saying, 'If everything here is yours then does it include this?'

He opened a tour booklet and inside was what looked to be an ounce of cocaine. His words to Chugg were simple and direct. 'Listen, you fat bastard, out on the footpath. I'll fucking talk to you when I'm ready.'

Chugg paced the footpath outside the police station until 3 am, when he was able to retrieve the necessary paperwork for the Chapman tour – minus the ounce of cocaine and the American currency. And Ian Saxon.

About a week later Chugg was in Brisbane, backstage with Kylie Minogue before a performance. The phone rang and it was handed to him by his tour manager. It was Chugg's wife telling him there were about twenty police officers outside their house. What should she do?

'For fuck's sake, go to the door and let them in,' Chugg barked into the phone.

The police began taking Chugg's home apart, presumably looking for either drugs or documents that would tie Saxon's activities directly in with Frontier's. They were tipping out sugar containers, testing flour and combing the space above the ceiling.

Meanwhile the forces of the law had already smashed down the doors of the Frontier office in William Street, not far down the road from the epicentre of organised crime in Kings Cross. The police removed dozens of files relating to tours, particularly but not exclusively those that Saxon had worked on. How were they to know that Ian Saxon was the only high-level drug dealer working for the touring company?

The police had search warrants, but it being a Saturday evening when they raided, no one was there to open up for them. 'They were mainly looking for money because Ian had told them that the money he was laundering was rock'n'roll money,' Chugg said.

Maybe Saxon was just being mischievous, he was desperate, or he didn't say it at all, but it seemed like he was quick to throw Frontier Touring Company under a very big bus as a diversionary tactic. Saxon allegedly said that he was laundering 'rock'n'roll money'. There's a lot of it around and myriad players so it would be jumping to conclusions to connect his activities with those of Frontier Touring.

Obviously the Saxon incident was a huge story at the time. This was big-deal organised crime, a long way from small-time street crime. The tabloids loved it – what's not to like for them? Drug dealing, rock'n'roll and big-name show-business artists, and Frontier Touring being the biggest Australian tour promoters at the time to tie in with it. You know: 'Kylie Minogue tour promoters caught up in alleged multi-million-dollar drug bust'. Read all about it!

The story was everywhere.

'Saxon didn't put a cent into Frontier,' Chugg insists, 'and we didn't know just what else he was up to.' According to Chugg, the police had been following Saxon for a long time prior to the arrest. 'When we brought Jimmy Buffett out for the America's Cup [in 1983], Ian was the tour manager because he was a mate of Jimmy's. I went over to Perth and Ian and I shared a room … That trip was when he did one of the big deals – and they were listening to our conversations, bugging the rooms. [After Saxon's arrest] they ended up going through all our stuff – all the tour receipts and accounts.'

This is an interesting comment on a number of levels. It suggests – if accurate – that the police had been on to Ian

Saxon for at least six years before arresting him. That's a long time to be observing high-level drug activity and not moving on it. And it proves to me that if anyone else in Frontier was involved, the police had ample time to mount a case against them, which they didn't and haven't. Case closed.

Reflecting on what went down, Chugg said years back, 'It turned everyone's life upside down, and the poor prick – he's still out in Long Bay. They've got him in solitary because everybody tries to kill him to get the money that doesn't exist – but they think it does.'

Chugg devoted an entire chapter in his memoir to 'the Saxon matter' as we'll call it. He writes that he felt partly to blame for Saxon's downfall: 'He wanted to move to Italy. I convinced him to stay in Australia to be tour manager for singer Tracy Chapman. He was arrested three days before the tour started.'

Later, Chugg goes into detail about the aftermath of Saxon's arrest and expresses his annoyance and anger that Saxon was so closely connected to Frontier in the media.

Michael Gudinski dismissed the subject quickly when it was raised with him but saw the Saxon incident as symptomatic of the reality that managers and promoters are constantly asked to supply drugs for artists touring this country. 'We've always kept out of that stuff,' he said. 'It's a no-win situation.'

That's all well and good but it would appear that not everyone in the upper echelons of the Australian music industry follows that advice. Stories have circulated in the music world for years of four or five powerful figures who formed a consortium to have their own drug courier bring significant quantities of cocaine in and out of the country.

After he was released from prison, Ian Saxon and I built an occasional friendship on social media and not long after my 2015 book on Michael Gudinski appeared, he contacted me asking for my address. Naturally I asked why and he responded somewhat curtly, 'Just send me your postal address.'

A few weeks later a nice card arrived from Saxon in New Zealand with a note requesting a copy of the Gudinski book. Inside the card was a crisp $100 note and Saxon had written, '*This is proceeds of crime – send the book and what's left over after the postage is yours.*' His sense of humour was not extinguished by his prison years.

Ian Saxon died in 2023 in Auckland and along with his death went the stories he carried about drugs, music and his wild years.

CHAPTER 19

MONEY LAUNDERING

As I've been discussing, pretty much every aspect of the music industry is rife with opportunities for crime and for criminal figures to operate and profit, especially when it comes to cash and money laundering. It's not all about men with guns, drug trafficking and huge piles of bank notes, increasingly there is a white-collar-crime element to it: people in front of computers establishing highly complex company structures and moving money around within these structures.

As the music industry has become more and more digitised, organised crime entities have spent time and resources working out how best to milk the new digital world order for maximum illegal gain – and they're very sophisticated about it. It's a very different world from Abe Saffron's day where computers were mostly a futuristic concept and music was only disseminated via physical records and cassettes. Even when CDs dominated, to think that most music would be bought and sold digitally, well – what planet are you on?

As described on epgdlaw.com, 'Money laundering is the process of making illegally-gained proceeds, also known as dirty money, appear legal, or clean. This is typically done by moving the money through a series of transactions or "layering" to obscure the funds' illegal origins. The process often involves moving the money through multiple bank accounts or shell companies, or even using it to purchase assets such as real estate or artwork. The ultimate goal of money laundering is to make the money appear as though it came from a legitimate source, so that it can be used without detection by law enforcement.'

There are many ways that this can occur in the music business. One common method is by using the proceeds of illegal activities to fund an artist's career. As an example, an individual may use money from drug trafficking to pay for studio time, music videos, tour costs or other business expenses. This can make it appear as though the money is being earned legitimately, when it isn't.

So when a new artist appears and they've recorded at state-of-the-art studios and have incredibly expensive-looking videos early on, well, they may be independently wealthy, they may have access to the proverbial Bank of Mum and Dad Inc – or there may occasionally be something else going on in the background.

It has been suggested that another way money can be laundered through music artists is by using them as a front for illegal activities. For example, as described on website epgdlaw.com, 'A criminal organisation may use a music artist as a cover for their illegal activities, using the artist's name and image to legitimise their business dealings.

'Money laundering can also happen through the sale of music royalties or other revenue streams generated by the artist's music. This can be done by creating a complex web of shell companies and bank accounts to move the money through, making it difficult to trace the money back to its illegal origins.' There are people who can do this sort of stuff in their sleep.

I want to be clear here, not all artists are complicit in behaviour and activity involving their name, likeness, creativity or money. It is very common for some artists to be involved in this kind of illegal activity and not be in the slightest bit aware that third parties are using these artists' names and fame for their own ends.

Money laundering is of course highly illegal and those engaging in it face the potential of prosecution on so many levels. It's also a highly risky way to move money around – and increasingly difficult but not impossible.

In Abe Saffron's day, cash was king. As I said earlier, there was no online banking, and far less advanced scrutiny of bank accounts and transactions. It was much easier in those days but it's clearly not impossible in today's comparatively modern and sophisticated world.

Whichever way you look or engage in it, it's a high-risk caper with significant penalties involved. Does it deter individuals and criminal organisations from being involved in it? Of course it doesn't, and it probably never will. And part of the reason so much of this activity takes place in and around the entertainment industry is that it's perceived to be glamorous.

If you have several hundred thousand dollars' worth of dirty or dodgy money that you want to have legitimised and you have a choice of doing it through a construction company or an entertainment business, there's a good chance many people are going to choose the latter. The perks are – for most people – better. A truckload of bricks and some steel girders or front-row tickets for major entertainment events and names on the guest list for after-show parties? What ya gonna do?

Let's start with live music concerts and touring. While there is limited cash involved these days there was for decades an enormous amount of cold hard coins and bank notes involved in all aspects of this business – ticket sales, artist merchandise, food and drink sales, payments to artists and support crew. All of it was cash, baby.

There are so many avenues for illegal activity here. Ticket and merchandise sales can easily be inflated. It's this simple – a concert promoter reports much higher ticket sales than actual attendances and mixes in so-called dirty money with legitimate earnings.

That's the most obvious way that money can be laundered but there are other methods involved. Most people don't imagine that record labels could be involved in such activities. Sure, they handle in many cases millions and millions of dollars but of course they account to artists and pay that money to those to whom it is due.

Labels appear to be completely legitimate business activities but they can be used to hide illicit transactions.

Royalties are defined as the payments made to artists for the use of their music, but can be manipulated. Artists and releases can literally be invented. As far as accounting figures are concerned, Fictitious Artist A sells 765,000 units at Y royalty rate. Money flows around and around with the business structure but none of it goes to Fictitious Artist A, who clearly doesn't exist.

This is complex fraud that involves skilled financial manipulation, but it is almost impossible to get away with it when equally skilled financial auditors examine the books.

The advent of digital streaming presented its own challenges and of course new opportunities for criminal figures hovering around the music industry. It is claimed that criminals can exploit streaming services by artificially inflating the numbers of streams. The cynics would ask why anyone would bother given the paltry percentages paid to artists, but if you do it enough times these minuscule amounts do begin to add up to something that might attract criminal elements.

Inflating streams can be done via bots or 'click farms', that generate fake plays and therefore increase royalty streams payable. When the money is paid by the streaming platform, it appears to be legitimate and provides the opportunity to launder that money elsewhere.

An infamous example from the music festival world is the Fyre Festival. It was even the subject of a 2019 documentary, 'FYRE: The Greatest Party that Never Happened'. The event was promoted by rapper Ja Rule and entrepreneur Billy McFarland and was the most spectacular of all fraudulent luxury (promised but not delivered) music festivals. Lurking behind the actual disaster that unfolded at the time was significant proof of misleading investors and diverting funds.

Music festivals and big events of any nature are a goldmine for money launderers. There are so many revenue streams, and to an extent still a relatively large amount of cash involved, particularly with food and drink stalls – and who's counting how many of these are dotted around a festival site? And is someone really counting how many tents and camping spaces were officially hired and paid for?

The sheer volume of transactions when there are 5000 people or maybe in excess of 50,000 at a festival combined with what was once nicely described as 'the often-chaotic nature of festival accounting', makes it an environment where it is comparatively easy to disguise funds and subsequently launder them.

Certainly, at its most basic level, a significant percentage of money generated by festivals is never destined for an interaction with the tax department. Stories abound about how in years past promoters and their associates would walk from stand to stand at festivals collecting their share of money for the hire of food and drink stands in large green garbage bags.

I'm not saying that this was rife, but it's pretty easy for festival organisers and promoters to introduce less-than-clean money into their financial system. Or, as mentioned, claim a higher than true attendance by using the excess cash to launder money, or the reverse and then take a big swag of cash and move it elsewhere.

Management companies are also potentially involved in such activities. These individuals or companies are usually the central hubs for all sorts of financial transactions connected to every aspect of the careers of the artists they manage.

It's comparatively easy for an unscrupulous manager to inflate their fees for services to an artist and use the excess amount to launder money. Also it's highly possible that they could negotiate a fee of, say, $150,000 for an artist to play a private function for a corporate client but tell the artist that the figure was only $85,000. Or if money needs to be moved around, they can create significant transport, artist payment and support staff invoices for events that didn't actually take place there by obscuring where money has actually gone.

It's not impossible to create fake artists or collaborators and use those entities by funnelling illicit funds via payments for non-existent work.

And of course, temporarily (in theory) 'borrowing' money owed to artists and using it for other purposes is, shall we say, a little more common than it should be.

Managers are in a position of significant trust and most respect that, but the opportunities are there. Like with Abe Saffron – if an opportunity is there to make money, someone will step up to do just that, legally or illegally.

CHAPTER 20

THE OLD AND THE NEW

I couldn't possibly write about Kings Cross without using John Ibrahim's 2017 memoir, *Last King of the Cross*, for information and inspiration. It's an action-packed recount of Ibrahim's life and times, and comes with some rather poignant and nuanced observations on the changing nature of the Cross – from the days when Abe Saffron was the main game in town through to the more recent past.

At the end of his book Ibrahim reflects, somewhat romantically and through some significantly rose-tinted glasses, on the suburb and particularly the main drag. He recalls that he was first stabbed at Sweethearts, which was directly over the road from Porky's, and above that was an illegal club where he was shot. He recalls Pinocchio's restaurant, the Budget Hotel and Hampton Court.

'I look around at the history of my life, written in large neon letters, and I remember what was exciting and important about the Cross,' Ibrahim writes. 'The availability to everybody of everything and anything that might be happening. I loved it, hanging with the guys, talking shit. It's where I felt most comfortable. I did it when I was a teenager, on the outer of the ring, and worked my way to the centre of it all.'

In the book Ibrahim gives us an insight into the changes to the Cross. He described how around 2009, things started looking up for the suburb, with renewed interest from younger people. His various businesses were flourishing. 'But, wouldn't you know it, as soon as I get some clean air, the Nine Network starts spruiking its new *Underbelly: The Golden Mile* series, which covers Kings Cross 1988–99, with me in the thick of it.'

That changing Cross still had some of the glamour of the old days – and Ibrahim talks about Stevie Wonder, Leonardo DiCaprio, Beyonce and Jay-Z and the clubs they went to. But he also highlights the change for many – from chasing money to chasing drugs and power.

When Ibrahim reflects on Kings Cross today in his book, he is not alone in feeling as though much of its original character is gone or in the process of being eroded. As he describes, clubs have closed and the 2014 lockout laws following two one-punch killings meant the government went on the warpath about alcohol and violence.

'Looking at Kings Cross today, there's not much left of my so-called kingdom. Most of the clubs have closed: the fear campaign and lockout laws have driven most of the punters away.' Restaurants and bars were doing it tough and developers moved in to replace hotels with apartments. As he colourfully says, 'Sydney is having its mouth washed out with soap. I'm no longer a teenager with a liquor licence, standing on the door. The bureaucrats are now running the show. An era has passed and me along with it.'

If only the walls could talk … Kings Cross has seen it all. But John Ibrahim has seen a lot too, so reading about it all in his memoir has been enlightening.

He is a highly successful businessman and I want to note the fact that I am discussing him in this book is not suggesting in any way that he runs his businesses other than professionally and legally. Thanks for the stories, John.

* * *

In 2025, of course there's nonetheless still criminality in and around Kings Cross, but much of its epicentre has shifted and spread all over the urban landscape. In the past the Sydney drug trade was centred around the Cross, Redfern and Cabramatta, now it's everywhere. You can dial a dealer and get a delivery directly to home … so I am told! And the same goes for criminality in all its forms. *Go west young men and women of the criminal classes* appears to have been the adage, and much criminality is now centred in the sprawling, often lower-socioeconomic suburbs on Sydney's ever-expanding boundaries.

The wannabe Abe Saffrons of this day and age are brash, arrogant, exuding a presence of being bulletproof (and repeatedly shown that they're not) and very much schooled in the eye-for-an-eye ethos. Shoot one of ours and we're coming for you muthafuckas.

Gone is the old-school charm, if you can call it that, which permeated the world around Saffron. Family members are no longer off-limits. Sure, things were often brutal and tough but rarely so bloody, brazen and (frequently) so unthinking and plain stupid.

By comparison with what happens today, the old-school guys appeared civilised. Okay, that's a stretch, but it was mostly contained brutality. It's easy to romanticise violence when you're removed from it. One can only wonder at what Abe would make of the class, or lack of it, in 2025.

There is no official data on gangs and gang membership in Australia. The term itself is debated by criminologists, and it is often exploited politically and sensationalised by the media. But street gangs and motorcycle gangs and far right extremist groups do exist. In the last decade media attention has from time to time focused on something labelled postcode wars.

Street gangs affiliated with their suburb or local district areas are usually identified on cultural lines. North, south, east, inner and western Sydney, each has their own manifestations and some form coalitions while others foster intense rivalries. There are names like 21 District, Section 60, KVT. In Mount Druitt, NF14 rules the streets, and the New South Wales Police allege that locally formed drill rap group OneFour were part of NF14 and a larger organised crime network. That's a claim OneFour deny.

This is an area where music might just break the path to jail and in 2014, via a community-funded program that provided free time in a recording studio, five young men formed OneFour. They have repeatedly denied their involvement in gang violence and say their name came about because of the year they started making music. The police disagree and say it's a nod to the street gang NF14. Their lyrics, true to the rap drill genre, barked revenge against rivals and dark criminal escapades, but so does a lot of rap and hip hop music, so the spotlight on this band is particularly intense.

OneFour are now acknowledged as the first Australian Pasifika drill rappers. And their popularity has been building. By 2018, their distinctive music started to reach a wider audience and by the time they released their debut album *Against All Odds* in November 2020, it peaked at number seven on the Australian ARIA charts and number eight on the New Zealand equivalent.

The problem for the young musos, who consistently reiterate that they are musicians who love their craft, was the New South Wales Police didn't like OneFour's lyrics. Arguing that the words were evidence of participation in a street gang, namely NF14, and some pretty serious criminal activity and violence, OneFour and other rappers came under the scrutiny of Strike Force Raptor.

Raptor was established in 2009 to focus primarily on outlaw motorcycle gangs and organised crime, but its focus was expanded to include street gangs and the drill music scene. Raptor investigators became convinced that OneFour with their angry prose were inciting vengeful violence and implicating the members in broader criminal enterprises. It wasn't just the moral argument of incitement; it was alleged participation. The group again deny this.

Consequently, New South Wales Police were hellbent on doing everything in their power to stop the group performing, even trying to remove their lyrics from streaming services.

Despite the lack of live performance, OneFour's popularity and profile continued to escalate.

Then in the opening months of 2024 the New South Wales Police uncovered a plot to allegedly kill four of OneFour's Sydney-based members. The band weren't as popular to all, it seemed.

So far five members of the alleged murder cell have been identified. Those arrested have been charged with conspiracy to murder, kidnap and commit armed robbery together with other serious firearm and drug offences.

At the time of the arrests and breaking news, the *Sydney Morning Herald* reported the head of the Organised Crime Squad, Detective Superintendent Peter Faux, saying the murder cell had 'done surveillance on the intended victims; they're following the intended victims on social media. They are extremely committed and are extremely organised.'

The members of the murder cell were not first timers. Police alleged they were linked to a series of kidnapping plots, and $1 billion worth of cocaine. Yes, you read that right – $1 billion worth of cocaine. One billion.

There is neither any evidence nor any suggestion that any of the members of OneFour are connected to organised crime. But the planned hit shows that someone was mighty pissed off about them.

So OneFour had managed to get themselves on the wrong side of some pretty nasty characters. If the police hadn't stepped in, things may not have ended well for the young rappers.

Did they seem concerned? Not in the slightest. In fact, the opposite.

As reported in the *Sydney Morning Herald*, 'When the murder plot was initially exposed, OneFour responded with a defiant post on Instagram of group members with the 50 Cent song 'Many Men (Wish Death)' playing in the background.' OneFour have, at the time of writing, 345,000 followers on Instagram. Not bad for a group that has posted only 162 times and follows just 195 others.

In June 2025, the band launched a new album and announced an Australian tour.

* * *

It is easy to legally harass musicians from disenfranchised backgrounds, but a look, lyrics and a pointed finger do not a criminal make. And like I said earlier, OneFour have consistently denied any gang affiliation. While they concentrate on their music, we know that there are professional criminals and others qualified to do a whole manner of jobs who also chose to participate in criminal activity. A side hustle if you will, albeit a dangerous one. Some who chose their risky second job are bankers and some are trying to make it as musicians.

But there is no evidence at all that the music itself is causative of bad choices. Maybe, just maybe, it's easier to enlist low-level foot soldiers for a bigger criminal enterprise from the ranks of the disenfranchised and marginalised –

some of whom make music. I suspect Abe may have learned that lesson long ago. But, like I said earlier, the more things change the more they stay the same. Money and drugs will always bring players who think they are somehow bigger than the game.

CHAPTER 21

WALKING WITH GHOSTS

Everything changes. I have said it before in these pages and I'm saying it again. That's just the way it is. The way it will always be. Recently I asked a musician based in the Lower East Side of Manhattan how he felt about the gentrification of his locale and he looked at me and said, 'Everyone asks that and to be honest everyone I know is sick of talking about it – of course things are different from how they were ten or twenty years ago and I'm sure it's the same in Sydney.'

And it is. As I was completing this book, I took a train to Kings Cross for a wander around the area with writer Duncan McNab, who has written very fine books on criminality in Sydney, including ones on Roger Rogerson and Abe Saffron, the latter being the yardstick that I relied on heavily for this book.

We met on the corner of Macleay and Orwell streets, right near where the Roosevelt still stands after an ever-changing history, including housing radio station 2KY and for a period the offices of free Sydney music/what's on magazine *Drum Media*.

I remember visiting the *Drum Media* offices a few times in that era and marvelling at the wonderful art deco surrounds but being oblivious to the building's previous incarnations. Today it's back as the Roosevelt, as it has been since 2012. The bar's website proudly explains its connection with Abe Saffron and the glamorous world of Kings Cross in what many consider to be its heyday.

The Kings Cross of my era in the 1980s and '90s has largely disappeared. The Manzil Room entrance now leads to expensive apartments; Benny's is an upscale restaurant; the Sebel Townhouse is apartments; and long gone are the Rex, Sweethearts, Pinocchio's and many, many other institutions.

In some cases the façades are still there. Duncan pointed out where Juanita Nielsen lived and various other houses that still stand that were at the centre of the development struggles in the 1970s.

The Coca-Cola sign still dominates the landscape and much of the surviving architecture is beautiful, reminding us of another time and place.

We walked past the old Chevron Hotel where the Hoodoo Gurus had played when I was their manager and where I'd seen Jimmy Barnes and many other Australian rock icons perform. We tried to work out exactly which building used to be the Sheraton where the Beatles had stood on a balcony and waved. We walked past where the Macleay Street bookshop had done business for decades. There's now another bookshop – further away from the Cross and on the other side of the road. It won Bookshop of the Year at the recent Australian book publishing industry awards

The streets – even on a Sunday afternoon – still showed evidence of working girls and boys, drug addicts and the homeless. But of course, homelessness and drug addiction isn't limited to Kings Cross. And what I saw at the Cross was largely overshadowed – at least in daylight – by the bright, happy, moneyed clientele at the seemingly endless array of cafes and restaurants, most of them pretty upmarket.

The old Cross is still there if you look hard enough – but only just. A few months earlier I'd visited the El Rocco jazz club and walked down the steep steps to the area where the mid-week jam session occurs. Squint your eyes and both the audience and the musicians on the low stage could have been from the 1960s – some of them clearly were. The vibe, as they say, was still there.

Kings Cross and the streets that Abe Saffron and his associates walked remain, though most of the clubs from that era have naturally disappeared and been replaced by other, more contemporary ventures. Buildings have been pulled down but a surprising number still stand. Spruikers still ply their trade at night, the lights shine bright and there's still enough neon to dazzle.

The rock'n'roll scene is less evident in this area than it was in the past. It's moved to Newtown, Enmore, Darlinghurst, Marrickville and other inner-west and suburban areas.

There's still a ridiculously large amount of money being made and moved around in the world of rock'n'roll and associated entertainments. Some of it flows through legitimate channels – and much of it as always doesn't.

Some is declared, much is laundered, drugs are still bought and sold and the proceeds shifted around through complex company structures or, if possible, in the same cold, hard cash that never appears on any tax return.

Heroin users aren't as visible as they once were. But the drugs are there, and I suspect they always will be. The times have definitely changed, but in some ways, the more things change the more they stay the same.

Did I witness any criminal activity while walking through Kings Cross that day? I could make a case for the price of the salad wrap and coffee at a cafe we visited. But that would be churlish. I didn't see it – but just like during the reign of Abe Saffron – I know it was there.

ACKNOWLEDGEMENTS

Naturally a bunch of fine humans provided insight, information and support during a project like this. First up I'd like to thank Duncan McNab, whose book on Saffron was my central resource for this book. I joked with Duncan a number of times that it was hard to write a version of Saffron's world with his book looming so large. Beyond that Duncan answered absolutely every email query quickly and always with additional information and insights. And towards the end of the project we spent a lovely few hours wandering around Kings Cross. Thanks, Duncan.

I'm lucky – very lucky – to have such a fine publisher as Vanessa Radnidge, who initially went for the idea and did a magnificent job of keeping me focused on the core story as I made seemingly every effort to disappear down another non-essential rabbit hole. Jacquie Brown steered the whole process with patience, insights and an endless array of suggestions and requests which have ultimately made for a vastly better book than if I'd been left to my own devices. I was fortunate to have not one but two crazily talented copyeditors work on the manuscript. Editors are wired differently to us mere mortals. I am in awe of them. Thank you, Jo Lyons and Deonie Fiford.

Others to whom I owe a big thanks are Graham Steele and Wayne Sole. Wayne kindly lent me his copy of Alan Heffernan's memoir, thereby saving me a large fortune even if I could find a copy of it. Jeff Apter, who has just written a fine book on Lee Gordon, answered all my queries and supplied extremely useful information.

My buddies in music Chris Pepperell, Frank Cotterell, Steve Stavrakis and John Foy gave me information about Saffron's excursions into record shops. Bob Yates and Glenn A. Baker provided helpful information, as did the very talented writer John Dix in New Zealand. Murray Lee engaged in many discourses on criminality. He also supplied a number of highly informative and thought-provoking essays and academic studies.

I hope to write as well as Mark Dapin when I grow up, and thank him for writing such fine books about criminality which fuelled my approach to writing this book.

My buddy George Enrique Munoz is the king of second-hand bookshop scouring and found me so many extremely useful books on criminality. And in fact I would be remiss to not thank the second-hand booksellers of Australia.

And to Trevor – just Trevor – who responded to an early reach-out on Facebook about David Hickie's *The Prince and the Premier*. I'd lost my copy over the years, or it might be buried in my storage, and it is a rare and expensive book. He drove over to my home and gave me his copy. That was the point when I realised I'd better get writing. It was the karmic message to stop procrastinating.

Susan Lynch is central to my very existence. My heart and soul. She has been there for seven, and now eight, books as a sounding board, motivator and inspirer. She'll roll her eyes when I say I couldn't do it without her – but I couldn't.

SOURCES

Introduction: Bright lights, big city

My friend and publisher Matthew Kelly has been reminding me for more than 20 years – regardless of the subject of the book I'm working on – to read and re-read *Not For Publication* by Chris Masters (ABC Books 2001), and in particular the opening essay, 'My Gangster'. It was particularly good advice with this book.

Part One: Abe's world

This is obviously not the first book to have been written with Saffron at its core. My total go-to text for my attempt was Duncan McNab's superb, incredibly researched and insightful *The Usual Suspect: The Life of Abe Saffron* (Pan Macmillan, 2005). It's the essential biography of Saffron, one which Saffron read before his death and corrected errors in. As noted elsewhere, Duncan answered each and every query from me – and there were many. It's hard to imagine this book existing without his research, help and friendship.

Mr Sin: The Abe Saffron Dossier by Tony Reeves (Allen & Unwin, 2007) was also an invaluable text which I referred to constantly.

Gentle Satan: My Father, Abe Saffron by Alan Saffron (Michael Joseph, 2008) was also invaluable for Alan's opinions and perspectives on various Abe-related matters, and it is of course the only inner-family insight that we currently have.

Also very useful was 'King of the Cross: Sydney crime boss Abe Saffron's secret friends and properties' by Kate McClymont (*Sydney Morning Herald*, 31 May 2007).

Chapter 1 Saffron's building blocks

Duncan McNab's biography was the essential source here, as well as *Under the Influence: A History of Alcohol in Australia* by Ross Fitzgerald and Trevor L. Jordan (ABC Books, 2009).

Chapter 2 Kings Cross beckons

For insights into Kings Cross throughout the decades, I gained valuable nuance and information from a number of books.

In the Gutter … Looking at the Stars: A Literary Adventure Through Kings Cross, edited by Mandy Sayer and Louis Nowra (Random House Australia, 2000), is a wonderful collection of Kings Cross–centric fiction, non-fiction and poetry.

Also indispensable was Louis Nowra's magnificently detailed and informative *Kings Cross: A Biography* (NewSouth Books, 2013).

The following were also very helpful:

The Good Old Bad Old Days: Woolloomooloo, Potts Point, Kings Cross, Elizabeth Bay, Rushcutters Bay by Warren Fahey (Bodgie Books, 2017).

Pictorial History of Kings Cross by Anne-Maree Whitaker (Kingsclear Books, 2012).

Razor: A True Story of Slashers, Gangsters, Prostitutes and Sly Grog by Larry Writer (Pan Macmillan, 2001), is the definitive book on Tilly Devine, Kate Leigh and their world.

Wild Women of Sydney by George Blaikie (Rigby, 1980).

Chapter 3 The Roosevelt

Bumper: The Life and Times of Frank 'Bumper' Farrell by Larry Writer (Hachette Australia, 2011) told me everything I needed to know about this notorious policeman.

Chapter 4 The Times They Are A-Changin'

Bodgie Dada & The Cult of Cool by John Clare and Gail Brennan (UNSW Press, 1995) is a magnificent examination of Australian jazz since 1945 and should never be out of print. Same goes for the accompanying double CD of the same name.

The Mayor's A Square: Live Music and Law and Order in Sydney by Shane Homan (Local Consumption Publications, 2003) was particularly useful as it covers the Sydney live music scene from the 1950s onwards.

I also learned from 'The El Rocco: An era in Sydney jazz' by Bruce Johnson (*Jazz Magazine*, 1983).

Chapter 5 Saffron, Sinatra and Lee Gordon

Alan Heffernan's self-published *Big Shows: The Lee Gordon Years* (2003) is an extremely hard-to-find – and expensive if you do – insider's look at the world of Lee Gordon. I took valuable information from it.

For this section, I also consulted biographies of Johnny O'Keefe, including:

Johnny O'Keefe: Rocker. Legend. Wild One. by Jeff Apter (Hachette Australia, 2013).

The Wild One: The Life and Times of Johnny O'Keefe by Damian Johnstone (Allen & Unwin, 2001).

Off The Record: Life With and Without Johnny O'Keefe by Marianne Renate (Pan Macmillan, 1998).

I read the exhaustive transcripts of Peter Cox's interview with Lou Nanlohy, 3 February 1993, which provided some colour.

I have no trouble reading about and listening to Frank Sinatra, so it was no chore to investigate James Kaplan's exhaustive and definitive two-volume biography, *Frank: The Voice* (Doubleday, 2010) and *Sinatra: The Chairman* (Doubleday, 2015). To suggest that these are a (Robert) Caro-esque endeavour is no understatement.

I also consulted the following:

'Lee Gordon' (*Nostalgia Central*, https://nostalgiacentral.com/pop-culture/people/lee-gordon/).

Lenny Bruce: 13 Days in Sydney by Damian Kringas (Independence Jones, 2010) provided valuable insights into Gordon, Saffron and Sydney in the early 1960s. It's a terrific book.

Information about Wayne Martin came from 'Founder of Pink Pussycat Club and friend to the stars' by Tim Barlass (*Sydney Morning Herald*, 14 February 2019).

Chapter 6 Nightclubs, sleaze and an iron fist

Aside from the aforementioned books, *Sydney Noir: The Golden Years* by Michael Duffy and Nick Hordern (NewSouth Books,

2017) is a marvellous book about Sydney and Kings Cross in the 1960s and 70s. It's a gem.

I also consulted:

Sex and Thugs and Rock 'n' Roll: A Year in Kings Cross, 1963–1964 by Billy Thorpe (Pan Macmillan, 1996).

'Chequers, a swinging hotspot in sixties Sydney' by Greg Ray (*Photo Time Tunnel*, 8 November 2018).

'Chequers owner leaves his stamp on Sydney' by Michael Gormly (*CityHub*, 10 February 2009).

'Nightclub owner played host to superstars' by Pat Sheil (*Sydney Morning Herald*, 2 March 2009).

Chapter 7 Kings Cross becomes dangerous

All of the aforementioned fed into this chapter, as did *For Facts Sake* by Bob Daisley (Thompson Music, 2013).

Chapter 8 The seventies and sexual freedom

He Did It Her Way: Carlotta – Legend of Les Girls (Ironbark, 1994) and the excellent introduction from collaborator James Cockington provided invaluable insights into Les Girls, Saffron and other goings-on in Kings Cross.

Madam Lash: Gretel Pinniger's Scandalous Life of Sex, Art and Bondage by Sam Everingham (Allen & Unwin, 2010) was greatly helpful.

Damned Whores and God's Police: The Colonisation of Women in Australia by Anne Summers (Penguin Books, 1975) was a key reference in trying to understand Saffron's relationship with his wife and other women.

There was a small bit of information about Saffron and Adelaide in *Don Dunstan: The Visionary Politician Who Changed Australia* by Angela Woollacott (Allen & Unwin, 2019).

Chapter 9 The lingering Juanita legacy

There has been so much written about Juanita Nielsen, and she features prominently in many of the already mentioned books I used. But the single best book aside from those is *Killing Juanita: A True Story of Murder and Corruption* by Peter Rees (Allen & Unwin, 2004). Start looking for Juanita here.

The Prince and the Premier: The Story of Perce Galea, Bob Askin and the Others Who Gave Organised Crime Its Start in Australia by David Hickie (Angus & Robertson, 1985) is a recognised classic of literature about criminality in Australia – and an expensive one to buy if you don't have a copy and need one. It is *the* book on organised crime in New South Wales from the 1940s to the 1980s. Anyone writing a book such as mine owes a debt to Hickie and his research.

The following were helpful:

'Juanita Nielsen's suspected murder brought Arthur King back to Kings Cross after his terrifying ordeal' by Michael Dulaney (*ABC News*, 31 July 2021).

'Who killed Juanita?' by John Moyle (*Sydney Sentinel*, September 2021).

'Fact or fiction: credibility of Juanita Nielsen doco's star witness called into question' by Neil Mercer (*Sydney Morning Herald*, 3 October 2021).

Chapter 10 Bourbon, Beefsteak and Bernie

The Politics of Heroin: CIA Complicity in the Global Drug Trade by Alfred W. McCoy (Lawrence Hill Books, 1991).

Chapter 11 Anderson's fireworks

'"Big Jim" of the underworld dies, aged 73' (*Sydney Morning Herald*, 12 July 2003).

'James McCartney ("Big Jim") Anderson' (http://www.milesago.com/people/anderson-jim.htm).

'To the end, "Big Jim" insisted it was all lies' by Neil Mercer (*Sydney Morning Herald*, 22 July 2003).

Chapter 12 Luna Park

I met Martin Sharp a number of times (once at his home with Tiny Tim) and regret never asking him about Saffron.

Martin Sharp: His Life and Times by Joyce Morgan (Allen & Unwin, 2017) is a fine biography.

Sharp (1942–1979) and *Sharper (1980–2013)* by Lowell Tarling (ETT Imprint, 2016 and 2017) are super detailed looks at the artist's life and times.

The following were helpful:

'ABC ghost train series "misleading" in linking Wran and Saffron' by Lisa Visentin (*Sydney Morning Herald*, 30 August 2021).

'The premier, the crime boss and the ABC' by Margaret Simons (*Inside Story*, 2 September 2021).

Chapter 13 The end of Abe

I looked at *Bugged! Legal Police Telephone Taps Expose the Mr Bigs of Australia's Drug Trade* by Bob Bottom (Sun Books, 1989) and Richard Walsh's *Sydney Morning Herald* article, 'It's a crime to think any other way', 4 October, 2005.

Chapter 14 Abe's legacy

The library of books about Australian crime and criminals is vast. For this book, I particularly looked at:

Mr Big: Lennie McPherson and His Life of Crime by Tony Reeves (Allen & Unwin, 2005).

The Dodger: Inside the World of Roger Rogerson by Duncan McNab (Pan Macmillan, 2006).

The Real George Freeman: Thief, Race-fixer, Standover Man and Underworld Crim by Tony Reeves (Michael Joseph, 2011).

Catch and Kill Your Own: Behind the Killings the Police Don't Want to Solve by Neddy Smith (Ironbark, 1995).

I also drew from these articles:

'Saffron's long lost son' by Kate McClymont (*Sydney Morning Herald*, 9 October 2011).

'Saffron's son: Dad paid off Askin and lent Packer money' by Kate McClymont (*Sydney Morning Herald*, 28 July 2008).

Part Two: Music's underbelly

To understand the relationship between criminal behaviour – both organised and otherwise – in the music industry, I have read widely. The essential books on the subject that I consulted were:

Hit Men: Power Brokers and Fast Money Inside the Music Business by Frederic Dannen (Times Books, 1990). On the back cover, it proclaims: 'Payola, Corruption, Drugs, the Mafia: An Everyday Story of the Record Industry'.

Stiffed: A True Story of MCA, the Music Business and the Mafia by William Knoedelseder (HarperCollins, 1993).

And Party Every Day: The Inside Story of Casablanca Records by Larry Harris (Backbeat Books, 2009) is the story of Casablanca Records (home of Donna Summer, KISS, The Village People, etc.) and a whole lot of strangeness.

Godfather of the Music Business: Morris Levy by Richard Carlin (University Press of Mississippi, 2016) tells the story of Morris Levy. The book title is accurate.

Dangerous Rhythms: Jazz and the Underworld by T.J. English (William Morrow, 2022) is a wonderfully detailed look at the history of and relationship between jazz and the underworld.

Have Gun Will Travel: The Spectacular Rise and Violent Fall of Death Row Records by Ronin Ro (Doubleday, 1998) is a jaw-dropping account of the iconic rap and hip-hop label and every possible element of criminality.

I Fought the Law: The Life and Strange Death of Bobby Fuller by Miriam Linna and Randell Fuller (Kicks Books, 2014) examines the alleged murder of rock singer Bobby Fuller.

The Mansion on the Hill: Dylan, Young, Geffen, Springsteen and the Head-On Collision of Rock and Commerce by Fred Goodman (Times Books, 1997).

They Fought the Law: Rock Music Goes to Court by Stan Soocher (Schirmer Books, 1999).

Off the Charts: Ruthless Days and Reckless Nights Inside the Music Industry by Bruce Haring (Carol Publishing, 1995).

Howling at the Moon by Walter Yetnikoff (with David Ritz) (Broadway Books, 2004).

Me, the Mob, And the Music: One Helluva Ride by Tommy James (with Martin Fitzpatrick) (Scribner, 2010).

Hitmaker: The Man and His Music by Tommy Mottola (with Cal Fussman) (Grand Central Publishing, 2013).

Moguls and Madmen: The Pursuit of Power in Popular Music by Jory Farr (Simon & Schuster, 1994) is a pacy story of guns, lawsuits, gangs and greed in the music industry.

Also insightful was the now legendary profile of Tommy Mottola, 'Tommy Boy' by Robert Sam Anson (*Vanity Fair*, December 1996).

Chapter 15 Kings Cross vibes

Louis Nowra's book on Kings Cross was again very useful here.

Chapter 16 Organised crime and the music industry

Information on Steve Marriott's relationship with organised crime came from *All or Nothing: The Authorised Story of Steve Marriott* by Simon Spence (Omnibus Books, 2021), an authorised biography of the artist – and also from conversations with Peter Noble, who promoted the tour I write about during the preparation of his self-published memoir, *Winners Never Quit* (2025).

Blood, Sweat and Beers: Oz Rock from the Aztecs to Rose Tattoo by Murray Engleheart (HarperCollins, 2010) is a wonderfully evocative look at the pub rock culture in Australia.

The information on Paul DeMarco came predominantly from 'Former Rose Tattoo drummer admits to role in gun racket with Sam Ibrahim' by Stephanie Gardiner (*Sydney Morning Herald*, 16 November 2016).

Chapter 17 Beyond Sydney

I relied on two books for the story of the Whiskey Au Go Go massacre:

The Whiskey Au Go Go Massacre: Murder, Arson and the Crime of the Century by Geoff Plunkett (Big Sky Publishing, 2018) is an extremely detailed look at the tragedy.

The Night Dragon by Matthew Condon (University of Queensland Press, 2019), like all of Condon's books about criminality in Queensland, was insightful and informative. I also looked at his *Three Crooked Kings* (2013), *Jacks and Jokers* (2014) and *All Fall Down* (2015).

I also drew from these articles:

'50 years ago, the Whiskey Au Go Go firebombing killed 15 people. We still don't know the full truth' by Isabella Ross (*Mamamia*, 14 July 2023).

'Convicted McCulkins' killer Vincent O'Dempsey denies involvement in fatal Whiskey Au Go Go firebombing, Brisbane inquest told' by Talissa Siganto (*ABC News*, 16 May 2022).

'Brisbane venue closed until April due to firebombing attack' by Tione Zylstra (*The Music*, 4 February 2025).

For information on John Wren and Festival Hall, I drew from 'Family of Melbourne crime boss John Wren to sell Festival Hall site' by Michael Bleby (*Financial Review*, 16 April 2019).

Chapter 18 Wheeling and dealing

For this section, I relied heavily on *Hey, You in the Black T-Shirt: The Real Story of Touring the World's Biggest Acts* by Michael Chugg (with Iain Shedden) (Pan Macmillan, 2010), which – like Chugg – is pacy, anecdote-filled and opinionated.

I want to single out *The Dark Side: The Explosive Story of Corruption, Greed and Murder in the Australian Drug Trade* by Clive Small and Tom Gilling (Allen & Unwin, 2017), which took my understanding and knowledge of the world of Ian Saxon and his associates and connections to a whole different level. This book is the business – not just on Saxon but the Australian drug trade and criminality in general. It's a beacon in the literature about this world.

I also read:

'Saxon, drugs and rock 'n roll: the outlandish tale of two Auckland brothers' by Tony Wall (*Stuff*, 16 June 2016).

The Best Years of Our Lives by Richard Clapton (Allen & Unwin, 2015).

There is a library of books about Mr Asia and related matters. I particularly looked at:

Crims in Grass Castles: The True Story of Trimbole, Mr Asia and The Disappearance of Donald Mackay by Keith Moor (Penguin Books, 2009).

The Mr Asia Connection: The True Story of Underbelly's Terry Clark by Richard Hall (Five Mile Press, 2010), originally published as *Greed* (Pan Macmillan, 1981).

Mr Asia: Last Man Standing: Inside Australasia's Most Notorious Drug Syndicate by James 'Diamond Jim' Shepherd (Pan Macmillan, 2010).

For information on Dragon and their world, I referred to *Chasing the Dragon: The Life and Death of Marc Hunter* by Jeff Apter (Hardie Grant, 2011).

I also read:

'Clark more than just a nasty killer' (*Southland Times*, 22 May 2010).

'Paul Hewson – In the Dragon's lair' by Glen Moffatt (*Audioculture*, 1 September 2014) is a wonderful piece of research.

'Ian Saxon aka Ian Saxon & the Sound' by John Dix (a very fine music writer) (*Audioculture*, 26 October 2016).

'Drug trafficking, money laundering bust sees five men, including Melbourne music promoter, arrested in joint NSW Police-FBI investigation' (*ABC News*, 11 September 2015).

For information on OneFour, I referred to:

'[Dr]illing in the name of: the criminalisation of Sydney drill group ONEFOUR' by Murray Lee, Toby Martin, Jioji Ravulo and Ricky Simandjuntak (*Current Issues in Criminal Justice*, 2022, *34*(4), 339–359).

'Sydney man accused of ONEFOUR murder plot' by Steve Zemek (*News.com.au*, 9 April 2024).

'Criminal conflict behind foiled rapper kill plot: cops' by Esther Linder and Miklos Bolza (*Canberra Times*, 11 January 2024).

'Rapper and accused Sydney gangster bailed with $1.8m pledge' by Alex Mitchell (*Sydney Morning Herald*, 30 July 2024).

'"Airtasker for crooks": Contract killings becoming big business' by Sally Rawsthorne (*Sydney Morning Herald*, 11 August 2024).

'Sydney police uncover alleged plot to kill OneFour rap group members' by Rafqa Touma (*The Guardian*, 11 January 2024).

'OneFour: Drill rap trailblazers spark debate over art and censorship' by Hannah Ritchie (*BBC News*, 27 January 2024).

'From being "Ladz in the Hood" to being "Welcomed to Prison": The story of OneFour' by Thaveesha Jinadasa (*ARC UNSW Student Life*, 30 November 2019).

'"Who wants war with Sydney's realest?"' by Osman Faruqi (*ABC News*, 13 December 2019).

'Gangland rapper Ay Huncho surrenders to police after major raids' by Fergus Hunter (*Sydney Morning Herald*, 16 December 2021).

'Prominent rapper "on the run" after raids targeting Alameddine crime family' by Fergus Hunter (*Sydney Morning Herald*, 15 December 2021).

'Onefour respond after police foil alleged murder plot' by Perry Duffin and Jessica McSweeney (*Sydney Morning Herald*, 11 January 2024).

'Third man arrested over alleged murder plot targeting Sydney rappers Onefour' by Angus Dalton (*Sydney Morning Herald*, 13 February 2024).

'Behind the ONEFOUR documentary: How filmmakers shared Western Sydney with the world' by Parry Tritsiniotis (*Triple J*, 1 November 2023).

Chapter 19 Money laundering

My key sources were:

'How the Mafia used to control the music industry' by James Mishra (*Click Track*, 20 March 2020).

'Multiple criminal gang members confirm they've used Spotify for money laundering in bombshell new report in Sweden' (*Music Business Worldwide*, 5 September 2023).

'How does the music industry launder money?' by Silvino Diaz, (*EPGD Business Law*, 10 February 2023).

'Money laundering in the music industry: An unseen symphony of crime' (*AML Watcher*, 29 July 2024).

'Kazaa offices raided in Australia' by Frank Ahrens (*Washington Post*, 6 February 2004).

'The life and crimes of the music biz' by Simon Napier-Bell (*The Guardian*, 21 January 2008).

'Founder of South Korean tech giant arrested over K-Pop deal' by Yan Zhuang, Jin Yu Young and John Yon (*New York Times*, 22 July 2024).

'Yakuza intractable in Japan showbiz' by Mark Schilling (*Variety*, 18 February 2012).

'Commentary: The music industry and the Mafia' by Dawoud Kringle (*DBDBD NY*, 12 December 2020).

Chapter 20 The old and the new

Last King of the Cross by John Ibrahim (Pan Macmillan, 2023) contains some wonderful, insightful observations on the changing nature of Kings Cross and its milieu. I relied on it heavily for this chapter – and loved reading it.

ADDITIONAL SOURCES

There are many (many) books on crime in Australia. Among those I referenced are:

Gangland Sydney by James Morton and Susanna Lobez (Melbourne University Press, 2011).

Gangland Oz: Yesterday, Today and Tomorrow by James Morton and Susanna Lobez (Melbourne University Press, 2017).

Leadbelly: Inside Australia's Underworld Wars by John Silvester and Andrew Rule (Floradale and Sly Ink, 2004).

Underbelly: A Tale of Two Cities by John Silvester and Andrew Rule (Floradale and Sly Ink, 2009).

Connections: Crime Rackets and Networks of Influence Down-Under by Bob Bottom (Sun Books, 1985).

Connections II: Crime Rackets and Networks of Influence in Australia by Bob Bottom (Sun Books, 1987).

Disorganized Crime by Richard Hall (University of Queensland Press, 1986).

On the fiction front, I learned a lot about this world from the novel *King of the Cross* by Mark Dapin (Pan Macmillan, 2009), which is a fabulous read.

I also drew knowledge from *Sydney Noir* edited by John Dale (Brio Books, 2018).

For a sense of the times, I loved *Suburban Noir: Crime and Mishap in 1950s and 1960s Sydney* by Peter Doyle (NewSouth Books, 2022). Same goes for *Bee Miles: Australia's Famous Bohemian Rebel, and the Untold Story Behind the Legend* by Rose Ellis (Allen & Unwin, 2023) and *Mr Blank* by Dean Manning (NewSouth Books, 2025).

Leviathan: The Unauthorised Biography of Sydney by John Birmingham (Vintage, 2000).

Sydney: A Biography by Louis Nowra (NewSouth Books, 2022).

I also watched and drew from to varying degrees:

Underbelly: The Golden Mile (Nine Network, 2010).

The Witch of Kings Cross: Rosaleen Norton – Scandalous Notorious Genius (directed by Sonia Bible, 2020).

Mr Sin: The Abe Saffron Story (directed by Hugh Piper, 2010).

The Night We Called It a Day (directed by Paul Goldman, 2003).

Blue Murder (Australian Broadcasting Corporation, 1995).

The Killing of Angel Street (directed by Donald Crombie, 1981).

Heatwave (directed by Phillip Noyce, 1982).

Two Hands (directed by Gregor Jordan, 1999).

Pure Shit (directed by Bert Deling, 1975).

Beyond El Rocco (directed by Kevin Lucas, 1990).

Croc-a-Dyke Dundee: The Legend of Dawn O'Donnell (directed by Fiona Cunningham-Reid, 2015).

hachette
AUSTRALIA

If you would like to find out more about Hachette Australia, our authors, upcoming events and new releases you can visit our website or our social media channels:

hachette.com.au

HachetteAustralia

HachetteAus